Okta Administration: Up and Running

Implement enterprise-grade identity and access management for on-premises and cloud apps

Lovisa Stenbäcken Stjernlöf

HenkJan de Vries

BIRMINGHAM—MUMBAI

Okta Administration: Up and Running

Commissioning Editor: Mohd Riyan
Acquisition Editor: Preet Ahuja
Senior Editor: Rahul Dsouza
Content Development Editor: Nihar Kapadia
Technical Editor: Aurobindo Kar
Copy Editor: Safis Editing
Project Coordinator: Neil D'mello
Proofreader: Safis Editing
Indexer: Priyanka Dhadke
Production Designer: Joshua Misquitta

First published: November 2020
Production reference: 1181120

Published by Packt Publishing Ltd.
Livery Place
35 Livery Street
Birmingham
B3 2PB, UK.

ISBN 978-1-80056-664-4

www.packt.com

`Packt.com`

Subscribe to our online digital library for full access to over 7,000 books and videos, as well as industry leading tools to help you plan your personal development and advance your career. For more information, please visit our website.

Why subscribe?

- Spend less time learning and more time coding with practical eBooks and Videos from over 4,000 industry professionals
- Improve your learning with Skill Plans built especially for you
- Get a free eBook or video every month
- Fully searchable for easy access to vital information
- Copy and paste, print, and bookmark content

Did you know that Packt offers eBook versions of every book published, with PDF and ePub files available? You can upgrade to the eBook version at `packt.com` and as a print book customer, you are entitled to a discount on the eBook copy. Get in touch with us at `customercare@packtpub.com` for more details.

At `www.packt.com`, you can also read a collection of free technical articles, sign up for a range of free newsletters, and receive exclusive discounts and offers on Packt books and eBooks.

Contributors

About the authors

Lovisa Stenbäcken Stjernlöf has been with Devoteam for over 4 years, working with multiple cloud vendors during that period. Starting out as a project manager, gaining certifications within G Suite and Salesforce, it was a natural step to start helping customers with their complete cloud setup, including Okta. Apart from customer work, she also has experience with management, both in resources and budgets. With several Okta implementations under her belt and an Okta Certified Professional in the bag, she now heads the Okta practice within Devoteam.

HenkJan de Vries has extensive experience with Okta, having been an Okta partner engineer for over 5 years. With a long history of both implementing and supporting many Okta customers, he understands what long-term requirements look like, but also day-to-day management within organizations. Currently, he is strategically supporting customers to reach all their Okta potential. HenkJan is a certified consultant and is currently part of the exclusive SME group within Okta. Besides his business-related reach, he also enjoys helping unknown and uncontracted customers on several community boards, and by doing so, he has been named an Okta Advocate in 2019 and an Okta Community Leader in 2020.

About the reviewers

Mike Koch is a senior systems engineer for a global retailer and has been in IT for more than 30 years, initially programming AS/400 systems in RPG and COBOL before moving into Windows Server systems engineering and administration, specializing in Active Directory and Exchange servers. He added identity management to his portfolio of skills when his employer switched from ADFS to Okta and discovered a real passion for the technology. He holds certifications from both Microsoft (old-school MCSE) and Okta (Professional and Administrator) and continues to serve as his employer's primary resource for Okta and their hybrid Active Directory, Exchange, and Office 365 environment. In 2020, Mike was tapped by Okta to be included in the inaugural launch of the Okta Community Leaders program, for his contributions to the Okta discussion forums and his willingness to share his knowledge and experience with the rest of the Okta community. He goes by the name @mikekoch on twitter.

> *To my wife, Elaine: Thank you for your love and support, and for putting up with the sometimes-crazy hours and late-night phone calls that come with always being on call. I love you.*

Ivan Dwyer leads product marketing for emerging products at Okta. Prior to joining Okta, Dwyer led marketing for ScaleFT, a pioneer in Zero Trust technologies that was acquired by Okta in 2018. An early advocate for Google's BeyondCorp, the marquee example of Zero Trust done right at scale, Ivan is a frequent speaker and writer on the topic of security, the cloud, and DevOps.

> *Many thanks to the authors for taking the time to write this comprehensive book, and for making the extra effort to become an expert administrator and end user across all of Okta's products.*

Packt is searching for authors like you

If you're interested in becoming an author for Packt, please visit `authors.packtpub.com` and apply today. We have worked with thousands of developers and tech professionals, just like you, to help them share their insight with the global tech community. You can make a general application, apply for a specific hot topic that we are recruiting an author for, or submit your own idea.

Table of Contents

6

Customizing Your Okta GUI

Section 2: Extending Okta

7

API Management

8

Managing Access with Advanced Server Access

9

Leveraging Access Gateway for Your On-Premises Applications

Other Books You May Enjoy

Index

Preface

Okta Administration: Up and Running is a book for anyone starting with Okta. The book covers Okta's features for the internal workforce. After finishing the book, you will have all the basic knowledge needed to have an Okta org up and running. We'll go over the different features, how to set up policies, best practices, and the most common terminology. The book gathers the information you need and connects the dots on how it all fits together.

Who this book is for

The book is for anyone new to Okta or anyone looking into the IAM space who wants to learn more about Okta's products. You don't need any knowledge beforehand, and we recommend you use a free Okta trial org and test out the examples from the book as you go along.

What this book covers

Chapter 1, *IAM and Okta*, is the chapter where we'll learn about Okta and its features. This information will serve as the foundation with which to approach this book and pick up the skills we require to integrate Okta into our systems and learn to use it in the best way possible.

Chapter 2, *Working with Universal Directory*, is where we go through Universal Directory, the foundation on which other pieces are mounted. In this chapter, you'll learn everything you need to know about how to integrate other directories, configurations for users, and how to set up groups.

Chapter 3, *Single Sign-On for a Great End User Experience*, is where we will look at Okta's SSO functionalities and how they will help your end users. We will look at how you can utilize the Okta Integration Network, but before that, we will look into the different connections you can create with various applications. We will also look at the difference between Okta- and application-initiated sign-on flows, as well as IdP discovery.

Chapter 4, Increasing Security with Adaptive Multi-Factor Authentication, is the chapter where we will look at Okta's capabilities in MFA, as well as the more advanced features of having your MFA adaptive. We'll look at how to set up policies and best practices around that.

Chapter 5, Automating Using Life Cycle Management, is an introduction to how we can use some of the knowledge we gained in previous chapters and use it for a complete user lifecycle. We will look at how we can use integrations for user provisioning, such as setting up an HR as a user master. We will also go deeper into editing a user's profile, for instance, with expression language. We will also go through how to use groups for automation, as well as Okta Hooks.

Chapter 6, Customizing Your Okta GUI, introduces the different features end users can utilize. After that, we'll go into how we can customize the end user dashboard with a logo and colors. We will go through what different administrator settings there are to configure the dashboard. While in the admin settings, we will also take a look at how to modify what is sent from Okta, such as emails and SMS messages. Lastly, we will investigate how you can customize the login page, and how to host the login with a widget.

Chapter 7, API Management, introduces you to how to work with the API management of Okta and access the APIs of external applications. This can be both for an organization or Oktas APIs, and also to access self-developed OpenID Connect applications.

Chapter 8, Managing Access with Advanced Server Access, discusses how you can extend Okta's core products to your server fleet. In this chapter, we will go through why a product like Advanced Server Access is needed as well as going through what you need to do to set up and manage ASA.

Chapter 9, Leveraging Access Gateway for Your On-Premises Applications, goes through the last of Okta's products, Okta Access Gateway. For many organizations, legacy on-premise applications are a problem when the organization wants to modernize IT. To have a unified identity platform like Okta, giving end users access with Single Sign-On, the optimal case would be to include all applications. Here, you will gain more knowledge on what Access Gateway is and an overview of how to deploy it. You will learn how to deploy a sample application to your environment and then you will get some insight into how to manage it.

To get the most out of this book

We recommend you follow the different steps and instructions in the book in a non-production org of Okta. If you don't have one, you can sign up for a free trial.

Download the color images

We also provide a PDF file that has color images of the screenshots/diagrams used in this book. You can download it here: `http://www.packtpub.com/sites/default/files/downloads/9781800566644_ColorImages.pdf`.

Conventions used

There are a number of text conventions used throughout this book.

`Code in text`: Indicates code words in text, database table names, folder names, filenames, file extensions, pathnames, dummy URLs, user input, and Twitter handles. Here is an example: 'While the first part is required to make sure the API call is accepted and correct using -H as a statement for the headers, the second part simply states the actual creation of the group with the accompanying details.'

A block of code is set as follows:

```
{
  "id": "00g1emaKYZTWRYYRRTSK",
  "created": "2015-02-06T10:11:28.000Z",
  "lastUpdated": "2015-10-05T19:16:43.000Z",
  "lastMembershipUpdated": "2015-11-28T19:15:32.000Z",
  "objectClass": [ "okta:user_group" ],
  "type": "OKTA_GROUP",
  "profile": {
    "name": "West Coast Users",
    "description": "All Users West of The Rockies"
  },
```

Bold: Indicates a new term, an important word, or words that you see onscreen. For example, words in menus or dialog boxes appear in the text like this. Here is an example: 'To create a new token, click the **Create Token** button.'

> **Tips or important notes**
> Appear like this.

Get in touch

Feedback from our readers is always welcome.

General feedback: If you have questions about any aspect of this book, mention the book title in the subject of your message and email us at customercare@packtpub.com.

Errata: Although we have taken every care to ensure the accuracy of our content, mistakes do happen. If you have found a mistake in this book, we would be grateful if you would report this to us. Please visit www.packtpub.com/support/errata, selecting your book, clicking on the Errata Submission Form link, and entering the details.

Piracy: If you come across any illegal copies of our works in any form on the Internet, we would be grateful if you would provide us with the location address or website name. Please contact us at copyright@packt.com with a link to the material.

If you are interested in becoming an author: If there is a topic that you have expertise in and you are interested in either writing or contributing to a book, please visit authors.packtpub.com.

Reviews

Please leave a review. Once you have read and used this book, why not leave a review on the site that you purchased it from? Potential readers can then see and use your unbiased opinion to make purchase decisions, we at Packt can understand what you think about our products, and our authors can see your feedback on their book. Thank you!

For more information about Packt, please visit packt.com.

Section 1: Getting Started with Okta

In this section, you will learn what IAM and Okta are, and why they're important. You will also learn everything you need to know about Okta's basic features: **Universal Directory (UD)**, **Single Sign-On (SSO)**, **Adaptive Multi-Factor Authentication (AMFA)**, and **Life Cycle Management (LCM)**.

This part of the book comprises the following chapters:

- *Chapter 1, IAM and Okta*
- *Chapter 2, Working with Universal Directory*
- *Chapter 3, Single Sign-On for a Great End User Experience*
- *Chapter 4, Increasing Security with Adaptive Multi-Factor Authentication*
- *Chapter 5, Automating Using Life cycle Management*
- *Chapter 6, Customizing Your Okta GUI*

1
IAM and Okta

Okta is an important, platform-agnostic set of services to help organizations with efficient and modern **Identity and Access Management (IAM)**. One of Okta's most important strengths is its ability to work with a variety of platforms and integrate its features and services into various platforms' own solutions to provide seamless IAM. This strength has made Okta the leader in its field, and important to us when managing our organization's systems, to ensure easy and efficient user account management.

In this chapter, we'll learn about Okta and its features. This information will serve as the foundation with which to approach this book and pick up the skills we require to integrate Okta into our systems and learn how to use it in the best way possible. In this chapter, we'll explore the following topics:

- The origins of Okta
- Exploring Okta
- Okta's basic features
- Okta's advanced features

Exploring the origins of Okta

Okta was started by Todd McKinnon (CEO) and Frederic Kerrest (COO), former Salesforce employees. They saw that the cloud wasn't just a product for the big leagues. They predicted it would be necessary for anyone who would want to grow their business. They started the business in the middle of the 2008 recession, with Andreessen Horowitz investing as one of the first capital injections for Okta in 2010. In 2017, Okta went public with its IPO and valuation of $1.2 billion.

The name Okta is derived from the unit of measurement for clouds covering the sky at any given moment. On the scale, 0 okta is a clear blue sky and 8 oktas is completely overcast. The wordplay of Okta (in Greek, *octa* is 8) and the fact that Okta wants to cover all of the cloud access by becoming the identity standard, thus creating a completely overcast sky (8 oktas), is well thought out.

Since Okta came into the space of IAM, they have steadily grown to the leading vector and have been on top for the last three consecutive years, bypassing giants such as Oracle, IBM, and Microsoft. Their take on being completely vendor-neutral has allowed them to gain customers big and small, across all verticals. This particular focus makes sure that Okta can allow all applications, without being tied to or biased toward any relationship or partnership. This gives the customer complete freedom in choice, setup, and a combination of tools.

In recent years, Okta has been socially active, taking the 1% pledge—committing time, product, and equity to give back to the community, but also supporting non-profit efforts in different ways. As Okta understands what it is like to start up and grow, during their annual conference in 2019, they announced an investment fund of $50 million dollars under the name Okta Ventures to help other start-ups in the identity and security sector to ramp up and grow.

Understanding IAM and Okta

IAM has the following components:

- Manage the roles of individual users within an organization.
- Manage the privileges they have to access company resources while using context.
- Configure scenarios to determine whether access is granted or denied.

Beyond this simple definition, IAM can do much more:

- It orchestrates the user's life cycle during their time within the company.
- It is constantly determined whether access is allowed within company policies and rules to gain access to needed resources, content, and data, using the best available security features.

The time of perimeters is behind us. Organizations can no longer just trust their networks and secure access mainly through their infrastructure. Nowadays, access is needed from every device to every application, at any given moment, with any reason or intent. This shows that security needs are dynamic and their requirements are evolving.

The outdated directory is being replaced by different tools, and all have to be maintained, secured, and fortified outside of the comfort of the company's network. This is bringing a lot of extra consolidating and rethinking around the concept of using the cloud, but also, how to manage it all for the workforce.

Thus, a new era started, where new IAM solutions were born in the cloud and existing solutions started a shift toward the cloud. This didn't mean that every organization all of sudden dropped its network and pushed everything and everyone to the cloud. Vendors had to become hybrid, delivering tools to connect the ground to the cloud with integrations. By consolidating the two, slowly the shift started to pick up pace and organizations began to understand the possibilities of using tools such as Okta as their IAM solution.

Exploring Okta

A complete user and system management setup isn't just in one product, nor is it one vendor. A complete view of all sections within and outside of the organization is best done by utilizing different tools.

This combination and their deep integrations make it possible to create a fine-knit layer of security and insights on top of everything, flexible enough to allow exceptions, but strong enough to fight off anything considered harmful to the users, content, data, or organization.

An IAM system can be seen as a collection of different elements and tools to deliver this. It can be considered that the following functionalities are part of, but not limited to, an organization's toolkit:

- A password vault to store and maintain access to applications and systems. This can be advanced by using protocols that allow **Single Sign-On** (**SSO**).

- Provisioning integrations to create and manage user identities within directories, applications, databases, and infrastructure.

- Security enforcement applications to secure access to applications, as well as securing the data of these systems and others.

- Unified reporting systems that allow fine-grained insight into the array of tools to create oversight and better knowledge of what is happening within and outside of the corporate network.

Okta is capable of delivering all of these functionalities for organizations large and small across any business vertical and within cost-effective boundaries.

By staying true to their form, they are capable of excelling in being non-vendor focused and an agnostic system. Allowing any application vendor to create integrations with Okta, and delivering applications broadly on request from customers, Okta has been able to grow their reach to over 6,500 pre-built and maintained integrations. While creating these integrations, Okta also invested heavily in delivering more and more functionality toward ground-to-cloud visibility and launched their Okta Access Gateway product.

Looking further than users, the world consists of more and more IoT, and the need for machine-to-machine management is becoming a much larger element within organizations' business models. By adding API Access Management and **Advanced Server Access** (**ASA**), Okta created more functionality to fill the needs of every aspect of the IAM situation within any organization.

Let's now take a look at the things that set Okta apart in the IAM space.

Zero trust

As organizations shift away from on-premises, making sure the workforce can decide how and when they access the data they need, Okta makes it possible to incorporate forward-thinking concepts, such as zero trust. A zero-trust framework has no physical or non-physical entities within or outside of the corporate perimeter that are trusted at any given moment in time. This allows the insight and control to manage users, identities, infrastructure, and devices accessing business resources and data. Threat detection and remediation are part of the cycle to make sure that this concept is enforced.

The zero-trust principle of least-privileged access can be incorporated into the organization's security policies. It allows users and machines to only get enough access for that moment and that task. This can be hard to manage on a case-by-case basis (for example, allowing and denying access to individual corporate content and files) but by understanding the concept, it is good to use the rule of thumb to only give out need-to-access privileges. A couple of examples are as follows:

- A support agent needs administrator rights in a system but might not need full super admin rights. Role-based access can be applied here.
- A machine reading data from a database needs read-only access, not write access. This would reduce the risk of an attacker being able to change or delete data.

Acquiring an IAM tool is not by default enough to make sure your organization lives up to a zero-trust approach, but it is a starting point for many organizations. When it comes to IAM and zero trust, Okta divides the journey into four stages of maturity.

Stage 0 – fragmented identity

An organization in this stage typically has **Active Directory** (**AD**) or some other on-premises structures as a user directory. Cloud applications might be used, but there is no integration to the directory. Passwords are not consolidated, but rather separate logins are everywhere. Security is done on a case-by-case basis, or rather, app by app:

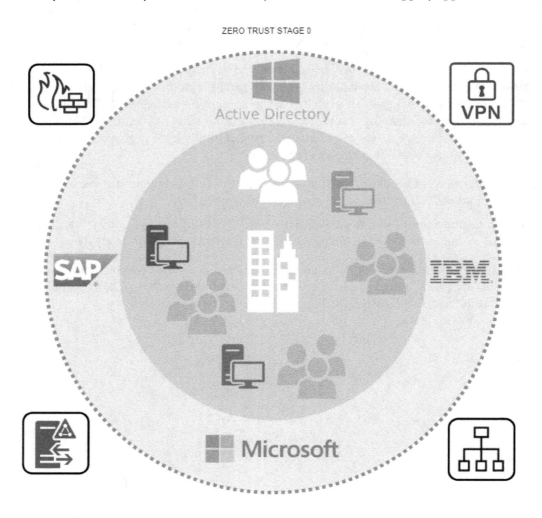

Figure 1.1 – In stage 0, most services and devices will reside within the corporate infrastructure. All applications and access are managed with networks and directories

Once users break free from or break through the corporate firewall, the need for more control over who can access what, and when, where, and how, allows the organization to move into the next stage.

Usually, more traditional organizations fall into this category. Their history is more based upon older infrastructure and the move toward the cloud is slowly happening. Companies with on-premises servers, fierce reliance on firewalls, and VPN access are often found in this stage.

Stage 1 – unified IAM

Once you open the gates, there is no coming back to a perimeter-based security practice. It's important to make sure certain access is managed for employees, partners, and contractors. Delivering unified SSO relieves the user of the responsibility to create, maintain, and manage strong passwords for each application, portal, and infrastructure. By adding **Multi-Factor Authentication (MFA)**, the organization is capable of creating more policies that incorporate different activities to confirm the user's identity while accessing corporate content. Examples of this can be as follows:

- Using an application such as Google Authenticator or Okta's own application, Verify, for a one-time code
- SMS with a one-time code
- Biometrics such as a fingerprint reader or a YubiKey

An outline of what stage 1 can look like is as follows:

Figure 1.2 – In stage 1, you will see a shift. Users will access corporate data outside of the network. Slowly, SaaS will make its way into the organization. Even so, old structures will still stay in place to maintain legacy and non-cloud access

You will find organizations of every trade in this stage. Moving to the cloud is part of their strategy. They will most likely start to embrace **Software-as-a-Service (SaaS)** options above their own capabilities. This is where perimeters start to fade and the call for more flexible security and management is needed.

Stage 2 – contextual access

Contextual-based access plays a large part when you want to expand your zero-trust initiative. Understanding your users, their devices, location, systems, and even time and date can be of importance to accelerate your dynamic zero-trust parameters. By incorporating all these components, you now allow your security team to widen their view of a user's posture and activities and set fine-grained policies and rules that are applicable to that user.

Having such deep control and the capability to interact on such a low level with users fits perfectly with the concept of zero trust. Of course, automation is the magic sauce. Using all these different elements in your security risk assessment is the first step, setting policies on top of that is step two, but automating it all and having the systems grow stronger is what adds even more value and is step three.

Within this stage, usually, you will see that corporate APIs and systems have, or leverage, APIs that need to be protected as well. Allowing API access management assures that even your systems are only allowed access, based on the least-privilege framework:

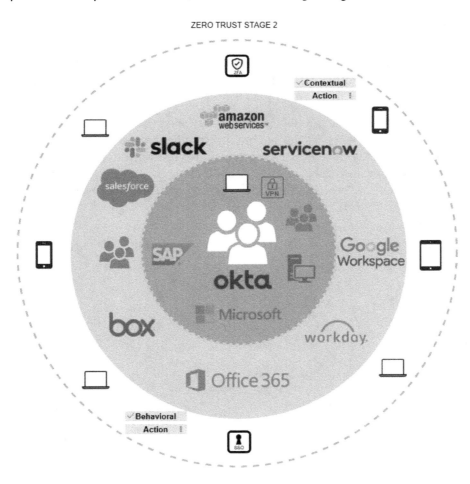

Figure 1.3 – In stage 2, organizations will most likely adopt more and more cloud services. The identity will become the perimeter and identity providers will become part of the primary components. Outside access to corporate content and data is no longer complimentary; it has become mandatory

It can be considered that organizations have a complete roadmap for themselves set out in regard to their zero-trust initiative. Cloud-driven, cloud-native, and cloud-born organizations will quickly adopt it and can be found a lot in this stage. The more traditional organizations in this stage have come a long way; they truly were able to reinvent themselves.

Stage 3 – adaptive workforce

When system automation increases, risk-based analysis can be added. This is when we are capable of creating a fully flexible and adaptive workforce. The incorporation of more security systems becomes a large addition to the whole security practice. Usually, additional values from third-party applications such as **Mobile Device Management (MDM)**, **Cloud Access Security Broker (CASB)**, **Security Information and Event Management (SIEM)**, and other connected systems will deliver even more user and machine context that can be used within policies.

Unknown vectors are detected, and policies start to act upon these discoveries. Adding alternative access controls when it's needed or required allows more security. While security might go up, the users' access can now be more controlled with the help of seamless access methods. Passwordless and factor-stacking methods are a more common situation in which users are prompted to show who they are, based on the risk they present to the systems that are controlling access:

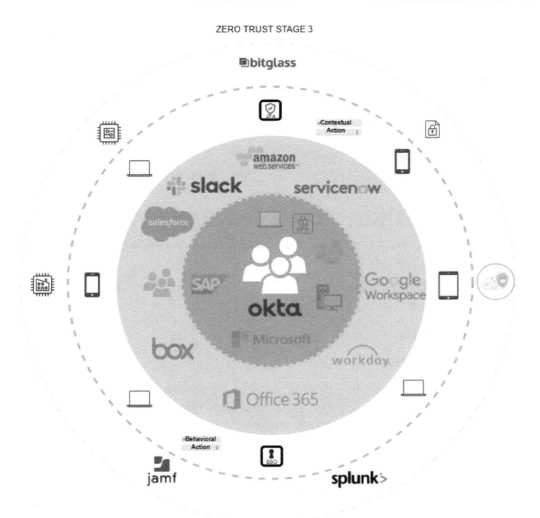

Figure 1.4 – In stage 3, interconnectivity with every endpoint will become the norm. Automation is added on top of data and content security. Least-privileged access can be maintained based on log consolidation and API management

Organizations that fall into this category will be front-runners in this initiative. They not only understand it, but they have also implemented it and made it their mantra. High-tech organizations with global workforces and dynamic management will fit this picture perfectly.

So, how would you start your own organization's journey to zero trust?

- Start with researching the concept.
- Do an assessment of your own organization.
- See what solutions you can keep and what needs to change and mitigate this.
- Get your users on board.

Now that we've learned the steps to take with your organization toward a zero-trust approach, let's look at the basic features in Okta that we can use to start our journey.

Discovering Okta's basic features

Okta has a lot of different products, and organizations can pick and choose as they see fit. The most commonly used are the following:

- **Universal Directory (UD)**
- **SSO**
- **Adaptive Multi-Factor Authentication (AMFA)**
- **Lifecycle Management (LCM)**

It's not always obvious in the administrator portal where one product starts and another one ends. This will be clarified in this book. The products will all be explained with practical examples in the coming chapters, but here is an initial overview.

Universal Directory

UD can be considered as the foundation of any Okta setup. UD is the directory of your users and groups. Users can be mastered by Okta, by other directories, or by an HR system. For organizations with multiple directories, such as AD, LDAP, and an HR system, Okta offers a complete 360 view of the users and their attributes. Users can be sorted into groups created in Okta and imported from a directory or an application. With Okta's Attribute Mastering feature, the attributes of any user can be mastered by different sources.

Single sign-on

SSO lets us connect applications and lets our users access them through Okta. End users will only have to log in to Okta once, and can thereafter access any application they have assigned to them. This is done with integrations based on SAML, WS-Federation, OpenID Connect, or with a simple **Secure Web Authentication** (**SWA**) where Okta stores credentials and passes them along to the application in a secure way. In the **Okta Integration Network** (**OIN**), more than 6,500 integrations are available, and more are added every day. If the required application isn't available in the OIN, customers can create their own integrations. This will be described in depth in *Chapter 3, Single Sign-On for a Great End User Experience.*

Multi-factor authentication and adaptive multi-factor authentication

Included in Okta's SSO product are basic MFA features. You can easily set up policies to let your users utilize different kinds of factors after entering their password. Using the basic IP settings, you can set up network zones that protect your users and block bad actors from the outside.

Many third-party MFA solutions can be integrated with Okta, allowing you to leverage existing and perhaps currently deployed solutions into your Okta MFA policies.

If the basic features of MFA aren't enough for you, Okta's Adaptive MFA product brings even more advanced options. With AMFA, you can set the context to your MFA policies. Context can be location awareness, device fingerprinting, or impossible velocity. Okta's device trust options allow you to integrate with your third-party MDM systems to generate even more context around your users and devices.

Lifecycle management

So far, the Okta products we've looked at have focused a lot on end user experience and security. LCM is all about automation, easing up friction between HR and IT. With LCM, organizations are better set up for audits. For instance, with your Okta instance set up— with groups, rules, integrations, and system logs—and access given, it's easy to show when a user had access to what. With the Group Rules feature, it's clearer what employees have access to. This will streamline work for the HR and IT departments, allowing them to do the work by creating the user only once in the organization's systems. The creation and management of users has never been this easy. Automatic account creation also minimizes mistakes caused by human error. A predetermined setup allows the organization to invest time upfront to create and set up the provisioning, and after that, it will automatically run based on the user's identity and profile.

With Okta's LCM functionality, you can also automate access control in certain applications. This allows you, with minimal interaction, to manage users with the correct role, license, and group access.

Workflows

Workflows is a part of the advanced LCM product. With Workflows, you can automate many business processes using a simple *if this, then that* methodology with no-code configurations. Okta provides a library of connections to many popular cloud applications, and workflows can also integrate with custom APIs. Some examples of where Workflows can be used include the following:

- On- and off-boarding enhancements
- Resolving conflicts when new users are created
- Sharing reports on a monthly basis.

Okta's basic features help us manage the most general day-to-day tasks associated with IAM. However, it also has some specific, advanced features to help us manage our systems better.

Okta's advanced features

If your organization needs to go deeper than general IAM, you might need to look at Okta's more advanced features.

Okta Advanced Server Access

Okta ASA lets us extend our zero-trust practices toward server accounts. Okta can manage access to both user or service accounts to Linux or Windows servers across different cloud vendors, such as GCP, AWS, and Azure, or on-premises servers. In Okta, your admins get a great overview of who has access to what and can see individual logins in log reports. ASA works with a lightweight agent and is installed in your infrastructure landscape.

Okta Access Gateway

Okta Access Gateway (OAG) makes it possible to implement modern cloud-based access management to legacy on-premises applications. With this product, you can gather all your identity needs in one place, making it easier to manage. It's easy to integrate, with templates and native on-premises integrations. By replacing your current **Web Access Management (WAM)** system, you can bring your applications to your users in a modern and non-restrictive way. Additionally, you can also secure those apps even more with extra MFA functionality.

API Access Gateway

Leveraging Okta's API Access Gateway allows the developer of your tools, systems, and platforms to be securely managed by Okta, while they can focus on their primary tasks. Adding security and allowing scopes to grant access into your own systems are managed by Okta. The shift of responsibility goes from the developer to the security and operations team. Focusing on management with out-of-the-box integrations and authorization servers is core to Okta's API access management.

Summary

In this chapter, we learned basic details about IAM and how Okta works as a great solution to any IAM needs. We've learned about the scenarios in which Okta emerges as an IAM solution. Finally, we learned about the features of Okta and how they work with various platforms to give us dynamic control over user accounts within our organizations. All of this information forms the basis of our understanding for the rest of the book, where we will take a deeper look at Okta and how to make use of all its features.

In the next chapter, we will learn how to work with UD by setting it up and configuring it. We will learn how to add or import users and explore the most important features and policies to help us use UD efficiently.

2
Working with Universal Directory

Universal Directory is the base of Okta, the foundation on which other pieces are mounted. Your users and applications will be an intricate part of Universal Directory. Groups will be vital for you to keep organized and make your Okta org as low-maintenance as possible. In this chapter, you'll learn everything you need to know to integrate other directories, configurations for users, and setting up groups.

Let's jump right in and start to look at what companies might have been using before, and how that can work with Okta.

We will explore the following topics:

- Connecting your infrastructure with directory integrations
- Importing and creating users
- Using groups in the best possible way

Directory integrations

If your organization is fairly new, there is a big chance that it was born in the cloud. Probably, you're only using cloud services and your user directory is in one of your applications, perhaps your collaboration platform. You will probably want to use Okta as your new identity directory going forward. But for other organizations, your users may have been living in a separate directory for ages, and you might have multiple hardware and infrastructure connections to that directory. Many organizations like this are not ready to leave their **Active Directory (AD)/ Lightweight Directory Access Protocol (LDAP)** behind. Not to worry, Okta can integrate with multiple directories and synchronize users, groups, attributes, and passwords.

Previously, this directory setup was sufficient, but with the shift in perimeter explained earlier, this becomes a problem when companies are moving toward cloud applications. Many cloud applications have their own directory within them, but the administrator's overview of who has access to what is lost. It is possible to still use AD or LDAP, but with custom API integrations, the upkeep will become hard to manage.

Instead, organizations can keep their AD/LDAP and use Okta as a directory between it and their cloud applications, using standard integrations, maintained by Okta.

Microsoft AD and various LDAP directories are handled differently, and in the following sections, we will guide you through how to install and configure these integrations.

Microsoft AD integration

For Microsoft AD, there are three different on-premises components to be used for different use cases:

- The Okta AD agent
- The Okta **Integrated Windows Authentication (IWA)** web application
- The Okta AD Password Sync agent

Let's go through them, one by one.

Importing users and groups with the Okta AD agent

The Okta AD agent is a lightweight agent to be installed on any Windows server to handle user authentication, provisioning, and deprovisioning between your AD and Okta.

To set up the AD agent, start by logging in to Okta from a browser on the Windows server where your directory lives. Go to the **Directory** tab in the admin console, and choose **Directory Integrations**. If you have had previous directory integrations, you will see them listed here. Choose **Add Active Directory**. On the next page, you will see the requirements:

- Install on Windows Server 2008 R2 or later.
- Must be a member of your AD domain.
- Consider the agent a part of your IT infrastructure.
- Run this setup wizard from the host server (you already did this).

When going through the installation, you will enter your Okta URL and your AD credentials. The best practice is to use a service account that has administrative rights. The agent creates a read-only integration account and connects to Okta through an outbound port 443 SSL connection. Usually, no firewall or network changes will be needed.

> **Tip**
> Test logging in to the host machine with AD credentials and access the internet via a browser. If that works, no change is needed in firewall or network settings.

From the Okta side, setup requires Okta super administrator access and will establish a security token. The token is only valid for one agent and can be revoked whenever needed. The token created at setup is authenticated by Okta, and the agent verifies the service by validating the **Secure Sockets Layer** (**SSL**) certificate for the URL. In terms of the domain controller, the agent will be authenticated using the read-only account for integration that was created during the installation.

After your agent is installed and verified, you can start importing your users. From **Directory | Directory Integrations | Active Directory**, you choose the settings to set your preferences.

If you check the **Enable delegated authentication to Active Directory** selection in the **Delegated Authentication** section, you let AD authenticate users when they sign in to Okta. You find this section by going to the **Provisioning** tab and selecting **Integration**. For organizations using AD for other services as well, this is an easy way for users to manage fewer passwords. It also makes for easier onboarding and adoption of Okta, where users don't have to remember anything new.

In the **Import settings** section, in the different menu selection to the right, you will see the following options:

- **User OUs connected to Okta**: You can add or remove **Organizational Units (OUs)** used to import users.

- **Group OUs connected to Okta**: You can add or remove OUs used to import groups.

Under the **To Okta** tab, you can find the following settings:

- **Schedule import**: In this section, you can select with what frequency you want to import users from your directory. You can use **Do not import users** to only allow manual importing and not have the schedule run at all.

- **Okta username format**: The format of the username must match the username you used when you imported users; otherwise, you might cause errors for active users:

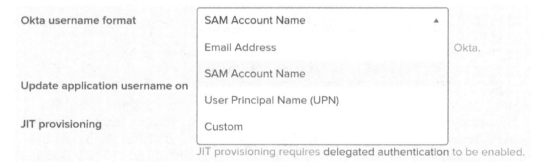

Figure 2.1 – Options of Okta username format

- **Just in Time (JIT) provisioning**: If you check **Create** and update users on login, a user's account in Okta is automatically created the first time they sign in to Okta using their AD credentials. For existing users, any account and group updates will be synchronized during new logins.

- **Activation email**: By ticking this box, you avoid sending out an email to end users to activate their account upon import. This should be your default setting on your first import since you might have other items to set up in your new Okta instance before you're ready for active users.

- **Universal Security Group support**: Select this option to avoid domain boundaries when importing group memberships.

- **Import Safeguard**: This setting prevents user accounts from being accidentally lost during import. The values set up here have an effect on the app and an org-wide impact threshold.

In the **User Creation & Matching** section, you set the settings that decide whether a user imported from AD is matched with an existing user in Okta. With the matching rules, you will establish how to map an imported user to an existing user. This is an important step to ensure you don't get duplicates of the same user in Okta; it is especially important if you import users from other places, such as applications.

To determine that an imported user is matched, you can choose from the following options:

- **Okta username format matches**.
- **Email matches**.
- **The following attribute matches**: You can choose an attribute from the drop-down list. The chosen attribute must match for it to be deemed an exact match.
- **The following combination of attribute matches**: You can choose combinations of attributes from a list; each combination you chose must match for it to be deemed an exact match.

You can also set rules that partial matches will be considered a match. For example, that could happen when a user's first and last name matches but the username or email don't.

Lastly, you have to decide what will happen when these matches are identified; that's done in the **Confirmation Settings** section. If you have a matched user, you can select **Auto-confirm exact matches** and/or **Auto-confirm partial matches**. If you don't select any of them, you have to manually confirm each import. In this section, you also decide what to do to new users that were imported, without being matched with an existing user in Okta. You can select **Auto-confirm new users** and/or **Auto-activate new users**. If you leave both unchecked, the users will be confirmed once they are manually activated by an administrator.

These parameters can be set up to your own needs and preferences for your own setup:

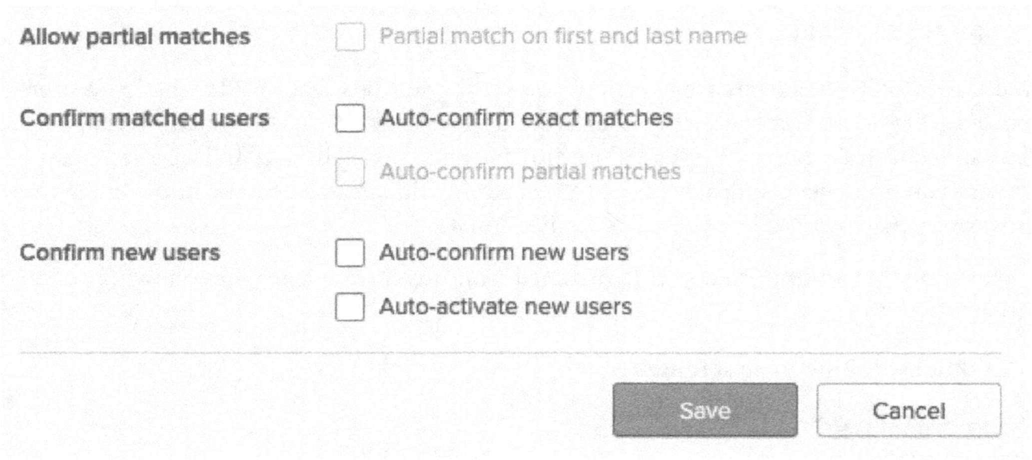

Allow partial matches	☐ Partial match on first and last name
Confirm matched users	☐ Auto-confirm exact matches
	☐ Auto-confirm partial matches
Confirm new users	☐ Auto-confirm new users
	☐ Auto-activate new users

[Save] [Cancel]

Figure 2.2 – Options of Okta username format

Don't forget to hit **Save**!

Now that we've looked at how to import users, let's look at how to set up **Desktop Single Sign-On (DSSO)**.

Simple sign-on with the Okta IWA web application

This agent is what you need to enable DSSO for your users. DSSO means that you are authenticated to Okta and any applications integrated with Okta by signing in to your Windows network.

> **Tip**
> The on-premises agent should use SSL. This is important not only for security reasons but also as it's required for application authentication—for instance, for Windows 10 universal applications.

These are the prerequisites for installation:

- The Okta AD agent must be installed and configured, and **Delegated Access** must be enabled.
- Ports 80 and 443 must be enabled on the server where you're installing the agent.
- Windows Server 2008 R2, or higher.
- .NET 4.5.2 up to .NET 4.6.x and ASP .NET 4.5.

- Make sure TLS 1.2 is enabled on your server.

- IIS 7.5 or higher must be installed on the server.

- The Okta AD agent 3.0.4.x or higher must be installed, but it's not required to be installed on the same server.

- If your organization has more than one domain, you may need to configure UPN transformation.

To install the IWA web application, make sure you're logged in to Okta as a super administrator. In the admin console, go to **Security | Delegated Authentication | Active Directory**. In the DSSO section, you will find the link to download the agent. To go through the installation, follow these steps:

1. Double-click on the file and click **Run**, then **Next**.

2. In the next dialog box, choose **Create** or use the Okta service account, then hit **Next**.

3. You will see a screen for **Register Okta Desktop Single Sign On**, where you will select an environment: **Production**, **Preview**, or **Custom**. Then, enter your Okta domain name, and once again hit **Next**.

4. After that, you will log in to Okta, using your super administrator account.

5. You will be prompted to approve access to the API. Click **Allow access**.

That's it! Click **Finish** and then reload the AD page you started on.

Easy login to apps with the Okta AD Password Sync agent

In an earlier section, we looked at the **Delegated Authentication** feature. In this scenario, passwords are not passed along over to Okta; AD is simply handling the authentication of users when they login to Okta. But in some cases, a downstream application needs a password to authenticate users. In this scenario, Okta checks the password entered with AD and also checks whether the user is assigned an application using the synchronized AD password. If the user doesn't have any applications in need of the password, Okta caches the password for 5 days. If the user has an application using the synchronized password, the password is synchronized to the application and also stored in Okta for the application; the password is cached in Okta for 5 days.

Since you just installed the DSSO agent, the Password Sync agent makes sure any changes of the password in AD are synchronized in Okta. If a user changes their password on the computer sign-on screen, the password has to be synced between AD and Okta. The user might have to sign out then sign in to Okta again to be able to access the application with the synchronized password.

To install, go to the admin console, then **Security | Delegated Authentication**. On the menu on the right-hand side, scroll down and click the link to download the synchronize password agent. After that, do the following:

1. Start the installation and follow the steps.

2. You will have to enter your domain name, in the format `https://mycompany.okta.com`. Don't forget the `https://` part!

3. At the end, you will pick your installation location, then hit **Install**. After that, click **Finish**.

4. Restart the server.

So, how do you configure the agent? On the server, navigate to **Start | All Programs | Okta | Okta AD Password Sync | Okta AD Password Synchronization Agent Management Console**. There, you can validate the URL. If it's valid, a success message appears under the field. If you want, you can also set the level of logging for the agent.

> **Note**
>
> The Password Sync agent must be installed on all domain controllers. Also, don't forget to enable delegated authentication!

Okay, that's all for any basic AD integration. Let's now look at how it's done for an LDAP directory.

LDAP integration

For other LDAP directories, there is a separate agent. Let's look at how to install it. The instructions are different depending on whether it's a Linux or Windows server. We will go through the Windows installation. Make sure you are logging in to Okta on the host server and with a super administrator account. Within the admin console, go to **Directory | Directory Integrations**. Choose **Add Directory | Add LDAP Directory**.

As with the AD integration, you get the requirements listed on the first page. Once you have made sure you fulfill them, click **Set up LDAP**:

1. Click on **Download Agent**, then choose the **Download EXE** installer and download it to your server.

2. Double-click the file and run the installer. If you get prompted to allow the agent to make changes on the computer, answer **Yes**.

3. Click **Next**, then agree to the license agreement, then click **Next** again.

4. Pick your location to install the agent, then click **Install**.

After that, you get to insert information on the configuration side:

- **LDAP Server**: Input your host and port in the format host:port.

- **Root DN**: The distinguished root name of the directory, where users and groups are searched.

- **Bind DN**: Administrator login credentials to bind the integration.

- **Bind Password**: Administrator login credentials to bind the integration.

Click **Next**. In the next window, you get to enter a proxy server for your LDAP agent, if you wish. After that, you need to register your agent with your Okta service by entering your Okta subdomain. Hit **Next**. After that, you will enter the username and password of your Okta admin account, then click **Sign in**. You will have to allow API access, then you just have to click **Finish**!

Now it's time to apply the settings. Navigate to **Directory | Directory Integrations**. The agent for the integration you just installed should be listed as **Not yet configured**:

- **LDAP Provider**: In this dropdown, you can select what provider you have, and the fields will be automatically filled. If the one you use isn't on the list, you just enter information in the fields manually.

- **Unique Identifier Attribute**: This value gives you the unique immutable value for the users and groups imported; only objects with this value will be imported from LDAP to your Okta org.

- Verify that it's auto-populated correctly from picking the LDAP provider.

- **DN attribute**: Also, this one comes for free if you pick an LDAP provider; it gives the attribute on all objects containing the **Distinguished Name** (**DN**) value.

Go down to the user section to continue configuration:

- **User Search Base**: In this field, you enter the DN of the base user subtree, so basically where you want to import your users form.

- **User Object Class**: Okta needs the object class of the users it should import.

- **User Object Filter**: You get this for free when selecting an LDAP provider at the top. The default is **Object Class**.

- **Account Disabled Attribute**: Input the attribute used to indicate whether a user is active or disabled.

- **Account Disabled Value**: This is to input the value that indicates whether the account is locked (for instance, **TRUE**).

- **Password Attribute**: In this field, you enter the user password attribute.

- **Password Expiration Attribute**: This is usually a Boolean value and it's inserted for you if you pick an LDAP provider. If yours isn't on the list, check your LDAP server documentation for this value.

- **Extra User Attributes**: This is optional, but you get a chance to enter any other user attributes to import.

You will then finish the group or role section; typically only one of them is used. In the **Validation** configuration section, you want to configure the following:

- **Group Search Base**: This is the root of the group structure Okta will search in, using the DN — for example, `ou=groups`, `dc=example`, or `dc=com`.

- **Group Object Class**: By adding this to Okta's query, it will filter what type of groups you want to import — for example, `groupofnames`, `groupofuniquenames`, or `posixgroup`.

- **Group Object Filter**: Okta prefills this by default with the object class of the group.

- **Member Attribute**: Here, you can specify the attribute containing all the member DNs.

- **User Attribute**: Normally, this field is empty. Okta will classify user memberships at runtime. If you explicitly use `posixGroup`, it is recommended to configure the value with `memberUID` and the user attribute with `uid`.

In the role section, the following fields are available:

- **Object Class**: The object class of a role.
- **Membership Attribute**: The attribute indicator as part of the DN string — for example, `cn=ADMIN`, `ou=roles`, `dc=example`, or `dc=com`.

To make sure your setup is correct, you can validate the settings by taking the following steps:

- Okta username format: What you enter here generates the username your users will use when they sign in to Okta. This needs to be in the format of an email.
- Enter a username to validate your setup. Okta will query the LDAP and you can validate that all returned data is correct.
- Click **Test Configuration**. You will get a **Validation Successful!** notification on the username you entered.

Click **Next**, and then **Done**, and with that, your LDAP integration configuration is done!

Now that we've learned about directory integrations, let's look at users and other means of mastering them.

Everything about users

In Okta, there are three different kinds of users: Okta mastered, directory mastered, and application mastered. These three have some different characteristics, so let's have a look at them.

The basics with Okta mastered users

If you don't have any external directories, your users might be created and mastered in Okta. There are different available options to create users: one-on-one in the administrator console, via a CSV upload, or via the API.

Let's start with adding a single user:

1. In the admin console, navigate to **Directory | People**.

    Before we move on and add our user, we can take a look at the **People** section. At the top, you have some quick actions, such as adding a user, resetting passwords, or multifactor. In the left pane, you get a quick overview of your users — how many you have added, how many are active, and whether any users are staged or pending to activate their account. You also get a quick overview of whether or not any users need their password reset or are locked out of their account. In the middle, you get a list of your users; you will see 25 per page.

2. Click **Add Person**, and a new dialog box appears. We'll go through the fields:

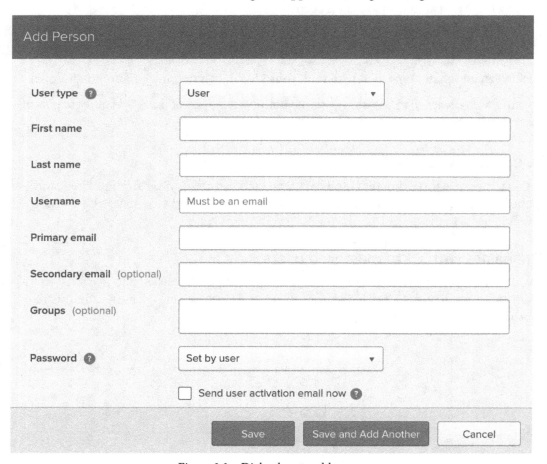

Figure 2.3 – Dialog box to add a user

As the default, the only available option for **User type** is **User**. If you have other kinds of users in your Okta directory, such as contractors or partners, you can set this here.

Creating a new user type

To create a user type, go to **Directory | Profile Editor**. In the top-right corner, you will see a green button for **Create Okta User Type**. Adding the new user type name and its variable name creates a copy of the default **User** user type and its 31 default attributes.

Back to creating a new user. An Okta mastered user has four required attributes, which you enter here:

- **First name**
- **Last name**
- **Username**
- **Primary email**

You also have the option to add a secondary email. This can be used as a backup if the user loses access to their primary email and needs to reset the Okta account.

If you have groups set up in your Okta org, you can assign the user to multiple groups in the next field. In the last drop-down menu, you get to select whether you want the user to set their password on activation or whether you as an administrator set it. If you select the latter, you get to enter a password, and also choose whether the user is required to set a new password on their first login. Your last selection in creating your new user is to check the box if you want to send an activation email to the user directly. Then, click **Save**!

Another option to create users is with a CSV file.

Tip
This method is most useful for creating multiple users at once.

In the **People** section under **Directories**, you can find the option to use a CSV file under the **More Actions** dropdown. From the dialog box, you get a template to use for the import. The CSV file contains columns for a lot of attributes, but as with when you create a user from the **Add Person** button, you need to enter at least the required four base attributes. In the CSV file, the variable names, rather than the attribute names, are displayed. If you want a translation between the two, you can check it out in the Profile Editor, and pick the Okta profile. But for the four base attributes, it looks like this:

- `login`: Username
- `firstName`: First name
- `lastName`: Last name
- `email`: Primary email

After you're done with the CSV file, import it through the dialog box. If you have any errors, it will let you know, and you can go back and correct the file. If the import runs successfully, you can click **Next**. In the next window, you get to pick how to import the users. You can select to either automatically activate new users or **Do not create a password and only allow login via Identity Provider**. Click **Import users**. You will see a list of new, updated, and unchanged users. If there are any errors, you can see what they are by downloading the offered error report. As previously mentioned, it's also possible to create users through Okta's APIs. This will be explored further in *Chapter 7, API Management*.

Enriching user profiles with attributes

As previously mentioned, you can see a user's complete list of attributes in the Profile Editor. There, you can also add attributes to the Okta default user. Navigate to **Directory | Profile Editor** and select the profile you want to edit, and then click the pencil icon. You will see the full list of attributes. Use the **Add Attributes** button to prompt a new window:

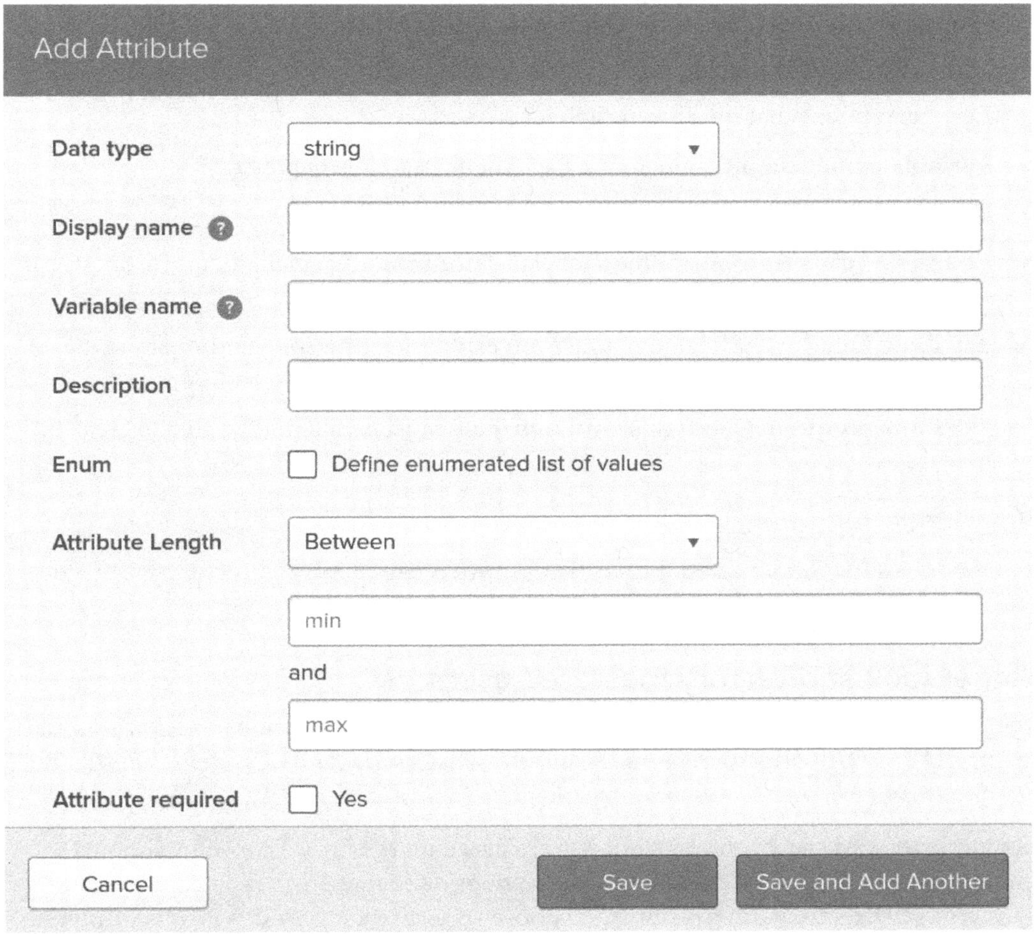

Figure 2.4 – Dialog window to create a new user attribute

Let's input some information:

- **Data type**: For this section, you will be able to put in some information:

   a) **string**: Zero or more characters, such as letters, numbers, and punctuation marks

   b) **number**: Floating-point decimal in Java's 64-bit double format

   c) **boolean**: Values true, false, or null

   d) **integer**: Whole numbers in Java's 64-bit long format

   e) **array of strings**: Collection of strings in sequence

f) **array of numbers**: Collection of numbers in sequence

g) **array of integers**: Collection of integers in sequence

- **Display name**: What the admins will read.

- **Variable name**: The attribute name that will be used for mapping.

- **Description**: Enter a description for your attribute.

- **Enum**: You can create an enumerated list — for instance, small, medium, or large if your attribute is T-shirt size.

- **Attribute Length**: As the name hints, you can decide how long and/or short the attribute entry can be.

- **Attribute required**: Check this if this attribute must be filled to be able to create a new user.

Lastly, hit **Save**.

That's the basics for Okta mastered users. Let's move on and look at directory mastered users.

Another look at directory mastered users

In the previous chapter, we looked at how to integrate Okta with various directories. Apart from an AD or LDAP directory, users can also be mastered by an HR system. We will dig more into this in *Chapter 5*, *Automating Using Life Cycle Management*.

Users imported and synchronized from AD are based on the OU(s) chosen to import from. If you want to go back and check your settings or change them, you can navigate to **Directory | Directory Integration** and choose your directory. Under **Provisioning**, in the pane to the left, you see that you can set it up both to and from Okta. Under the **To Okta** section, you will find the settings you made during integration configuration, such as **Matching rules**. The last option, **Integration**, is where you can see what OUs you are importing both users and groups from.

If you want to trigger a new import, you can go to the **Import** tab in the current view and click **Import now**. You can select partial import or full import. For a partial import, the scan will only be for users created or updated since the last import. For a full import, all current data on a user is replaced with what's in the directory. Users not found in the scan (for instance, removed from the OU) will be denied access to Okta, but not deactivated.

Attributes for a user mastered by your directory can be found in the user's profile, and are read-only when mastered by an external directory.

Now you know everything about how directories are integrated, and also how users are mastered there. Let's check how that works for users from applications — new ways of working with application mastered users

If your organization has been using an application such as Google Workspace as your directory before introducing Okta, you can import your users from there. To be able to start the import, you need to integrate Okta with your application environment through **Okta Integration Network (OIN)**.

With your application integrated, you will start by navigating to the **Provisioning** tab of that application. In the **To Okta** section, you will be able to configure settings for imports and matches:

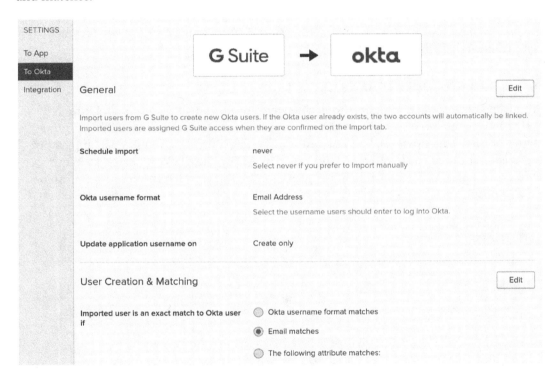

Figure 2.5 – Application to Okta settings

As with the AD integration, you get to select how to possibly match users imported from the application with existing users in Okta. You can also check what you want to do with matches and new users:

- Auto-confirm exact matches
- Auto-confirm partial matches

- Auto-confirm new users

- Auto-activate new users

By clicking **Edit** in the top section, you can select the interval of how often you want to automatically import users. If you'd rather import manually, you select **never**. Then, navigate to the **Import** tab. By simply clicking **Import users**, the integration will search for new or updated users. In Okta, you will see a division of exact and partial matches, as set in the previous tab.

If your users are living in an HR application such as Workday or BambooHR, they can be mastered by that. This flow will be explained more in *Chapter 5, Automating Using Life Cycle Management*.

Now that we have looked at what to do with different types of masters, we will look at how to set profile and attribute masters.

Profile and attribute mastering

With profile mastering, it's possible to decide what source of truth a user's attributes are dictated by. A user can only be mastered by one source at any given time. Different groups or types of users can, however, be mastered by different sources. If you have an application integrated that can act as a source of truth, such as AD or Google Workspace, as in our previous examples, you can enable in the provisioning settings that the application can be used as a profile master:

Figure 2.6 – Enable Google Workspace to master users

Simply click **Edit** and check the box to allow Google Workspace to master users. Note that it can be a problem for an application to master users if you also have the **Update User Attribute** feature in play.

Now, let's see how you set profile masters. Navigate to **Directory | Profile Masters**. If you have more than one profile master, you will be able to set the priority order:

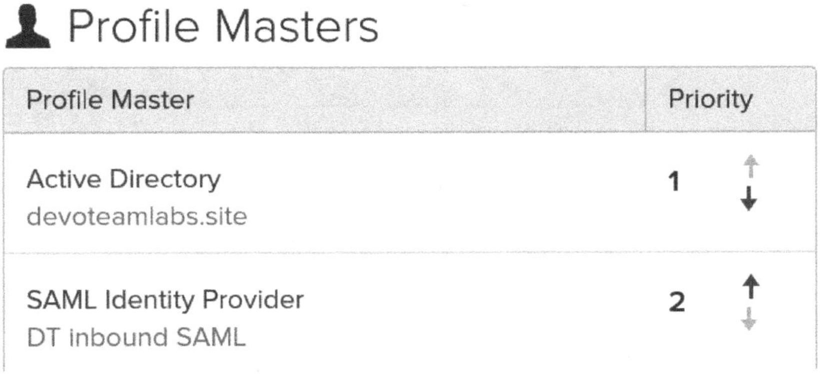

Profile Masters

Profile Master	Priority	
Active Directory devoteamlabs.site	1	↑ ↓
SAML Identity Provider DT inbound SAML	2	↑ ↓

Figure 2.7 – Different profile masters and their priorities

To change the order of the priority, simply click the arrows. For users assigned to AD, their profile is mastered by AD. For users not assigned to AD, their profile will be mastered by a SAML identity provider — in this case, Google Workspace. If a user is assigned to both, the highest master will be the leading one.

If this is not fine-grained enough for your organization, you can also use **Attribute-Level Mastering (ALM)**. With this feature, you can let data such as a name and email be mastered by an HR application, while the phone number is mastered by AD and the secondary email by the user themselves.

There are a few requirements for using ALM:

- Profile mastering is enabled.
- You have prioritized the different profile masters.
- Mapping is set through UD mapping.

You've already done the first two steps, so let's look at the last. Navigate to **Directory | Profile Editor**. Go to the Okta profile and find the attribute you want to edit. Click the **i** icon of the attribute and select under **Master priority** the mastering source of that attribute. This will only set the mastering of that attribute to that source, while others might have different mastering sources to abide by:

Figure 2.8 – Different options for attribute mastering

To override the inherited master, choose **Override profile master**. You will then get to pick an alternative master. When you are done, click **Save Attribute**, and you have now changed the master of that specific attribute for that mastered user.

You have now learned a lot about users, so let's move on to how to work with groups.

Using groups

Every user needs to gain access to mail accounts, fileservers, Wi-Fi, applications, and so on. Managing this on an individual case-by-case basis can become very time-consuming and repetitive work. Using groups solves this pain by allowing users to be managed in bulk. Access rights can be updated and changed, and all users within the group receive these updates as one. It simplifies the work, delivers more insight into the management of the directory, and issues are more quickly resolved in larger pieces.

Groups have existed for a long time, and the concept is still very relevant. That's why you can find group management in almost every application currently available. Okta is no exception and relies heavily on group management to consolidate user structures, application assignments, and policy enforcement.

Types of groups in Okta

Okta is always created with one default group, the **everyone** group. Even though this is a good name, the fact that it can't be deleted or renamed results in the group itself becoming hard to use in several instances. Assigning applications to this group allows everyone within Okta to gain access to the app. This includes any outside or third-party users that aren't part of the organization. Policies using this group mean that there is no distinction between users. In the hierarchy of policy setup, these policies should be considered last in the row, as it will catch everyone. Okta can manage several different types of groups:

- Okta groups
- Directory groups
- Application groups

Okta groups are the standard grouping method within Okta Universal Directory. These groups can be created from within Okta and can be managed to do multiple things. Users can be assigned to groups. Applications can be assigned, as well as managing any provisioning for the assigned users. Directories can be attached to the groups, allowing users to be provisioned into the directory:

Figure 2.9 – Group interface in Okta

Creating an Okta group can be done via the admin interface. You can name the group and add additional information to clarify the group's function. Once the group is created, it will receive a unique ID, which is not changeable and can be used in functions and API calls.

Groups can also be created by using Okta's API. Using the API allows the fast creation of groups, especially if you need to create a lot of them in a short amount of time. We will go through this more in *Chapter 7, API Management*.

Okta can show different types of groups. Directory groups will be shown once you have set up the group's OU within the directory integration. These groups will be visualized with a different icon in the group list than Okta groups. These groups don't allow user assignments from Okta; it is a visual of the group in AD and is only manageable by the AD. In the groups overview pane, you will find that the groups are prepopulated with users:

Figure 2.10 – Layout of an AD group

The users shown in those groups are users that are also in Okta. These identities have been connected, with the import and matching we've been through earlier, and therefore, the group can show the corresponding users in the integrated directory. If users are not shown in the group, but exist in the directory group within the directory itself, this means the user doesn't have a corresponding user identity in Okta. For instance, it may be that the user isn't in one of the OUs Okta is importing from.

Directory groups can be assigned with applications. This means that if you have a structure that works for you within your directory, you do not need to create Okta groups to recreate this structure. If you need to create more than the directory shows, adding Okta groups would be one choice; adding more groups through the directory is another. Depending on the situation, it can be advisable to leave the directory as is, and recreate the directory structure with Okta groups to have more options and capabilities. If you are thinking about replacing AD down the line, this can be a good approach.

Certain applications are capable of showing groups just like the directories do. By setting up provisioning and allowing group import, you can do this with applications such as the following:

- Google Workspace
- Office 365
- Slack
- Box
- BambooHR
- Workday
- Jira

The list is constantly growing, and Okta works hard to add more and more group integrations to allow even more and better management of users across all systems:

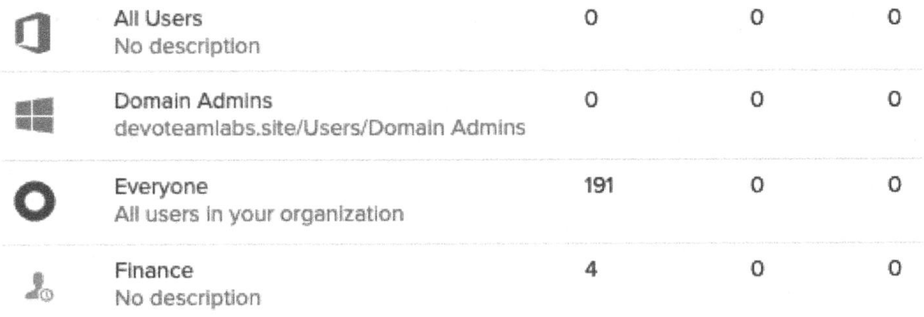

All Users No description	0	0	0	
Domain Admins devoteamlabs.site/Users/Domain Admins	0	0	0	
Everyone All users in your organization	191	0	0	
Finance No description	4	0	0	

Figure 2.11 – Different types of groups with the number of users in them

Application groups act the same way as directory groups do. User counts show the connected identities, and users can't be added to these groups. Applications can be assigned, but based on the fact that it's an application group, assigning other applications can be considered a bad practice.

Using AD groups

Okta has a deep integration with AD and handles AD groups based on their type:

- **Universal Security Groups (USGs)**
- **Distribution Groups (DGs)**

These two groups are imported and handled differently when it comes to user assignments.

Universal Security Groups

USGs can be imported through manual or periodic imports, and when an unknown user signs in to Okta for the first time, leverage JIT provisioning. Importing USGs can be done as full and incremental imports. If a user is unknown and signs in for the first time to Okta between imports, Okta will check whether the user is part of the domain, import any USGs that the user is part of within the synchronized OUs, and import the user with its corresponding profile. This allows Okta to always be up to date on any changes during events triggered by users when logging in.

If a user logs in to Okta and their USG is outside of the domain, the USG will not be imported, but the user will be added individually to Okta. If the second domain gets added later, or if the OU in which the USG resides is added for synchronization, any new USGs will be imported into Okta during a next scheduled import or manual import, or added when a user is JIT provisioned.

Once domains are added, Okta can see within these domains. With OUs that have been selected to synchronize, Okta is capable of joining users together that are part of different domains. Users that are manually moved out of the synchronized domain and/or OUs will no longer have access to Okta and integrated services. This method is commonly used by AD administrators.

Okta isn't capable of detecting nested groups within the synchronized groups. Okta will see the users of these nested groups as users within the parent group and treat them as such. If this happens accidentally, Okta will not be able to roll back the assignments. This can result in unwanted assignments. JIT provisioning will be able to resolve this problem and remove the user from the synchronized parent group. This does require oversight, as users themselves need to log in; an admin cannot do this for them.

Distribution groups

DGs are handled differently than USGs. Okta will handle user assignment like this.

Okta will synchronize the users assigned to USG in a connected domain during scheduled and manual imports, and during JIT provisioning. DG's will only allow synchronization during scheduled and manual imports, not during JIT provisioning.

This will mean that if a user is eligible to sign in to Okta, and hasn't been imported, their DG assignment in Okta have not been updated. This will result in login problems. Having the periodic import schedule set to every hour, which is the shortest import schedule, will in most cases be sufficient enough to resolve this problem.

Users that are part of a DG, and the DG is a member of a USG, will not inherit Okta access if the USG is not imported into Okta via a regular import.

Okta will not see the child DG, and thus its users, while JIT provisioning is occurring. Regular imports will be needed to allow membership of parent groups to be reflected in Okta.

Creating users in AD through Okta groups

User management can also be done from Okta. You can provision users into your AD by using dedicated Okta groups. This allows you to create group-assigned users in the corresponding OUs you set up synchronization with. This allows quick and bi-directional user management. It allows more granular management, and if your AD has specific OUs you want your users to reside in, you can attach all of these OUs to corresponding Okta groups. Each of these can have different setups and reasoning to do so.

Additionally, you can synchronize the users with extra AD attributes filled with Okta profile attribute values. This will synchronize valuable details across all your profile environments. Simply put, you can make sure your users have the correct details from and to the AD and Okta during any moment in their life cycle.

Pushing groups

Pushing groups is a functionality that lets you create or manage existing groups in directories and applications. To be able to do group push, the target application has to be set up with provisioning. While some applications have good integrations, others are limited. If the target app supports group push, the creation of new groups is possible. If the target app also supports enhanced group push, Okta can take control of existing groups in the app and there is no need to recreate the group structure. During this takeover of groups, Okta will overwrite the existing app group name with the Okta pushed group name. This might need further investigation within the application to see whether this is a desired outcome.

Certain elements to consider while setting up group push are as follows:

- The group push requires application provisioning.
- Group members assigned to the synchronized group have to be previously provisioned and assigned to the target application.
- Pushing AD groups require permission to create and manage users within groups based on the AD service account used in the integration.
- Okta won't allow groups to be pushed that are also used to provision users into the same target application.
- Usage of other application groups is allowed. Be careful with using other application groups or directory groups, as these can change based on internal management.

Setting up pushed groups can be done within the **Push Groups** tab of a target application. By clicking on the **Push Groups** tab, you are presented with a configuration window:

Figure 2.12 – Push group for an application

Clicking on the green **Push Groups** button allows you to start the setup of a pushed group. Okta allows you to do this manually by selecting a group by name, or even by using rule-based automation to add groups based on conditions:

Figure 2.13 – The Push Groups button

Let's set up a group push rule. First, we will explain how to do it manually, and then we will explain how to set up a rule-based group push.

Setting up a group push manually is done with the following steps:

1. Click on **Push Groups**.
2. Select **Find groups by name**.
3. Search for the desired group to push.
4. Optionally, select **Push group membership immediately**.

This allows you to work with different options. Depending on your integration, you can have either just the option to create a group or the option to choose between creation or linking to an existing group. In both scenarios, the options are the same:

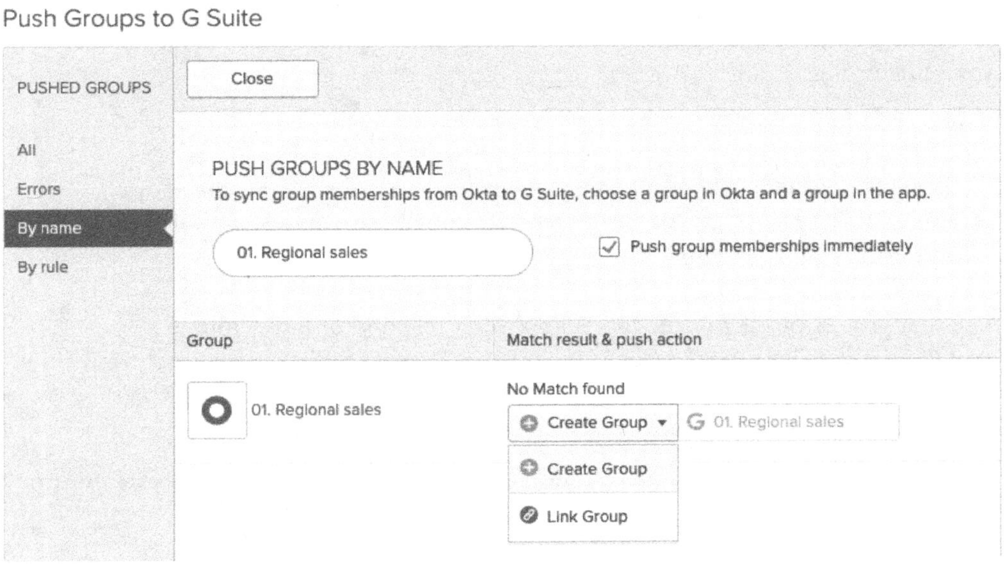

Push Groups to G Suite

Figure 2.14 – Push groups matching options

Choose to either create a new group or a link group.

If you select **New Group**, do the following:

- Create the new group.
- Set the desired application group name.

If you select **Link Group**, do the following:

- Select the desired group you want to link to.
- Click **Save**.

If you are going to use the group push with rules, the setup slightly differs. Let's see how that is done. Click on **Push Groups**:

1. Select **Find Groups by rule**.
2. Give the rule a name.
3. Create the rule with either name conditions or description conditions — for example, *Push all groups with 'Sales' in the name to the target app*.

Okta will immediately synchronize all found groups to the application

This will only allow new groups to be pushed.

Group push rules will find all groups across all applications and directories. This means it can have a huge impact if certain applications have similar group names that are found by the group push rule.

> **Tip**
> If you do have multiple groups with the same name from incoming directories, group similar named groups into a new Okta group with a more unique name, and synchronize that into the target application.

It can be that groups pushed to the target app won't respond or have trouble synchronizing users. Turning the push rule off and on will trigger a new synchronization. It is a common mistake that users are added to the pushed group but not to the provisioned group and are therefore not visible in the target app or directory.

Sometimes, new groups in the target app don't show for linking. Using the **Refresh App Groups** function will do a fresh import of the groups from the target app:

Figure 2.15 – Button to refresh groups

If for some reason you want to delete a pushed group, you can choose to deactivate the group push. This will stop any further synchronization of the group toward the target app or directory, but the current pushed group in the app or directory will keep existing with its current set of users. You can also choose to unlink the group; this will present you with the extra option of deleting the group in the target app or directory:

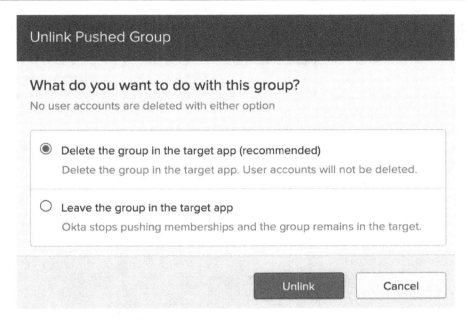

Figure 2.16 – Dialog window with options to unlink pushed groups

By selecting the recommended option, Okta will delete the group, and users in that group will not be deprovisioned or lose access to the application or directory. The group itself will no longer be available and functionalities within the application or directory no longer apply to those users based on the group pushed.

Bulk editing groups can also be done by selecting the option. Additional tick boxes will appear beside the groups. You can then either choose to deactivate the group sync or delete the groups from the target application or directory:

Figure 2.17 – How to bulk edit pushed groups

During the steps of setting up a pushed group, Okta allows linking groups from within Okta to the target application or directory. By default, the group will be named as the group it's linked too. Optionally, you can turn that off and allow the original name to exist within the target application or directory. It can be somewhat troublesome to find the correct links if those names differ a lot, but if there are justified reasons not to change them, this option will be your option of choice:

Figure 2.18 – Icon to access settings

Turning off this feature after you have already linked groups will not reinstate the original names of the target groups. These will stay changed. Only new groups pushed will follow this option:

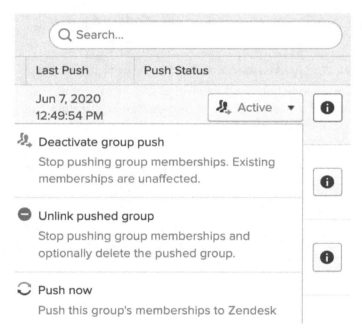

Figure 2.19 – Options for pushed groups

If you choose not to push immediately during the setup of a group push, you can force it to push in the main screen after saving the group push. This will trigger a forced push to the target group.

Deleting groups

Deleting a group can sometimes be a good habit to keep your directory clean. Having all these groups in the group list can create unwanted double entries and longer loading times, and make it harder to find groups using search.

The different types of groups can be deleted in different ways, but there are some common elements to consider:

- Okta groups can be deleted regardless of applications and user assignments.
- Application groups can be deleted in bulk through the **Integrations** tab of the provisioning settings by unticking the **import Groups** box.
- Application groups won't be deleted if still in use by group rules, policies, and push group mappings.
- Directory groups can be deleted by deleting or removing them from synchronized OUs in the directory. Okta will update accordingly during an upcoming import.
- Using the API, Okta and application groups can be deleted if previous points are considered.
- Application groups deleted through the API will be re-imported by the application on the next import.

By not being too dependent on imported groups, application groups won't have too much impact on the directory set up of Okta.

Important note

Additionally, nowhere in the group interface is it clear if the group is used for policies. Deleting groups can have an impact on how policies behave. Be aware and double-check whether the group is used in any way before deleting a group from Okta.

Assigning applications to groups

Setting up applications can be quite daunting, and doing it on a per-person basis is simply tedious work. Using groups can alleviate the pain and allow more structural management of app assignments. Any type of application can be added to any type of group in Okta. This allows granular management based on Okta, directory, and application groups.

Applications assigned to groups have no hierarchical priority, and management is done in one simple interface. Depending on the type of application being provisioned, or the sign-on settings being configured, the group can be used in different and combined methods.

The simplest method is to have **Single Sign-On (SSO)** applications added. Users are assigned to the application, based on their group membership, and will therefore follow the needed sign-on method, configured for that specific application.

Applications assigned to groups with provisioning will ask for more group-based configurations to make sure all assigned users receive the same provisioning into the application.

Lastly, you can combine sign-on methods with provisioning in an assigned application in a group.

As applications might need more than one group to configure their users, multiple groups can allow more granular management of, but not limited to, the following:

- Profile attributes
- Licenses
- Roles

In certain cases, using the combination of groups can be used to add multiple attribute values to the user while provisioning the user into the target application. Think of combining license types for Office 365 by using and assigning them through different groups, or combining multiple permission sets in Salesforce by having users be part of different groups to do just that.

Setting up the provisioning methods will be further discussed in *Chapter 5*, *Automating Using Life Cycle Management*.

Now that we've learned about different types of groups and how to use them, we will look at some best practices.

Some best practices for group usage

Here are some best practices on how to use the different types of groups in Okta.

Naming Okta groups

Okta groups only go one level deep, meaning there is no capability of nesting groups, or creating a hierarchy. To still allow this to happen, it is recommended to name your Okta groups with a number in the front of it. This will help in a few ways:

- Your groups will float to the top, as Okta will show the groups based on naming order.

- You can determine the structure of these groups.

- You can create a nested method by using decimal sub numbers.

This is demonstrated in the following screenshot:

Source	Name	People	Apps	Directories
⬤	00. Organization All apps for the whole org	104	7	0
⬤	00. organization - managed devices No description	1	2	1
⬤	00.1 Stockholm HQ Everyone @ HQ	33	0	0
⬤	00.2 New York office No description	36	0	0
⬤	00.3 All remote Remote workers across the globe	30	0	0
⬤	01. Sales No description	42	3	0
⬤	02. Marketing No description	27	1	0
⬤	03. Finance No description	24	1	0

Figure 2.20 – Suggestion on Okta group naming

As you can see here, you can mimic nested groups using numbering.

Structuring the groups

Creating structure in groups helps with better oversight, organization, and management of what they do and what they are used for. Reflecting your organization will make it easy to understand what access is based on, and normally, that organizational structure will be the cornerstone for any application setup needed. Trying to map out the deepest, smallest end groups will allow you to be as granular as possible.

Using the groups

Setting up a policy for how you will be using groups that make sense to your organization will help in your overall group usage in other ways as well. The same group used to assign sales applications can also be used for sales policies, and be pushed into applications as the sales group. This means that one group can do multiple things.

Specific application groups

In some scenarios, you can't simply automate within the organizational structure. But by numbering a group range specifically for applications, you can always find and structure it in a way that shows the different groups used for different applications. Usually, these are used for provisioning different licenses or roles. Creating a range higher up (for example, 70.XX for all specific apps) allows you to create group rules that send users to correct groups. Having that range will keep the Okta groups together, and stop them from floating into the abyss of all the groups imported into Okta.

Import only on a need basis

If you are setting up applications with provisioning, but you see no need for the groups to be imported, don't turn it on. Okta will be able to import quicker and the groups will not show up in your search queries.

Using directory groups

If you are heavily reliant on your directory, it may be the best move not to recreate the group structure again with Okta groups. Even though they might have some more benefits, managing two sides of the coin will allow more errors and more interpretation when troubleshooting. As AD and LDAP have a special relationship with Okta, it might be wise not to do so.

On the other hand, if you are looking for a way to divert from your directory, or legacy decisions have resulted in a messy structure, recreating a fresh and strong Okta group structure can be very helpful for your usage toward applications and other possible directories.

Using application groups

Usually, application groups already exist before Okta integrates with the app. Most of the time, the structure of the app has been owned by someone other than the IT or security team that is going to manage Okta. This can lead to fragmented and possible overuse of groups within that application. Using that as a structure to manage your users in Okta and toward other applications and directories is not considered a wise method; especially when the groups are used for policies, the application owner might *unknowingly* scramble the groups and in doing so remove access management.

Using the application groups to allow group push or group rules to synchronize users from an application group to an Okta group is considered the best way to use these.

If you are setting up the structure with our recommended naming convention, consider turning off the overwrite application group names, because this can have an impact. This is highly dependent on your situations and setup.

Summary

In this chapter, we learned about Universal Directory and what we can do with it. We looked at how to integrate with your existing directories, and you now have a full understanding of how to install and configure the different agents you might need. We have looked at the different kinds of users that Okta handles, and how to work with their attributes using profile mastering. Then, we took a deep dive into the different types of groups available, and how to use them to make your workload easier — for instance, for assignments. We finished off by highlighting some best practices when you set up and work with your groups.

In the next chapter, we will go into Okta's SSO capabilities and explain how to utilize the **Okta Integration Network**.

3
Single Sign-On for a Great End User Experience

Single Sign-On (SSO) is a very user-friendly feature. But it also has great security benefits that will make any IT administrator happy.

In this chapter, we will look at Okta's SSO functionalities and how they will help your end users. We will look at how you can utilize the Okta Integration Network, but before that, we will look into the different connections you can make with various applications. We will also look at the difference between Okta- and application-initiated sign-on flows, as well as IdP discovery.

We will look at the following topics in this chapter:

- Using Single Sign-On with Okta
- Using the Okta dashboard and Okta Mobile app
- The Okta Integration Network
- Using Secure Web Authentication applications

- Using SAML and OpenID Connect applications
- Managing inbound SSO
- IdP discovery

Using Single Sign-On with Okta

While we will talk a lot about logging into different types of applications and their security steps, Okta, of course, has its own sign-in options. This is, in general, the cornerstone of every end user's experience. Their sign-on to Okta allows no further password inputs in any application beyond Okta. This first encounter with Okta's SSO ensures that the user has identified themselves according to the setup policies and are now allowed to sign into any integrated applications down the road.

The login process for Okta is straightforward and doesn't ask for any high-level understanding of the process. Signing in is as simple as any other application, but on the backend, you will see that Okta allows for a much more granular methodology, making sure all sign-ins are checked against any policy that has been set up.

Every Okta org is created with an `Okta.com` subdomain. These subdomains are determined at the moment the contract is signed with Okta, and changing them is difficult for Okta to do. Making sure you have the right one that your users remember is key.

As Okta wants to keep security as strong as possible, you will find that any subdomain will show you a login screen. This is to fend off bad parties in search of Okta orgs to start doing password spray attacks. Your end users could therefore also end up on a dummy subdomain, so making sure that your org is identifiable to your end users is important. Using Okta's option to set a sign-in background and login widget logo will help to identify the correct Okta org.

The sign-on policies are created in hierarchical order. When the Okta org is created, a default login policy is added to ensure anyone can log in from the start. Adding more policies to reflect your organization is highly preferable. Okta has different policies for different needs.

The password policies allow the granular management of users' passwords being used in different groups, directories, and situations. Let's take a look at both policies and their settings.

Password policies

Password policies determine the strength and management of the end user's passwords. You can create multiple policies and base them on conditions. Users might need to update their password to comply with your new or updated requirements next time they update their password.

When going to the section **Security | Authentication**, you land on the **Password** tab. Here, you can set your policies and accompanying rules:

Figure 3.1 – Possible hierarchy of password policies

As these policies work based on groups and in a hierarchical way, while using your password, you will be checked against the policies in numerical order from top to bottom to see if your account fits the conditions. Once it does, Okta will either request an update of the password if you meet stricter conditions, or it will let you sign in.

A password policy contains two sections: the general setup and policy rules for self-service.

The general settings allow you to set a name, the group(s) it belongs to, the password strength, duration, and a visual aid for the end user:

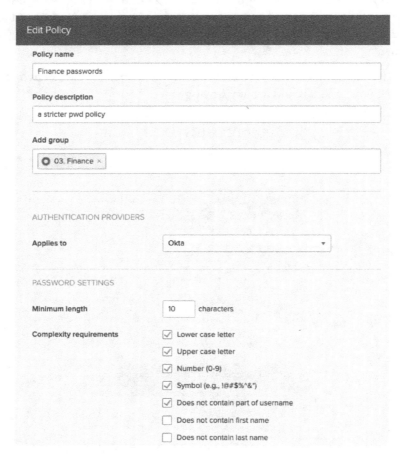

Figure 3.2 – Password policy settings

By adding a new policy or editing one, you will see the same settings window, allowing you to modify and set up the following:

- A policy name
- A brief description of the policy
- Assigned groups (this can be more than one)
- Application of usage, either Okta or Integrated Directory
- Minimum length of the password
- Complexity rules

Within **Complexity requirements**, there are many available options:

- Requiring a lowercase letter
- Requiring an uppercase letter
- Requiring the use of a number character
- Requiring a symbol
- Allowing or denying the use of (part of) a username
- Allowing or denying a first name in the password
- Allowing or denying a last name in the password

After this, the following configurations can be set:

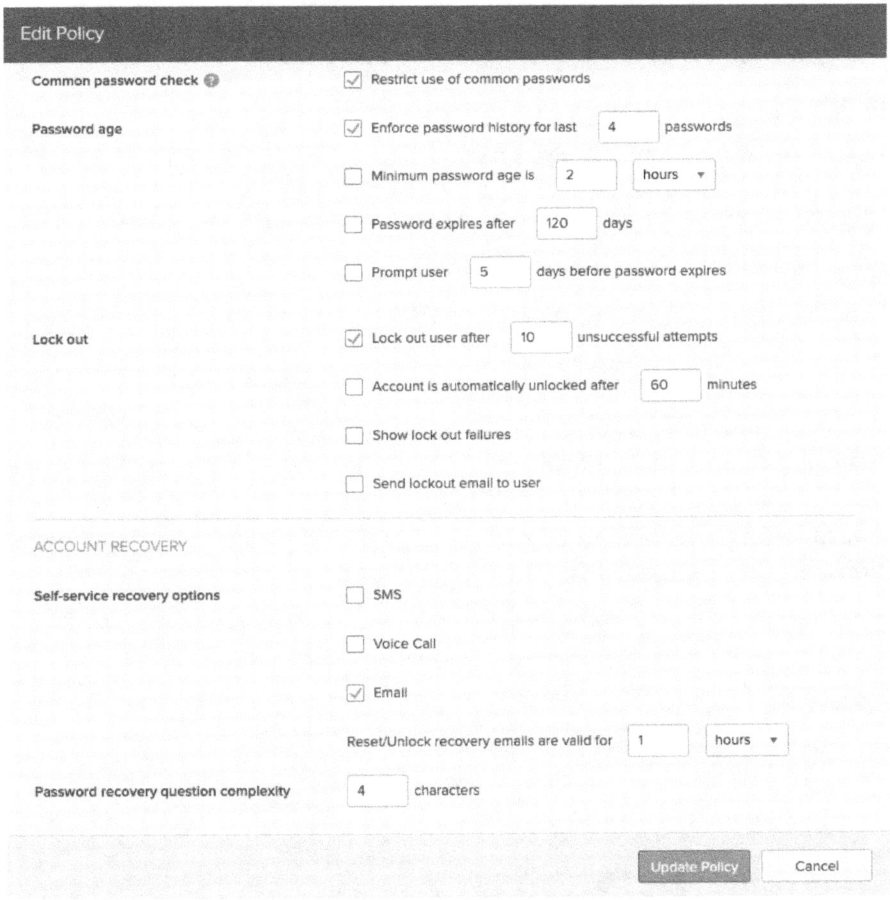

Figure 3.3 – Password complexity settings of a password policy

Start with **Common password check**, avoiding the use of common and easy to break passwords. Then move on to **Password age** conditions:

- Enforcing password history, denying the reuse of the same password
- Minimum password age, denying changing the password within a certain period
- Expiration period — the duration a password will be valid for
- Setting how long before the password expiration a user will be prompted within Okta's dashboard

After that, you will set **Lock out** settings:

- How many attempts a user can have before the account locks
- Allowing or denying automatic account unlocking after a preset duration
- Showing the number of failed attempts to log into Okta
- Sending a notification to the user when locked out

Lastly, you will set **ACCOUNT RECOVERY** options:

- Setting self-service recovery methods via **SMS**, **Voice Call**, and **Email**
- The duration of the validity of recovery emails
- The complexity of a password recovery question

> **Note**
> The complexity of the password recovery question isn't in regards to the question, but the length of the answer.

These password settings are then accompanied by password policy rules that allow setting the conditions for how users can self-reset their account:

Figure 3.4 – Password policy rule overview

Within a policy, you can add multiple rules to make sure all the different combinations are handled. Click the green **Add Rule** button to create an additional rule:

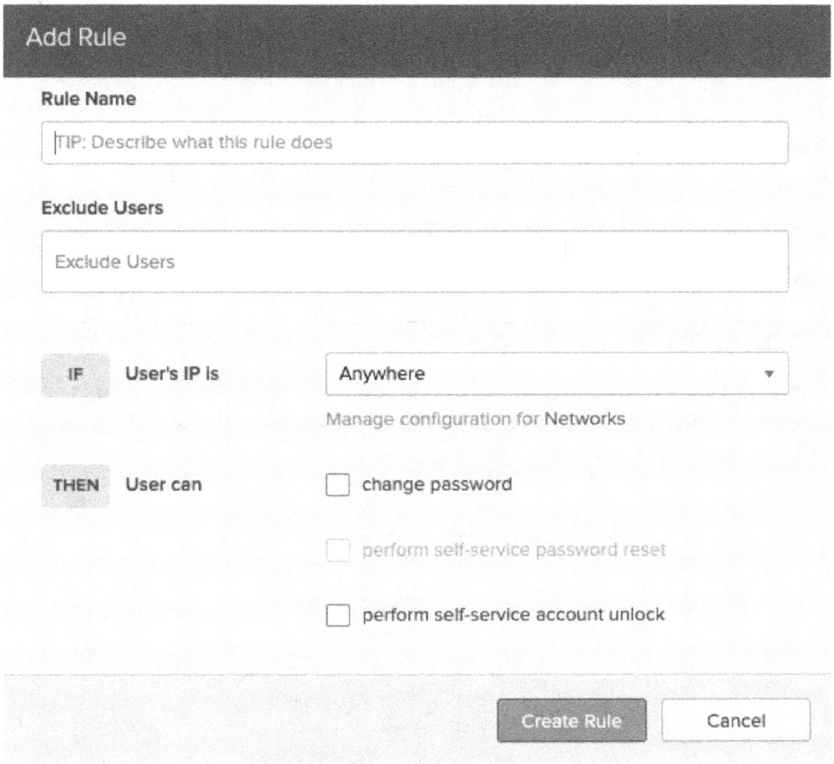

Figure 3.5 – Password policy rule settings

The rules contain the following settings as an IF/THEN set up:

- A rule name
- An option to exclude users from the rule

In IF User's IP is, you have following options:

- Selection of IP location: **Anywhere**, **In zone**, or **Not in zone**

Zones are managed within the zone's settings menu and will be explained more in *Chapter 5, Automate using Life cycle management.*

In THEN User can, you have following options:

- **change password**

  If **change password** is turned on, then **perform self-service password reset** will be available to be turned on.

- **perform self-service account unlock**

These rules allow room to manage the behavior of Okta towards end users.

After setting your password policies, your users need to follow sign-on policies to log in correctly. We will look at this section next.

Sign-on policies

Sign-on policies are rules that conditionally look at group assignments and rules that will grade the user's login attempts with a risk factor. Based on those conditions, a user is allowed, denied, or required to step up their security:

Figure 3.6 – Hierarchy of policies

Just like the password policies, sign-on policies are used in a hierarchal way and the user is checked from top to bottom until the conditions are met.

Setting a sign-on policy requires a group assignment. And the more the group is unique or filtered, the higher up the list it should be. If you have a policy at the top with a group that everyone is part of, no other rule will ever be hit.

To set up the policy, you click on the green **Add New Okta Sign-On Policy** button:

3.7 – Add New Okta Sign-On Policy

Then you will be presented with a small window with the following settings:

Add Policy

Policy Name

TIP: Describe what this policy does

Policy Description

Description

Assign to Groups

Assign to groups

Create Policy and Add Rule   Cancel

Figure 3.8 – Okta general sign-on policy settings

The window contains the following fields:

- **Policy Name**
- **Policy Description**
- Group assignment

After you click on **Create Policy and Add Rule**, you will be presented with the rule builder for that policy:

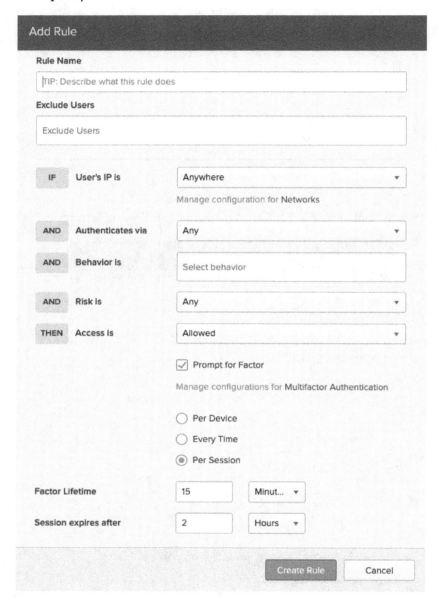

Figure 3.9 – Okta sign-on policy rule settings

In this window, you can use multiple conditions to check and set the security that is needed. This rule engine also works with an **IF**, **AND**, and **THEN** methodology.

The options are as follows:

- **Rule Name**
- Option to exclude users from the rule

Options under **IF** are as follows:

- **User's IP is**: **Anywhere, Inside zone**, or **Outside zone**

Options under **AND** are as follows:

- The user authenticates via any method or specifically via RADIUS.
- Their behavior contains conditions (see *Chapter 4, Increasing Security with Adaptive Multi-Factor Authentication*).
- Their risk is **Any, Low, Medium**, or **High** (these options are only available within the Advanced Lifecycle license, and are not visible if you don't have this license).

Options under **THEN** are as follows:

- **Access is**: **Allowed** or **Denied**

Additionally, you can add factor conditions. You can turn on or off whether prompting for a factor is needed, then decide when the rule will take place:

- **Per Device**: It will only prompt once per new device, or if the cookie is cleared in the browser.
- **Every Time**: The user is prompted every time they sign on to Okta, regardless of sessions and cookies.
- **Per Session**: This allows more granularity. Let's look at it.

You get two additional time-based options for the **Per Session** option:

- The lifetime of the factor itself — based on minutes, hours, or days
- The length of time the session expires after — based on minutes, hours, or days

Once you have set up your different policies for the different groups of users, you can ensure that the security is set based on the user's conditions.

Now that users are prompted to create a strong password based on the password policies, and they are allowed to access Okta based on the sign-on policies, the user can actually log in and start using Okta's SSO dashboard. We will go over what an end user can do on their dashboard in the next section.

Using the Okta dashboard and Okta Mobile app

Okta gives users a great experience by having a dashboard that all the user's applications are on. End users can arrange which apps go where and they can move them into different tabs to manage their environment even more. Okta's dashboard allows end users to set their personal passwords in applications and change and update these passwords later on. We will go through this in more detail later in this chapter. Depending on the settings, they can possibly also add personal applications through the personal application store, with over 5,000 applications. This only includes applications with passwords, because an end user cannot integrate Okta themselves with other applications using more integrable options.

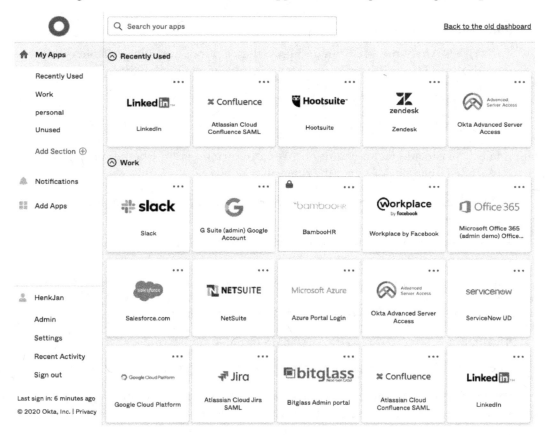

Figure 3.10 – End user's application dashboard

Once a new application is added, the user will see a notification bubble after they get onto the dashboard. If they don't read it, the notification will stay available in the menu on the left, under **Notifications**.

Within the same menu, the user can also edit their profile, which they can manage themselves. We will further deep dive into this in *Chapter 6, Customizing Your Okta GUI*.

The Okta Mobile app

The Okta Mobile app is the mobile version of the Okta dashboard. As an administrator, you can have users use the Okta Mobile app, determine which apps you want to have shown in the app, and choose what type of security on the phone is needed to be allowed access.

Logging into the Okta Mobile app for the first time requires the phone or mobile device to download the app from an app store: iOS — **Apple App Store**; Android — **the Google Play store**.

After downloading, you need to set up the environment details to get access:

Figure 3.11 – Login experience in Okta Mobile

Enter the following information:

- **Site Name** — your Okta domain name, as seen in the example in *Figure 3.11*

> **Important note**
> If you have an `okta-emea.com` domain, you will need to input the entire
> URL, otherwise, the app won't recognize your Okta org.

- **Username** — the full username of the user
- **Password** — the user's password

Once you have signed in, you will be asked to set a pin code. After you have done that, additional device related security, like Apple's Touch ID or Google's face unlock, can be added as a login method to sign into the Okta mobile app by the device itself. This allows strong authentication into the application.

After that is set up, you can access all your applications within the Okta Mobile app.

To hide an application from Okta Mobile, navigate to **Application** and click on the application you want to hide. In the **General** tab, under app **App settings**, click **Edit** and check the right box under **Application visibility**.

Now that we've looked at the end user side, we will go deeper into the administrator side.

Simpler administration with Okta Integration Network

For many organizations, a reason to start using Okta is to avoid the upkeep of multiple integrations. This was a problem Okta saw early on, and the **Okta Integration Network (OIN)** has been an important cornerstone of Okta for a long time. At this time, the OIN is gathering over 6,500 integrations to applications within a variety of product types. What's unique about this collection is that all protocols for SSO and APIs for provisioning are maintained by Okta. Integrations are not only for cloud apps but a collection of on-premise, web-based applications are also represented within these integrations. The integrations are for **Secure Web Authentication (SWA)**, **Security Assertion Markup Language (SAML)**, and **OpenID Connect (OIDC)** integrations. For applications supporting any of these methods, even if it's on-premise or VPN services, it's possible to integrate with Okta, even though there is no existing integration in the OIN — all of this will be explained below.

SAML has been around since 2002 and is considered the most commonly used SSO option by vendors and identity providers. SAML's protocols have gone through some iterations, from 1.1, 1.2, and the last and current standard, 2.0. There are still vendors that incorporated it when it was an earlier version. It's important to know that the older federations will work with Okta, but they are not cross-compatible with each other to set up and use.

As an administrator, there are two ways to interact with the OIN. You can go to Okta's website and search for different integrations, applications, or product segments. This is useful if you are thinking of selecting a new system, for instance, an HR system. Then you can easily go in and search for different applications and see what HR system has an integration that fits your needs.

But the way you will most frequently interact with the OIN is through the admin console. From there, you will navigate to **Applications | Applications**. By clicking **Add Application**, you will end up in what is basically a searchable catalog of all OIN-available integrations. The applications are divided into categories:

CATEGORIES

Featured	
API Management	6
Apps	6116
Apps for Good	9
CASB	3
Directories and HR Systems	13
Security Applications	662
Okta Applications	11
Okta Test Applications	14
VPN	22

Figure 3.12 – Available OIN categories

Most applications are available in the **Apps** category. Under **Directories and HR Systems**, you will find applications you can use as a directory source. You will probably search for an application. The tile of the application you want to integrate shows what available integration options you have, for instance, SWA, SAML, whether provisioning is enabled. The different integration types will be described later in this section:

Atlassian Jira Server

SAML, SWA, Provisioning

Figure 3.13 – Application tile when finding an integration

Clicking on a tile will bring you to a complete page about the integration. Here, you can read more about its capabilities. You will find the following:

- Overview — a description of the application
- Category — the OIN categories you will find this application under
- Last update — when the integration was last updated
- Capabilities — what protocol for access the integration supports as well as what provisioning features are available

Now that we have looked into the OIN, we will deep dive into the two different kinds of integration there are: SWA and federated (for instance, SAML).

We will specifically talk about the standardized ways to add an application that doesn't already have a preconfigured setup. Applications available in the OIN mostly come with extensive integration documentation and usually are well managed by both Okta and the SP

Basic integration with Secure Web Authentication

As mentioned earlier, there are a few different kinds of integration, and one of them is **SWA**. This integration type was created for any application that doesn't support federated authentication. That means that the application does not support or allow an SSO flow where a user's authentication token is trusted across multiple systems or platforms. With SWA, Okta stores a user's credentials in a secure way, with strong encryption and a customer-specific private key. When an end user clicks on the application tile, the credentials are sent to the application login page via SSL. When setting up SWA integration, you can configure the credentials settings in the following ways:

- The user sets the username and password
- The administrator sets the username and password
- The administrator sets the username, the user sets the password
- The administrator sets the username, the password is the same as the Okta password
- Users share a single username and password set by the administrator

The different configurations are quite self-explanatory, but we'll go through some things to think about.

The use case where users set the username and password would typically be used for an application you are already using in your organization, where the username and password already exists. It could also be for personal accounts you want to enable through Okta, such as LinkedIn.

The use case where the administrator sets both would be, for instance, when a company rolls out a new application. It provides strong administrator control, as the end user never sees their credentials. For this approach to work, the best thing would be to disable any possibility for end users to reset and change their password within the application.

These are the steps to get this configuration to work:

1. Create the user and set a password in the application.

2. In Okta, create the integration in OIN.

3. Navigate to the **Sign On** tab on the **Applications** page.

4. Edit the **SIGN ON METHODS** option.

5. Assign the application to the user and set the credentials.

It's good to know that, after this step, the password will never be visible in Okta again, to either the end user or the administrator.

For the option where the password is the same as for Okta, the application must have provisioning capabilities. After the account is created in the downstream application, the username is connected through provisioning.

The last option is when multiple users share one account. This could, for instance, be an organization's social media account. As an administrator, you set the credentials and by assigning the application to users, they get access without ever seeing the credentials. This adds multiple security measures, and when a user leaves the organization, they will not be able to access the application again after losing access to Okta.

For SWA applications to work, the user needs to install the Okta Browser Plugin. The plugin is available through the app stores of the main, commonly used browsers. For Internet Explorer, an administrator needs to give end users permission to download it directly from the Okta end user dashboard. The plugin is needed for security reasons. When an end user clicks on an SWA application, a new tab is opened. The credentials are collected from Okta through encrypted SSL and posted to the application. The plugin only works with trusted and verified sites:

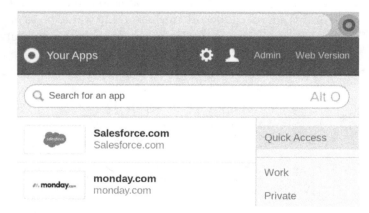

Figure 3.14 – Interface of the Okta Browser Plugin

The plugin can do a lot of things:

- Initiate an Okta login — If an end user clicks on an application in the Okta Browser Plugin but isn't logged into Okta, the user will be prompted to log into Okta on the application page.

- Automatically sign-in to apps — If the user is already signed into Okta and navigates directly to the application's login page, the plugin will fill in the credentials and sign the user in.

- Fill in credentials — If the user previously hasn't used an SWA app, and fills in credentials and then navigates to that application, the user will get to enter the data and save it to Okta.

- Update passwords — If a user is in an application and changes the password, the plugin can save the new password. It can also enter the previous password if needed for the password update.

- Switch users — You can easily switch the active user by clicking the person symbol and choosing the account to see.

- Admin console quick access — For admins, there is a link to go directly to the admin console, instead of to the end user dashboard.

For applications without an SWA application in the OIN, you can easily create one yourself with the templates available. There is also an integrations wizard, **Application Integration Wizard (AIW)**. Integration with the wizard is easy but doesn't work for all applications, so we will start going through the templates. There are three main template types:

- Template App
- Template Plugin App
- Template Frame Plugin App

Template Plugin App has subcategories:

- Template App 3 fields
- Template 2 Page Plugin App
- Template Basic Auth App

So how and when should we use them? Navigate to **Applications | Applications**, and click **Add Application**. Search for `Template` and click **See All Results**.

Use the Template App if your application supports authentication via a form POST. On the **General** settings page, you will enter the following information:

- **URL**: The URL of the form you are posting to. Note that this is not the URL of the page where you see the form.

- **Username and Password parameters**: Enter the parameters that contain the credential data.

- **Optional parameters**: Possibly more static data that is needed and sent during login.

- **Application Visibility**: Select whether the application should be visible to users.

- **Browser plugin auto-submit**: Select this option if you want to submit the user's credentials immediately when a user navigates to the applications.

The Template Plugin App and its subcategory templates are configured similarly, so we'll go through them together. Start the same way by searching for the Template application you want to set up on the **Add Applications** page. As before, in **General settings**, do the following configurations:

- **Application label**: The name you want to be shown to your end users.

- **Login URL**: The URL to the page where the sign-in form is visible.

- **Frame URL**: The URL for the actual frame.

- **Redirect URL**: If the URL to the sign-in page redirects you, enter that URL here.

- **Regular expression**: This is optional; you can define a pattern to restrict access to URLs.

- **Username field**: The CSS selector for the username field.

- **Password field**: The CSS selector for the password field.

- **Login button**: The CSS selector for the login button.

- **Checkbox**: The CSS selector for a checkbox (for example, this can be for a remember me or Agree to terms checkbox on a login page).

- **Next button**: The CSS selector for the button to direct you to the next page.

- **Extra field selector**: The CSS selector for the extra field (possible in the Template Plugin App 3 fields; this can, for instance, be a company name needed for login).

- **Extra field value**: Enter the value for the extra field.

As you might have noticed, the Template Plugin App is using the CSS selectors rather than providing parameters. So how do you find these CSS selectors?

- Open the page with the login form.

- Click in one of the fields, right-click, and select **Inspect** in the menu that appears.

This opens the Chrome developer tool. In the **Elements** pane, you'll find the ID and type needed for your CSS selector:

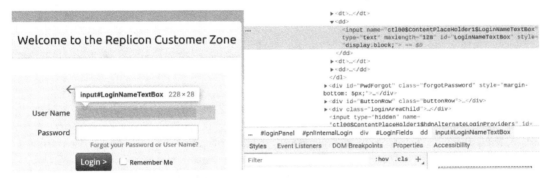

Figure 3.15 – Example of input to a CSS selector

That's the basic configuration possibilities of the different SWA applications. Let's move on to look at how to set this up using the App Integration Wizard **(AIW)**.

SWA with the AIW

An easy way to get integration with an application with SWA is to use the AIW, by navigating to **Application | Application**, and then clicking on **Add Application**. If you then click the green **Create new App** button, you will get prompted to choose SWA, SAML, or OIDC application integration. Choose **SWA**. When clicking **Next**, you will be prompted to fill in some information:

- **App name**: The name visible to your end users.

- **App's login page URL**: The URL to the login page.

- **App logo**: Optionally, you can upload a logo picture, which makes it easier for end users to navigate to the right icon on their dashboard.

- **App visibility**: You can choose to not show the icon to end users on their dashboard, and/or to not show it in Okta Mobile (mobile access).

- **App type**: If this integration is with an internally created application that is not intended to be used outside of the organization, check this box.

After these settings, you will be able to decide how the username and password are to be set, as per earlier instructions.

In general, if you want to find more information on adding applications, refer to https://help.okta.com/en/prod/Content/Topics/Apps/Apps_Apps.htm.

Using SAML and OpenID Connect applications

To fully embrace the capabilities of Okta's SSO, it is recommended to use federation protocols such as **Security Assertion Markup Language** (**SAML**) and **OpenID Connect** (**OIDC**). Both handle and look at login flows differently, but they share one common feature, they allow an application to delegate their authentication to an **Identity Provider** (**IdP**) such as Okta. This means that there is no reason to have a password in your application anymore. The user is no longer responsible for a strong unused password, but the application will refer to the IdP for authentication. We will be looking at both, to see what they have in common and where they differ.

SAML is a framework built upon XML and allows interactions between an IdP and **Service Provider** (**SP**), to communicate user authentication, entitlement, and attribute information. The flexibility of the XML allows it be modified and to send different relevant information based on the integration of the IdP and SP.

Every message is secured by using a signed X.509. During the setup of the SSO integration, a public certificate is given to the SP to verify any incoming requests. A SAML response sent by the IdP will be signed with a private key and can be verified against the uploaded public certificate. This allows the SP to check the origin and trust the IdP.

An example of what a typical login flow from the SP looks like is shown in *Figure 3.16*:

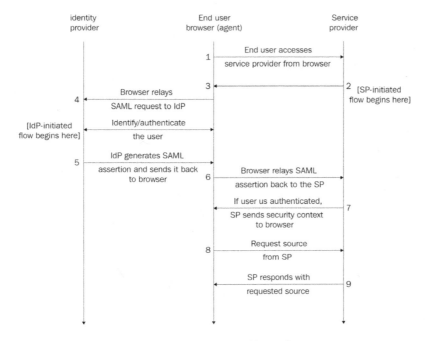

Figure 3.16 – SP-initiated login flow

While this figure starts with the user going to the SP (SP-initiated login flow), it can also be that a user starts at the IdP (IdP-initiated flow). They look similar, but the start of the request happens somewhere else.

While nowadays it's more and more common that authentication flows also require consent requests, for example, allowing access to parts of data in the underlying application, SAML doesn't have that built into its core. It can be custom-added into the login flow, but this only happens on the SP side and is usually not configurable for users and admins to turn on or set up.

For any application with SAML possibilities, but without available integration options in the OIN, it's possible to set up your own integration with the AIW. What this kind of integration does is to create the XML required for the SAML request. To be able to set this up, you will need information from your application provider, either documentation or via their support. To start setup, navigate to **Application | Application** and click **Add Application**. Click the **Create New App** button and on the pop-up window, select **SAML**, and click **Next**. On the first page, you will only enter the **General** settings:

- **App name**: The name visible to your end users.

- **App logo**: Optionally, you can upload a logo picture, which makes it easier for end users to navigate to the right icon on their dashboard.

- **App visibility**: You can choose to not show the icon to end users on their dashboard, and/or to not show it in Okta Mobile (mobile access).

Next, it's time to configure the SAML settings:

- **Single sign on URL**: This is the URL where the assertion is to be sent to with an HTTP POST. This can be called a SAML assertion consumer services URL in application documentation.

- **Audience URI (SP Entity ID)**: The unique identifier defined by the application, usually called an SP Entity ID.

- **Default RelayState**: This field identifies a specific application resource if an SSO has been initiated from an IdP. It's usually left blank.

- **Name ID format**: The processing rules and constraints for the assertion's subject statement for SAML. Leave as the default **Unspecified** unless your application requires something specific:

Figure 3.17 – Options for Name ID format

- **Application username**: Select the format you want the username for the application in — used for the assertion's subject statement.

- **Update application username on**: The only option is **Create and update**.

For **Application username**, there is a variety to choose from:

- Okta username
- Okta username prefix
- Email
- Email prefix
- Custom
- (none)

If needed there are an array of advanced settings:

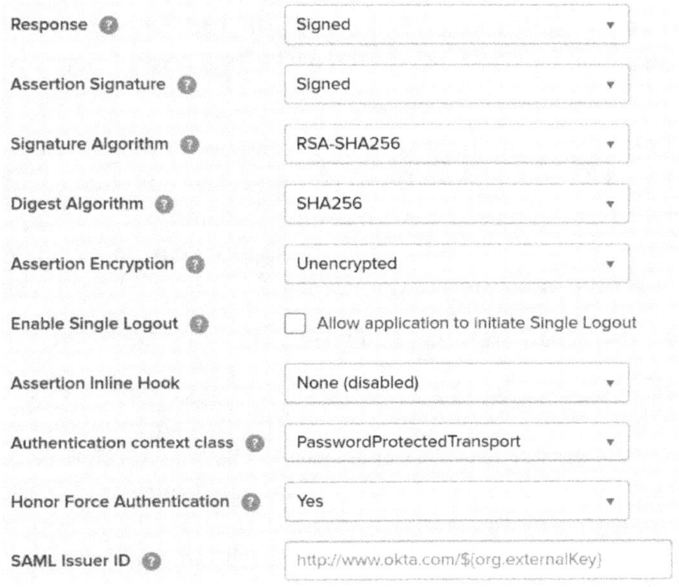

Figure 3.18 – Options for advanced settings

After that, you are able to set attribute statements, both per user and/or group. This can be used if the application needs any values set in a specific way or if any additional values are needed. To create these, you need to set **Name**, **Name format**, and **Value** or **Filter**:

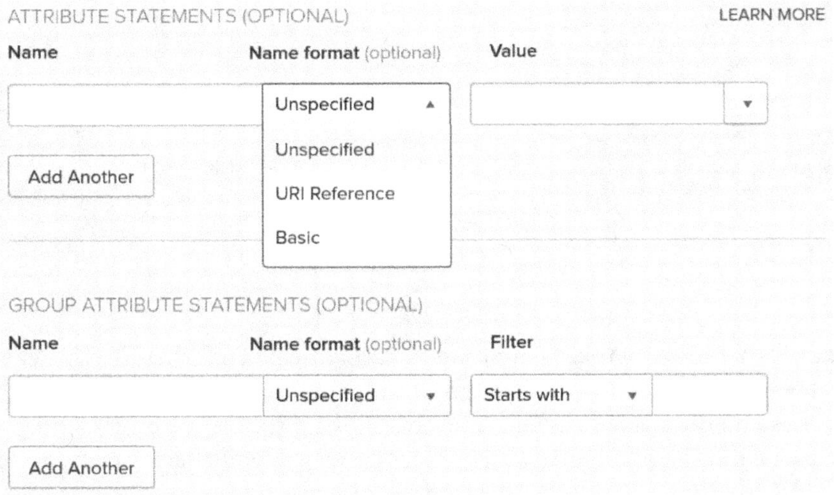

Figure 3.19 – Options to set attribute statements

It's possible to use Okta's Expression Language to change values. Read more about that in *Chapter 5, Automating Using Life cycle Management*. If you need to set more than one statement, you can use the **Add Another** button. If you need help or more information to fill in the statements, you can use the **LEARN MORE** link, which leads you to Okta's help site.

When you're done with all your settings, you can preview your SAML assertion before you start using it. If you have documentation from the application supplier, you can compare that against what you have set up the app with using this feature. If your application needs a certificate from Okta, you can download it from the right-side pane. When you're satisfied, click **Next** and you'll get the possibility to give feedback to Okta, before clicking **Done**.

Now let's take a look at OpenID Connect and how that is built and used.

OIDC is built on top of OAuth2.0, which is a framework to grant limited access to scopes of data requested by one service to another service. Think of an email plugin in Gmail asking for access to read, write, and delete contacts. While this doesn't seem like an authentication process, OIDC was created to use that platform to ask for and give limited access to accounts and by doing so creating a single sign-on method. Some very common and widely used OIDC methods are Google's **Login with Google+** or almost any other main social login option:

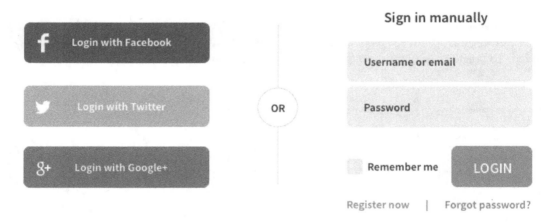

Figure 3.20 – Social logins using OIDC

The main idea is that identity tokens are used to authenticate with the IdP. This can be done through various OIDC flows (for example, implicit flow, authentication flow, hybrid flow). All of these methods have distinct ways of allowing secure communication between the relaying party and the IdP. During this process, the flow will check, verify, and secure the data and information while authenticating the user.

As there is no other way to log into the application other than using the IdP as the authentication server, it cannot overstep any additional policies and security features added to the flow. Okta is capable of adding policies as we already discussed. But if there's already a session ongoing for Okta, Okta can use application policies to add conditional risk assessment and add multifactor authentication to secure access to the application. This allows more checkpoints before someone accesses the requested application.

Setting up an OIDC application with the wizard can be done quite quickly. As before, you would navigate to **Application | Application** and click **Create new App**. Doing the initial setup is easy:

- **App name**: Enter the application name.
- **App logo**: Optionally upload a logo for the tile.
- **Login redirect URIs**: Where Okta will send the OAuth responses to. Due to how OIDC works, the URIs must be absolute. You can set more than one.
- **Logout redirect URIs**: Optionally, you can also set URIs for logout. There can be more than one. It's the same here — they have to be absolute.

By clicking **Save**, you have created the initial integration. You will now enter additional configurations on the settings page. The page opens automatically. There are a couple of different kinds of applications here, where settings differ a little. For web apps and single-page apps, you have the following settings:

- **Login initiated by**

Here, you have some available selections:

- **App Only**: There is no tile for the application for the end user to click; the application is instead started in the background.
- **Either Okta or App**: You get to choose the **Application visibility** option, then pick a **Login flow** option.
- **App Embed Link**: A link you can use to log into the OIDC client from outside of Okta.

Then you can move on to the following:

- **Initiate Login URI**: You can enter or change the existing link, to initiate the sign-in request

Click **Save**. If you need to, you can generate a new client secret. Do so by clicking **Edit** in that section of the page, then click **Generate New Client Secret**.

For native apps, you have your initial configurations in the **General Settings** section. In the section for **Client Credentials**, you can select an option for **Client Authentication**:

- Use **Proof Key for Code Exchange** (**PKCE**) (for public clients): This ensures that only the client that initially requested the token can redeem it and is recommended for native applications.

- Use client authentication: With this, the client secret is included in the client and sent with requests to prove the identity. This is not recommended for native distributed applications, since it's less secure.

As with web apps, you can generate a new client secret if needed.

That's all for integrations. Let's move on to inbound SSO.

Managing inbound SSO

Okta allows the use of external identity providers to log in to Okta, using their own user database and login methods. This can be a Microsoft, Google, or generic SAML application. You could have contractors or outside partners needing access to some of your applications that want their IdP to be the source to log in with. Using inbound SSO with Okta makes it possible to connect with other IdPs, and have their users login.

Even though Okta can easily connect to one of the aforementioned methods, we will focus specifically on connecting with a SAML IdP, allowing them to log in and have additional options to use:

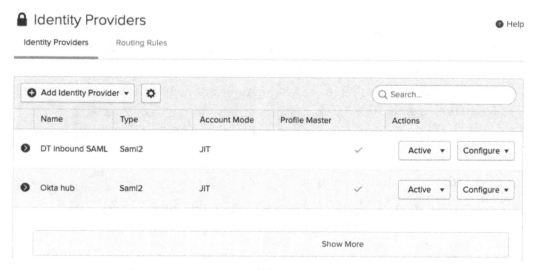

Figure 3.21 – Overview of identity providers configured

When navigating to **Security | Identity Providers**, you land on the overview page of all inbound SSO connections.

Clicking on the **Add Identity Provider** button will allow you to choose the type of IdP. We will be setting up a SAML IdP:

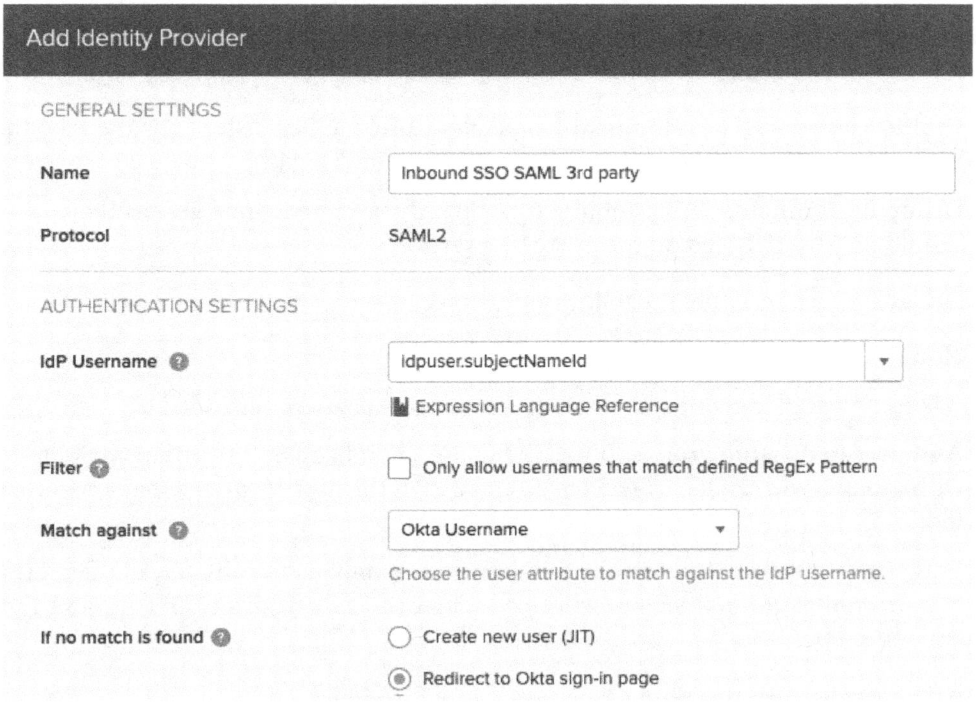

Figure 3.22 – Adding an identity provider

You will get a new window with settings to go through:

- **Name**: A name for the integration

- **Protocol**: A fixed value from the selection in the previous window

- **IdP Username**: An open field to add condition expressions to determine the IdP login name of the inbound user, or you can use the default values

- **Filter**: Allowing you to filter the inbound users using regex patterns

- **Match against**: Allowing you to choose the attribute you want the inbound username to be matched with to secure authentication

- **If no match is found**: Let's look deeper into this one

If no match is found, you get two options, where one has more features to it:

- **Redirect to Okta sign-in page**: Will send the user to manually authenticate into Okta.

- **Create new user (JIT)**: This option will open up more options to set.

Just-in-Time (JIT) provisioning was touched upon in *Chapter 2, Working with Universal Directory*. Let's look at the possibilities for how it works during IdP discovery:

- **Profile Master**: If JIT is allowed, you can allow users to be mastered by the inbound SSO and have their attributes updated every time they log in.

- **Group Assignments**: Provisioning users directly into predefined groups they should be part of, based on their SAML insertion.

For group assignments, we get the following options:

- **None**: No group assignment.

- **Assign to specific groups**: You can preset the groups users get added to.

- **Add user to missing groups**: If the SAML assertion has a SAML group attribute with groups, you can have Okta check and assign the user to groups that are in that filter.

- **Full sync of groups**: The same as missing groups, only Okta will sync all the groups fully from that group filter, but will also remove the user from any Okta groups that are not in the filter.

Back to the initial set up, there are a few more settings to finish off:

- **IdP Issuer URI**: The inbound IdP issues this URI

- **IdP Single Sign-On URL**: The sign-on URL provided by the IdP to log into.

- **IdP Signature Certificate**: A certificate provided by the IdP to upload into Okta.

If advanced settings are needed, you can open the advanced section and further set the values for **Request Binding, Request Signature, Request Signature Algorithm, Response Signature Verification, Response Signature Algorithm, Destination, Okta Assertion Consumer Service URL**, and **Max Clock Skew**.

Click **Add Identity Provider** to save the configuration.

After saving, the added identity provider will be on the list and active immediately. To complete the setup, you need to copy the ACS URL and Audience URI, and possibly the SAML metadata. These details can be added to the IdP setup:

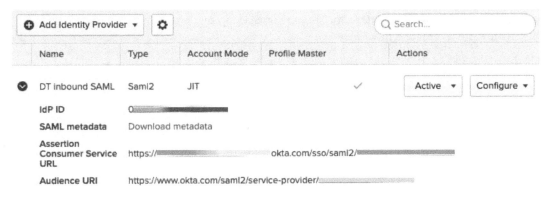

Figure 3.23 – Active identity provider

Depending on the inbound IdP, after configuration, it's wise to test the SSO into Okta, by having a user that is either in both systems or pushed from the inbound IdP through JIT and test the login.

Once this works, you can also use IdP discovery and route how a user needs to log in to Okta. We will discuss that in the following section.

IdP discovery

IdP discovery can also be called IdP routing rules, which might be a more telling name. With these routing rules, end users can be routed to different IdPs, depending on the context. The context can, in this case, be device related, IP or network zone context, or simply looking at the email subdomain. Rules can be set for each identity provider or combinations of user criteria. The rules are set in a hierarchy and if there is more than one rule that matches the current situation, the topmost will be used. Let's look into how to set this up.

The first prerequisite is that at least one IdP needs to be set up. Navigate to **Security |
Identity Providers**. If you don't have any set up, go back to the beginning of this section
to set one up. Even without an additional IdP, you can still set up routing rules for
networks, and if you have the IWA agent installed, you can set up rules for Desktop Single
Sign-on. Go to the **Routing rules** tab. There is one set up by default, where Okta is the IdP.
Click **Add Rule** to create a new one:

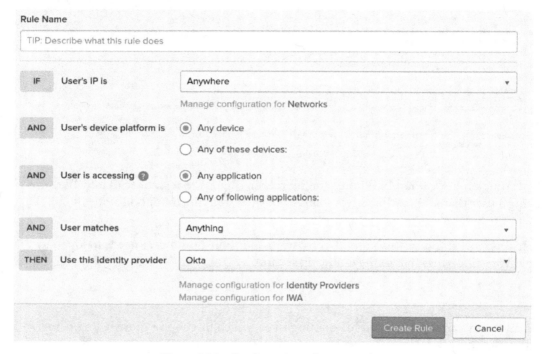

Figure 3.24 – Configuration of routing rules

Routing rules are **IF**, **AND**, and **THEN** statements:

- **Rule Name**: Give your rule a name that makes it easy to understand what the
  rule entails.

Under **IF**:

- **User's IP is**: If you want to use a zone here, you need to have that configured — see
  Chapter 4, *Increasing Security with Adaptive Multifactor Authentication*. Otherwise,
  you can set a rule that works in any zone (default).

Under **AND**:

- **User's device platform is**: Set any combination on mobile and desktop devices.
- **User is accessing**: It's possible to select one or multiple applications that this rule is targeting.
- **User matches**: Here, you select the login attribute that must match.

You will have the following options:

- **Anything**: It will apply to anyone.
- **Domain list on login**: If you log in from a specific domain, this rule applies to you. As the name implies, you can enter a full list of domains.
- **User attributes**: Select a user attribute, for instance, you might want a rule for a specific department.
- **Regex on login**: If neither the domain nor attribute is enough, you can combine them with any valid regular expression.

Under **THEN**:

- **Use this Identity Provider**: Select one of your available IdPs from the dropdown.

So, what are the use cases for these kinds of rules? For instance, if you use a hub-spoke model with multiple Oktas interconnected, or have multiple domains in your organization, you can easily set different IdPs for them. If you have both on- and off-network users, you might need to keep legacy authentication for off-network but use Okta for on-network. The sky is the limit.

As mentioned before, you can also have other social logins used as methods to sign into Okta. These options need to be set up in a similar way and require changes on the login page of Okta to be used. Or you can use these routing rules to use the normal login page, but have the user be transferred to their own social IdP for authentication. The choices are quite extensive.

Summary

In this chapter, you have been through the different integration methods supported by Okta, and how to integrate your organization's applications using the tools available. For your end users to access these applications via SSO securely, we've also looked into how to set password and sign-on policies and rules. To simplify login and the end user experience, we've also learned about inbound SSO and IdP discovery. We have also lightly touched upon the user dashboard and Okta Mobile application, to see how end users will integrate with Okta on a daily basis.

In the next chapter, we will go into the possibilities around multifactor authentication and the different settings and policies available.

4
Increasing Security with Adaptive Multi-Factor Authentication

Two-Factor Authentication (**2FA**) and **Multi-Factor Authentication** (**MFA**) are security features growing in many organizations to keep their users and data more secure. The two terms mentioned here are not the same, but rather an evolution from having two factors to having multiple factors. Instead of one type of factor, based on the context, users are asked to confirm who they are, by presenting something they know, such as their username and password, something they have, such as a physical card, token, or soft token on a device, and/or something they are, such as using biometrics. In this chapter, we will look at Okta's capabilities within this field, as well as the more advanced features of having your MFA adaptive. You will increase your skills in the following areas:

- Different types of factors
- Basic MFA settings
- Contextual access management

- Creating layered and app-specific policies
- Enrolling end users in MFA
- Securing VPN with MFA

Different types of factors

We will start by looking at the different types of factors that are available for working with Okta. These can be divided into three categories:

- Knowledge factors
- Possession factors
- Biometric factors

Let's look at them more closely.

Knowledge factors

Knowledge factors are the ones you need to memorize. First of all is your password, which needs to abide by the password requirements set up in Okta. Secondly, Okta allows a security question to be used as a knowledge factor. This factor is different from the security question used to do self-service resets and unlock features, explained in *Chapter 3, Single Sign-On for a Great End User Experience*.

By enabling the security question factor for your end users, they will receive a notification saying **Extra verification is required for your account** after their first sign on. End users are required to follow these steps:

1. Click the security question factor setup button.
2. Choose a security question and enter the password.

This security question answer has just a few limitations:

- The answer needs to be a minimum of four characters long.
- The answer cannot be the user's username or password.
- The answer cannot contain parts of the question.

With these limitations, you can expect that this type of factor isn't the strongest one available. But perhaps in certain situations it is a good way to allow users to log in with limited access.

The next category in line is possession factors.

Possession factors

Possession factors — that is, authentication by something you possess (something you have) — include the following:

- Okta Verify
- Google Authenticator
- SMS authentication
- Voice call authentication
- Email as a factor
- Third-party factors, such as Duo, an RSA token, and YubiKey

Let's look at these one by one.

Okta Verify

Okta Verify is an application developed by Okta. It can be used either with a **One-Time Password (OTP)** or with a push option. With OTP, the user opens the application and sees a pin code, and enters it in the browser. The six-digit pin code is generated by the industry standard. With push, the user only has to verify that they are trying to log in, by clicking **Yes, it's me** in the push notification.

Google Authenticator

Google Authenticator is an application developed by Google that has the same function as Okta Verify OTP. To use it, the end user needs to open the app and use the six-digit OTP to authenticate to get into Okta. After five unsuccessful attempts, the account in Okta is locked and needs to be reset by an administrator.

SMS authentication

Most people have experienced the *SMS authenticator*, where some sort of code is sent via SMS. As an administrator, this is a typical factor to enable, since end users are used to it and most people have a phone that can receive SMS. What would enrollment look like for your end users? End users will receive a notification saying **Extra verification is required for your account** after the first sign on. End users will need to follow these steps:

1. Click **Setup**.

2. Enter your phone number.

3. Confirm by entering the security code that was sent to that phone number.

After that, you're done!

> **Tip**
> Even though SMS is easy for your end users to handle and enroll on, it's not as secure as many people think. If this will be an active factor in your organization, you should also consider alternative factors to utilize. If the phone is lost or replaced, having extra factors to use to log in to Okta diminishes disruption for the end user.

Voice call authentication

Voice call authentication is a basic factor but is sometimes needed in some organizations. As a rule of thumb, this shouldn't be used if there aren't specific use cases for it. These could be that employees don't have a mobile device or that users are present in countries where cellphone data is limited. To set this up, users are, as previously described, notified that extra verification is needed:

1. Click **Setup**.

2. Click **Call** to push for a call and receive a confirmation code.

3. Enter the code, then click **Verify**, and then **Done**.

After voice call authentication, let's look at email as a factor.

Email as a factor

Email as a factor is exactly what it sounds like. End users will receive the OTP via email and they need to enter it on the login screen. If this factor is set as required, the user's primary email will automatically be used to send the OTP. The lifetime of the emailed OTP is set to 5 minutes. It can be increased by increments of 5 minutes up to 30 minutes. Just like the security question, email as a factor can be considered a weak choice, and should not be used as a basic factor.

Third-party factors such as Duo, an RSA token, and YubiKey

Okta supports an array of third-party factors, such as an RSA token, Symantec VIP, and Duo Security. These are set up differently, but with easy-to-follow instructions when enrolling the factors. For instance, a certificate is needed for setting up Symantec VIP. With the RSA hardware dongle, it's possible to use an on-premises agent from Okta, to enable on-premises MFA. The Okta agent then acts as a **Remote Authentication Dial-In User Service (RADIUS)** client and communicates with your RADIUS-enabled MFA server.

YubiKeys have a wide range of options and functionality, where they also use **Fast IDentity Online 2.0 (FIDO2)**. FIDO is a web API and uses cryptographic keys that are unique for every website. The authentication tokens cannot be compromised and the private keys never leave the end user's device. This eliminates all forms of password theft, as well as reduces the risk of phishing and replay attacks.

Biometric factors

Biometric factors — something you are — include WebAuthn FIDO2 (such as Windows Hello and Apple Touch ID). This is the most advanced and secure MFA option. End users with a MacBook with Touch ID or a Windows laptop with Windows Hello can simply identify themselves with their fingerprint on the reader or face scan. After the end user has enrolled with their machine to the Okta service, they will be prompted to authenticate with their biometrics at login.

In regards to any factor a user needs to enroll in, they will be prompted to do so based on the enrollment setup. Depending on the type of factor, instructions are given to make sure the user enrolls successfully.

We have learned what types of factors Okta support and how they are set up by the end users. Now, let's look at how to set them up from the admin panel and manage them from there. First, we'll discuss the basic features.

Basic MFA settings

Before deep-diving into Okta's adaptive functionalities, let's look at the basic settings that are available in the **Single Sign-On (SSO)** licenses. It's possible to set MFA both when signing in to Okta and when signing in to applications. Different levels of security and factors can be set for different logins. As an example, if Okta Verify is determined as safe enough to log in to Okta, biometrics might be added as a factor to log in as an administrator to a business-critical system. Before we can do anything, we have to enable the different kinds of factors available that you want to allow your end users to be able to enroll in. Navigate to **Security | Multifactor** in the top menu in the administrator console. On the first tab, you will choose which factors you want your end users to be able to use. Remember, any factors you enable aren't mandatory to all end users and are not active until end users actually enroll in them. You have your end users enroll in them by using policies. We will be able to create policies and assign them to different groups or users in the same way as we did for sign-on policies in *Chapter 3, Single Sign-On for a Great End User Experience*. The following screenshot shows the factor types:

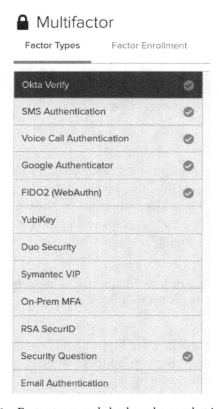

Figure 4.1 – Factor types and checkmarks on what is enabled

Click on any of the factors you want to enable. You will be able to read some information about the factor and then click **Deactivate** and change it to **Active**. For some factors, you have to add more information, such as security keys or certificates. Each type has instructions and is easy to enable.

When it comes to what factors to enable for your organization, there are some conditions to take into consideration. Security is, of course, very important. Factors such as hard tokens with FIDO2 are the strongest across different risk levels, but not the easiest to deploy among end users. In some organizations, employees don't receive a corporate phone, don't have a phone, or simply aren't allowed to use one during work. Setting up a factor such as **Voice Call Authentication** can be a problem in such scenarios.

After the factors you want to use are enabled, you will set how end users can enroll in them. There is always a default policy available. Navigate to the **Factor Enrollment** tab, then click **Add Multifactor Policy**:

Figure 4.2 – Hierarchy for multifactor policies

When clicking the **Add Multifactor Policy** button, you can add an additional enrollment policy.

> **Tip**
>
> Keeping your organization's structure in mind, you can set up policies to enforce enough security as per the requirements. Assigning department groups allows you to fine-grain access with accompanying factors based on requirements and level of access, all while combining different factors.

The setup of a factor is easy; you just have to enter the following:

1. **Policy name**: Give the policy a name that is easy to understand.

2. **Policy description**: Give it a description.

3. **Assign to Groups**: Add what groups should be assigned to the policy. When you start typing, you will see a list of available groups matching what you have written.

The last step is to select **Optional, Required**, or **Disabled** for the available factors. With the best practices tip preceding this, you would enter **Optional** or **Required** on only one factor and **Disabled** on the rest. Finish off by selecting **Create Policy**. After that is done, it's time to create a **rule** for the policy. The rule states under what conditions the policy will take place. Here is how to set it up:

1. **Rule Name**: Give the rule a clear name.

2. **Exclude Users**: If there are any users in the assigned groups that should be excluded from this rule, you can subtract them here.

After that, it's the usual **IF, AND**, and **THEN** statements:

1. **IF User's IP is**: Select **Anywhere, In zone**, or **Not in zone** from the dropdown. How to set up zones is explained later in this chapter.

2. **AND User is accessing**: Select a checkbox for Okta and/or applications. If you select applications, you will be able to set the appropriate application(s).

3. **THEN Enroll in Multi-factor**: Select from the first time a user is challenged for MFA, the first time a user signs in, or do not enroll.

Click **Create Rule**. As you can see, you can add multiple rules to a single policy, in order to have granular management of your users. You can activate and inactivate rules as you see fit; you can also edit them after creation if needed.

That's all you need to do to set up basic MFA for your organization. The multi-factors used in the basic settings are also what are used in Okta's Adaptive MFA functionalities. Let's look at what makes them adaptive.

Contextual access management

> **Important note**
> There are functionalities explained in this chapter — for instance, contextual access, dynamic zones, and behavior detection — that are only available with licenses for Adaptive MFA and Adaptive SSO products.

With Okta's contextual access, it becomes possible to use linear elements of different technologies to be combined into a more complete picture of the user's situation and requirements. Instead of assigning roles or groups to corresponding policies, Okta can act much more fluid with a multitude of vectors that are accessible and known by Okta during authentication moments.

By allowing this context to be used, Okta decides in a much more fine-grained method what to do and how to allow the user to sign in to Okta or the required application. Okta can build a risk assessment based on a stack of vectors, such as location, device, type of request, timing, and so on. From this, together with group assignments and roles, Okta can either ease or restrict access.

It is required that these requests are quickly assessed and automatically assigned to the user for that specific moment. Any delays can result in a different risk assessment because of changed conditions in any of the used vectors.

Part of the adaptive side of things is that users are notified about these decisions and changes. If the risk goes up during the process, users are informed that additional factors are required. If a login attempt seems suspicious, it will send an email to the user to allow them to assess the incident and notify Okta administrators if it seems necessary.

Allowing self-service resets not only relieves the IT and support staff from manually helping users but also allows the users themselves to better understand and have control over the situation. They can affect what happens and bring their own risk down by repeating vectors in the flow.

Think of a user always going to the office; their risk assessment can be set to low because of the following vectors:

- The WAN address of the office is added to a zone.

- The user logs in on a regular basis around the same time and on the same days.

- The user is using the same device, which is enrolled on their **Mobile Device Management (MDM)**.

- The user is using the same OS and browser.

Perhaps in this scenario, you would allow the user to access all applications, with a lower threshold for MFA.

But say this user wants to do the same work but with these vectors changed:

- The user is hopping from Wi-Fi to mobile data, thus changing IP addresses constantly.

- They're doing so based on different time zones, or different times.

- The user is using their own devices, such as an iPad, Android mobile, and a self-owned laptop.

- They are using different OSes and browsers.

The risk assessment will evaluate the situation to be riskier and will prompt the user to identify themselves using more secure login factors, have them stacked (for example, username, Okta Verify, and **Universal 2nd Factor (U2F)** token), and perhaps even deny access to more business-critical applications.

This way, the assessment is done using a lot of different elements. Their role within the organization and the assignment to different groups can help to create these policies and methods. Prompting the user to change passwords because their risk assessment became much higher, enrolling new factors, and receiving notifications allows them to go through this process completely self-managed and in control. They could decide not to do it at that point in time, and allow Okta to restrict their workspace for the time being. Once they comply with more secure requirements by enrolling, they can continue to work with all their available applications.

Eventually, Okta wants to make sure security doesn't come in the way of productivity. By allowing the user to do their own assessment, they are in control of the situation. They can decide whether they think it's required to fall in line with the restrictions, or whether they are going to forgo them and work with a more restricted workplace.

Implementing these context-aware policies requires an understanding of the different situations and needs of a user-focused approach.

At the beginning of the book, we spoke about the zero-trust approach, using Okta's contextual access management, which allows you to move into higher levels of zero trust. This doesn't mean that implementing contextual access management means you tick off the box to be in the zero-trust model and you can raise the flag. It means you are changing your focus from an organizational perimeter to a user-centric perimeter.

Now, let's see what dynamic application access is.

Dynamic application access

Okta also allows other vendors to integrate and use their vectors as part of the assessment. By having third-party MDM tools manage the device, you can generate a trust certificate exchanged with Okta. This device trust can then be used in application sign-on rules as an extra vector. This allows you to stack the security by using your Okta sign-on policies to assess the user's situation. Later, once the user wants to log in to applications, the device trust vector can be used as part of the assessment to allow or deny access to the application.

Beyond that, with the help of device trust, you can use custom SAML attributes to inform the application about the status of the device and have the application itself use that status for more granular limitation. This is called device context for limited access.

By using Dynamic Authentication Context, Okta can pass along information during the authentication flow and let the application determine the access limits for in-app behaviors.

For both device context for limited access and Dynamic Authentication Context, the **Service Provider** (**SP**) has to be able to consume these extra values during authentication. Based on this, the SP acts upon the values to do its own risk assessment and guide the user accordingly to its own policies set up for the different risk levels. This can require certain licenses or other add-ons to set up. Salesforce is one example that can consume and use this input to set its own policies and determine whether the user is allowed to change values, read information, or perform any other task, based on the outcome.

So, now that we have read the concept of Okta's contextual access, let's dive deeper into the different types of context vectors that are used in these processes.

Setting up network zones

Network zones within Okta are used through all policies. It is what Okta started with and is still relevant to this day. The usage of network zones is quite simple to explain: you are either are in a zone or not. The network zone is a security perimeter, used as a restricted access layer. A network zone can be a single IP address, one or more IP ranges, or geolocations. You can have multiple networks to be used in different ways. You can also categorize network zones as blacklisted, flipping the idea of being safe in a zone to not allowing access at all from that zone.

Depending on your situation, take the following into consideration:

- You can have static zones, or also dynamic zones.
- When creating rules for sign-in policies, while using notifications for VPN and incorporating **Integrated Windows Authentication** (**IWA**), the network zones can be used for more granularity.
- When a zone definition is changed, this will automatically update policies and rules. You can have a maximum of 100 zones configured.
- It's possible for each zone to contain up to 150 gateway IPs and 150 proxy IPs. This is excluding IP blacklist zones.
- Similarly, it's possible for IP blacklist zones to contain up to 1,000 gateways per zone and up to 25,000 per org.

Setting up zones is straightforward; you can find the settings for network zones under **Security | Networks**. You can create and specify all your network zones right here:

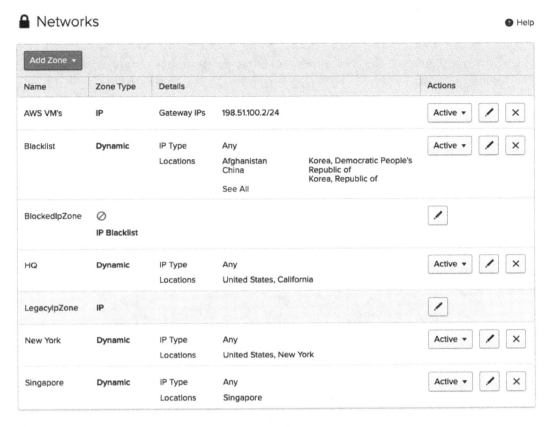

Figure 4.3 – Network zone overview

When you start creating your list, you will always start with two network zones that cannot be deleted: LegacyIpZone and BlockedIpZone. These are defaults within Okta.

> **Tip**
> When a new Okta org is created, these zones are created with it. As they aren't that descriptive, it might be wise to rename them so that it's clearer how you want to use them in your policies.

Setting up an IP zone

Any additional network zones can be added by using the green **Add Zone** button.

The dropdown will give you the choice to set up either an IP zone with ranges of IP or a dynamic zone:

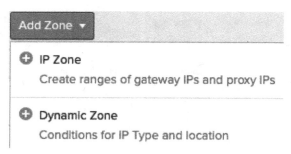

Figure 4.4 – Adding an IP zone

If we choose **IP Zone**, we are presented with the following options:

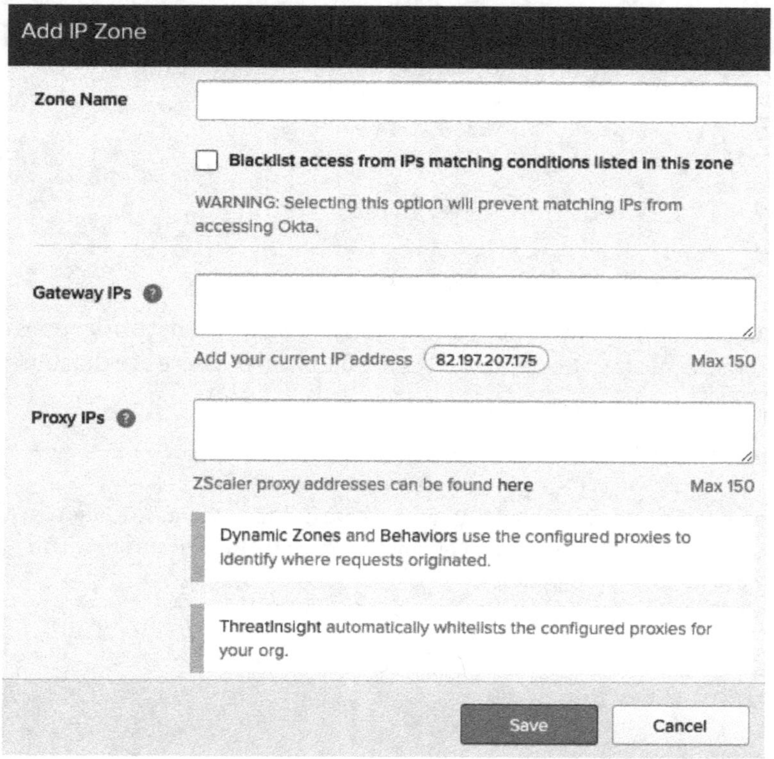

Figure 4.5 – The IP zone setup window

You can see the following fields in the preceding screenshot:

- **Zone Name**.

- A checkbox to turn this network zone into a blacklist, therefore blocking access entirely toward Okta.

- **Gateway IPs**: These can either be single IP addresses, ranges of IP addresses separated by hyphens, or **Classless Inter-Domain Routing** (**CIDR**)-notated IP ranges — for example, 216.119.143.01, 216.119.143.02-216.119.143.22, or 216.119.143.01/24.

- **Proxy IPs**: These can either be a single address, addresses separated by commas, ranges with hyphens, or CIDR notation.

By clicking **Save**, you add the new zone to the network zone overview. After this, you can start using the zones immediately.

Setting a dynamic zone

Setting up a dynamic zone is similar to the IP zone, only we get the opportunity to add geo zones as perimeters. That allows many more dynamic options in regards to the usage of these zones in policies and so on.

We start by clicking the **Add Zone** button and selecting **Dynamic Zone**:

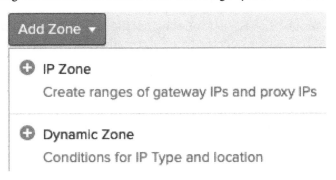

Figure 4.6 – Adding a dynamic zone

The following window shows a slightly different setup. We are now presented with a few options:

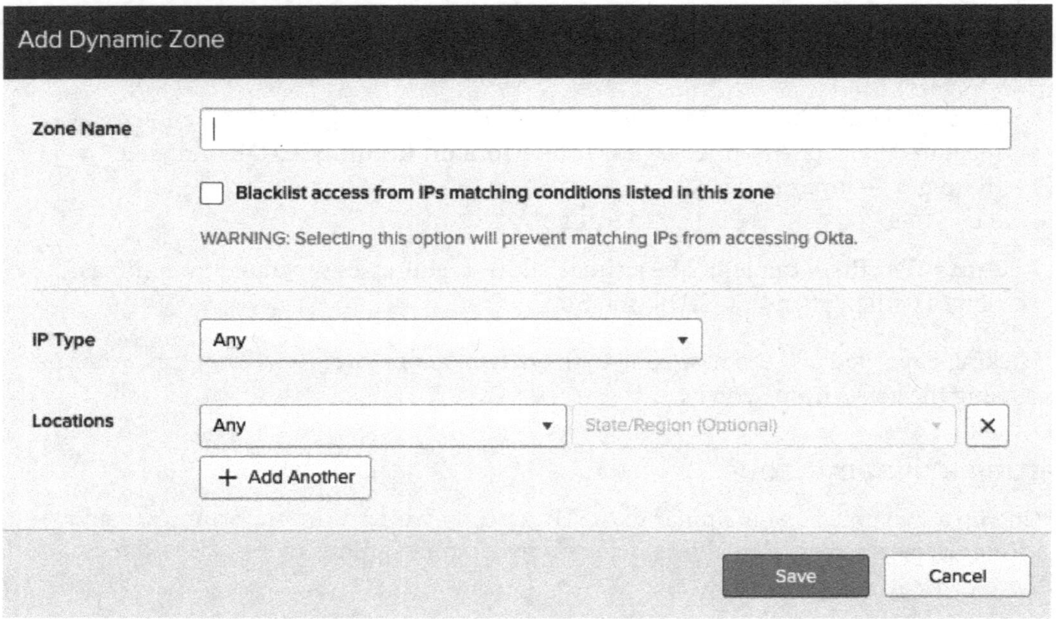

Figure 4.7 – Setting up a dynamic zone

For **Zone Name**, make sure the selected zones match the naming to avoid confusion using the zone. Examples of this can be country name, a specific office location, and so on.

Then, there is a checkbox to make this dynamic zone a blacklist.

After that, you have the choice to select an IP type:

- **Any**: To allow any type of IP
- **Any Proxy**: To allow any type of proxy
- **TorAnonymizer**: To filter untraceable IP addresses
- **Not a TorAnonymizer**: To exclude TorAnonymizers from the zones

Lastly, we can add locations. This allows a more geo-located approach:

1. First, you select the country you want to include in the zone.
2. You can further filter it down into states or regions.

After you hit **Save,** the zone can be used in different areas. It can be really helpful to filter a region, to manage at a more granular level. Let's say the workforce in New York needs access to Salesforce, but outside of New York, no one should be allowed access. You can create a New York zone to achieve this.

Let's look at some other dynamic elements that Okta uses to further the granularity of options.

Behavior detection

Behavior detection is an important part of the zero-trust path with Okta. Understanding the user's context is key. Okta allows you, as an admin, to use parts of this context in different multifactor policies. By adding these vectors, Okta is capable of setting risk scores and using them to tighten or loosen the policies.

Behavior detection has two components: trackable behaviors and definable actions based on changes from the user.

Trackable behaviors are as follows:

- Signing in from a new location, such as a country, state, or city
- Signing in from a specified distance from a previous successful sign-in location
- Signing in from a device that is new for the user — for example, a different laptop or mobile workstation
- Signing in from an IP address that is new for the user — for example, a mobile hotspot, home IP, or public transport
- Signing in after an impossible travel, which means it's deemed impossible for a user to have traveled between two geographical locations between two successive sign-in attempts

Examples of actions are as follows:

- Allow or deny access.
- Require the user to verify with an additional multifactor.
- Set the session lifetime.

Under **Security | Behavior Detection**, we can see all the behaviors Okta created by default and add any more or change the defaults to our own liking:

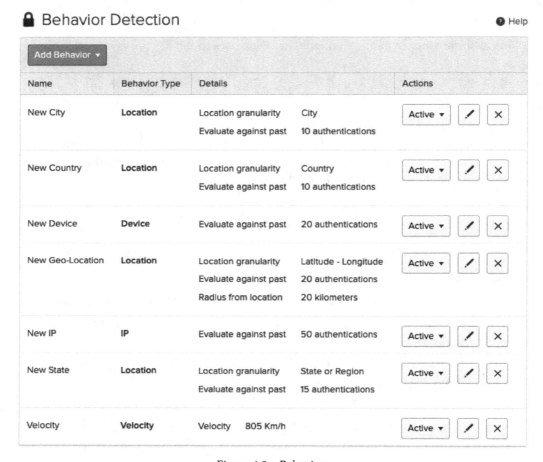

Figure 4.8 – Behaviors

Here you can *add*, *edit*, *delete*, and *set* behaviors to **Inactive** or **Active**. Let's go through them and see how they are used or act in Okta.

We can group these behaviors into four different types.

First, let's see location:

- **Country**: A country that hasn't been part of previous successful logins.
- **State**: A state that hasn't been part of previous successful logins.
- **City**: A city that hasn't been part of previous successful logins.

- **New Geo-location**: You can specify a location within a specified radius from a previous successful login. Anything outside of that would be new behavior.

Next, we will learn about devices:

- **New Device**: A device new to the specific user that previously wasn't used for a successful login. If you switch browsers on a previously used device, that would be considered a new device, since it's client-based.

Next in line is IP:

- **New IP**: When an IP address hasn't previously been part of a successful login, it would be considered new.

Lastly, we will learn about velocity:

- **Velocity**: A measurement of velocity used to identify suspicious logins. Velocity is evaluated based on the distance and time elapsed between two subsequent user logins.

Each of these types allows more granularity and can be added individually or combined into a single sign-on policy:

Figure 4.9 – Behaviors added to a policy rule

By adding this into a policy, you can add layers into steps of the risk assessment. Let's say we have sales teams on the move. They might go from town to town. Adding the state and city behavior to the sign-on policy allows validating their previous logins. New states and towns will be checked against the given amount in the behavior. If Okta then determines the risk as **High**, the user will fall into that rule of the policy.

We can create multiple rules per policy, setting the risk level to **Any**, **High**, **Medium**, or **Low**. Based on those conditions, we can have the user go through different sign-on flows.

Here, you can see different rules set up within a policy:

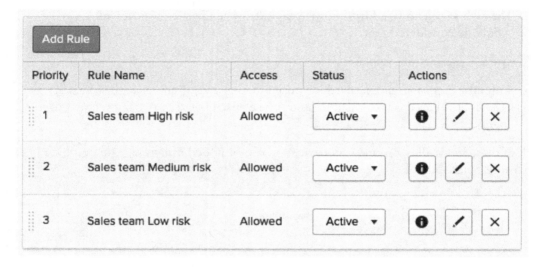

Figure 4.10 – Rules with behavior detection in a sign-on policy

As with any other policy, these work in a hierarchy, and the user will be vetted against them from top to bottom. Therefore, it is wise to start with the highest risk or strongest rule at the top and end with the weakest rule at the bottom.

By using rules within policies, you allow Okta to work for you and no longer force the users into one set of strict or loose policies and rules. You allow yourself to create more elaborate sign-on policies, which prevents the overhead of creating one for every scenario.

All of this is saved in the end user's profile. If for whatever reason it is necessary to clear this out, you can go to the user's profile and reset their entire behavior profile:

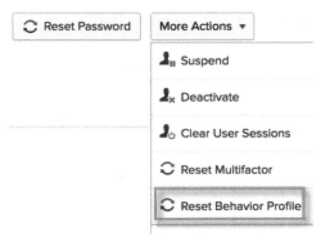

Figure 4.11 – Resetting the user's behavior profile

This will make sure the user will start recreating their profile with new information.

We covered a lot of ground within Okta's contextual access options, such as using external systems as additional vectors for risk assessment and working with different zones. Then, we talked about setting up policies with rules and additional behaviors to complete the grand scope of policy-making.

Now, let's take a look at using these same principles for applications.

Creating layered and app-specific policies

Another way of creating layered policies is by applying MFA to specific applications. You can choose to either do this for signing in to Okta, for signing in to the application, or both, as mentioned earlier. The reason why you might want to add MFA policies to an application, even though you have already enabled it to sign in, can be the following:

- An administrator of an application needs to authenticate with a factor with higher security than what is rolled out for signing in to Okta, to get access to that application.

- A C-level (top management role) user needs to authenticate with a factor with higher security than what is rolled out for signing in to Okta, to get access to an application with business-critical information.

- You need to enforce extra security for certain applications outside of the office network.

To add MFA to an application, navigate to **Applications | Applications**. Select the application you want to add an MFA policy to. Go to the **Sign On** tab and scroll down to the bottom, and select **Sign On Policy**. If you haven't done anything here before, you will only see a default rule, which says that anyone that is assigned to the application can access from anywhere. To add a new rule, click the **Add rule** button and follow these steps:

1. **Rule Name**: Give your rule a descriptive name.

   You can check the box under this to disable the rule on creation. This can be useful if, for instance, you need to communicate the change out to your organization before enabling it.

2. **People**: Select whether you want to assign the rule to all who are assigned to the application, or select who you want to assign it to.

   If you select the latter, you get to search for groups or users.

   > **Tip**
   > Try to assign to groups as much as possible, to achieve maximum automation.

3. **Zone**: Select whether the policy will be enforced without considering zones, or choose either **In zone** or **Not in zone** to be more specific.

   If you select **In zone** or **Not in zone**, you get to select any of your predefined zones by typing the name of the one you want to select.

4. **Client**: Use this section if you want to set up the policy for a certain kind of device.

    For devices where you have set up device trust toward any MDM system, you can also set if you want the policy to be set for trusted or untrusted devices. To set this up, navigate to **Security | Device Trust**. Different types of devices have different setups, usually with a two-step configuration. Some require a security key, while others require credentials:

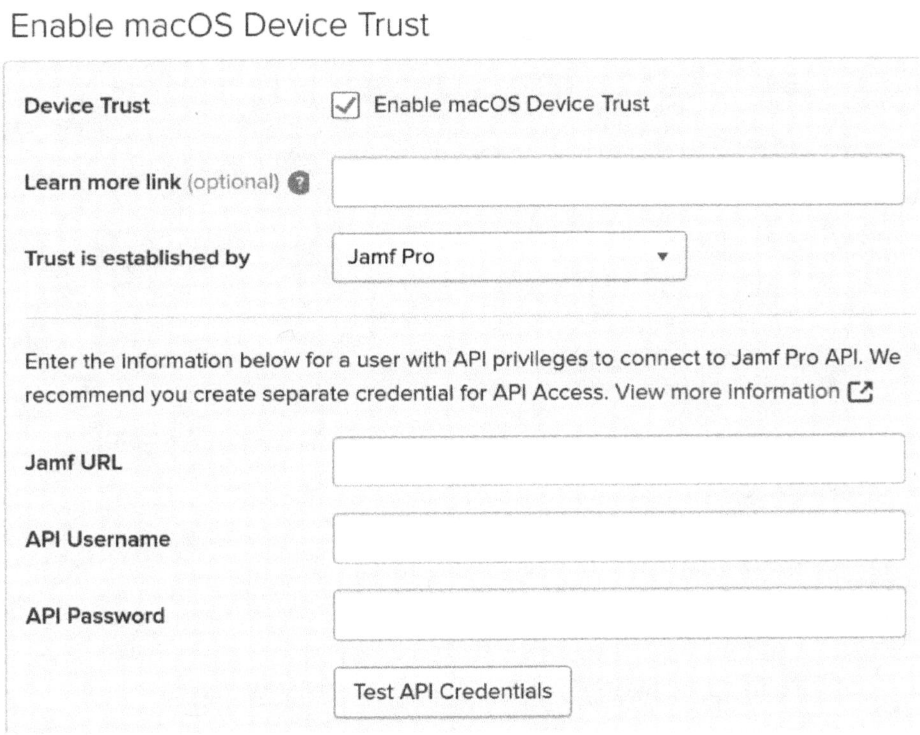

    ## Enable macOS Device Trust

Device Trust	☑ Enable macOS Device Trust
Learn more link (optional) ❓	
Trust is established by	Jamf Pro ▾

    Enter the information below for a user with API privileges to connect to Jamf Pro API. We recommend you create separate credential for API Access. View more information ⬀

Jamf URL	
API Username	
API Password	
	Test API Credentials

Figure 4.12 – Example of device trust setup for macOS with Jamf Pro (Mac MDM solution)

5. Lastly, you select how to allow access. Check the box to ask for multifactor, after which you set the frequency of how often to prompt for it.

    After you've clicked **Save**, you can prioritize the different policies by clicking the arrows in the list:

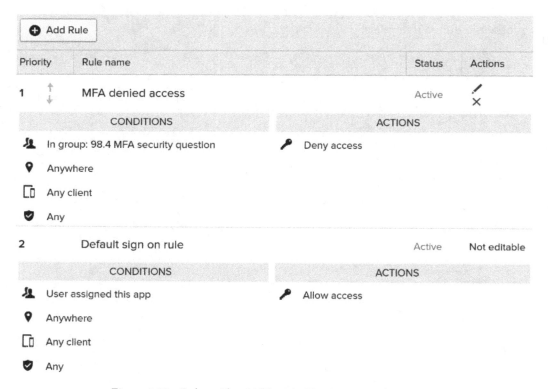

Figure 4.13 – Rules with possible prioritization using the arrows

The process is the same for any application. Now that we've looked at the administrator side, let's go into how it will look like for the end users.

Enrolling end users in MFA

We previously looked at how enrollment in different MFAs is working, but let's take a closer look at it from an end user perspective. We'll learn this with the help of an example: an end user enrolling in Okta Verify. After a new MFA policy is rolled out, end users will be prompted to enroll in one or multiple factors on their next sign-on. Let's look at how it would work when the user clicks **Setup for Okta Verify**:

1. At the first step, the end user will select what device they are using, and then be informed to download the Okta Verify application from the device's app store.

2. After doing this, by clicking **Next**, the user will scan a QR code on the screen with the Okta Verify application.

After the code is scanned, the setup is done, and the user will be sent back to the factor page. Here, they might need to enroll additional factors to complete enrollment entirely, if the policy is requiring the user to do so. If they are not required to do so, they can select to finish the setup, and proceed to log in to Okta.

We enrolled a factor, so now let's take a look at how to reset a factor.

Resetting multifactor

There can be situations where users need to reset their multifactor, as follows:

- The end user has a new device and needs to recreate an active Okta Verify or Google Authenticator account.

- Something isn't working with the end user's factor — for instance, they are stuck in a loop or the OTP code isn't working.

> Tip
> Make sure your end users enroll in at least two factors on setup. This should preferably be on two different devices or platforms (for example, Okta Verify and SMS, or a MacBook's TouchID and Google Authenticator). That way, they can reset one of them while using the other.

As an administrator, you can always help your end users reset their multifactor. Navigate to **Directory | People**, and find the user to reset multifactor. By clicking **Reset Multifactor Authentication**, you can select factors to reset or reset all of them.

But users can also help themselves. If a factor reset is planned, such as changing their device, they can go to **Settings** and scroll down to **Extra Verification**:

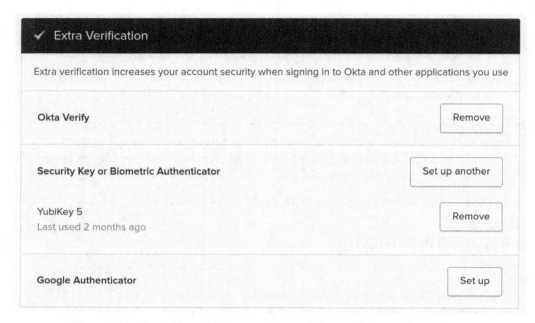

Figure 4.14 – Available multifactor options, and the possibility to change them

For instance, with Okta Verify, the end user can remove the **Okta Verify** option from this menu, and then with their next login, enroll into Okta Verify from the new phone, as before.

Now we understand Okta from an end user's perspective. It will benefit the administrators if end users learn how to enroll and reset factors. Now, let's take a look at using MFA with a VPN.

Securing a VPN with MFA

VPNs have been one of the standard ways to connect securely to applications and data behind organizational perimeters. As VPNs evolve, so do options to secure them. The credentials to log in can be compromised, and having additional security allows outside threats to be thwarted and secures what is usually most critical and sensitive behind the VPN.

Different VPNs' software and vendors deliver different types of integrations. Some might allow SSO to be set up, while others use directories such as Active Direcory or LDAP, and perhaps even RADIUS. In any of these methods, you can use Okta's login credentials to be the only set of credentials the user has and add MFA to the login process.

As we spoke about earlier in this chapter, we can utilize at least two categories in securing access: *something we know* and *something we have*, and perhaps even *something we are*.

Depending on the type of VPN software running, the client of the user might be able to visually allow the user to choose a token type:

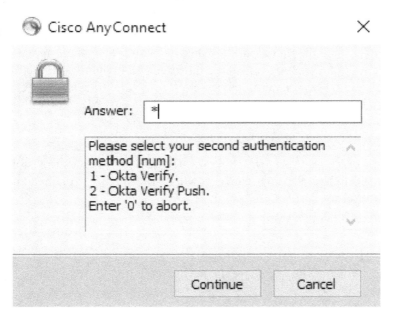

Figure 4.15 – Request for factor selection

As shown in the preceding screenshot, the user will be prompted to choose a factor, and the window will then switch to either a window to input an OTP or simply awaits confirmation from Okta based on the Okta Verify push response. The software might even use modern authentication and allow a browser login to be used. This can fully incorporate Okta's login flow.

In other cases, the VPN software might not allow this to happen and the user will have to input the password and string a token code to it in the password field. If it's allowed to use Okta Verify push, Okta will directly push the request and the user can verify it. During this process, the VPN authentication request will pause until Okta fully verifies the user's login and then allows the process to continue.

Of course, sometimes you have to make the best of the situation, and the user might need additional factors or need to switch over to other factors. This can be hard to manage, but with Okta's adaptive multifactor functionality, you have the full array of options ready to be used, and as an admin, you can make sure that the least amount of friction is used to deliver the highest possible security.

Setting up these rules depends on the VPN software. Some can be set up with application sign-on policies, while others might require Okta sign-on policies to be used.

Summary

In this chapter, we learned everything we need to know about using different kinds of factors, setting up policies for them, both for signing in and for specific applications. We also deep-dived into Okta's features around contextual MFA, where your factor policies can be adaptive. You now understand how to set up zones and how to use them in different settings. Lastly, we also looked at the possibility to use MFA for VPNs and similar solutions.

In the next chapter, we will look into Okta's life cycle management features, such as automations and workflows. Also, basic but powerful features such as provisioning and **Human Relations (HR)**-as-a-master concepts will be thoroughly explained and we will show how they are set up.

5
Automating Using Life Cycle Management

In this chapter, we will look at how we can use some of the knowledge we gained in previous chapters for a complete user life cycle. We will look at how we can use integrations for user provisioning, such as setting up a **Human Resources Information System (HRIS)** as a mastering service. We will also go deeper into editing a user's profile, for instance, with Expression Language. For the groups we learned about in *Chapter 2, Working with Universal Directory*, we'll now learn how to use automation to get them to work for us. Lastly, we will deep dive into the different kinds of hooks offered within Okta, as well as how we can utilize workflows.

These are some skills you will learn:

- Automating user provisioning
- Provisioning rich profiles
- Setting up group rules
- Setting up self-service options
- Using workflow capabilities
- Using Okta Workflows

Automating user provisioning

Previously, we've looked at several things that together become a complete user provisioning process. Groups, directory integrations, and so on, all come together for complete onboarding and offboarding. Let's look at how we can put it all together.

As mentioned in *Chapter 3*, *Single Sign-On for a Great End User Experience*, there are different kinds of integrations available in the **Okta Integration Network** (**OIN**), and many of the applications have **System for Cross-domain Identity Management** (**SCIM**) possibilities. SCIM is an open standard to use for managing user identity information. With SCIM, there is a defined schema and a REST API for **Create, Read, Update, Delete** (**CRUD**) operations. To say it more simply, SCIM is a protocol to store user information in a way that identity data can easily be shared with multiple applications.

Let's look at it with an example. If an end user quits, and an administrator deactivates their account in Okta, the user attribute **Active** is set to false, and the attribute is also updated in any SCIM connected applications.

This is a possible **Life Cycle Management** (**LCM**) flow, for applications supporting CRUD operations. When a new user is created with certain attributes, a new account can be created in downstream applications that have SCIM integration or other integration that supports the *create* operation. You will know this by looking at the capabilities of the integrations. Navigate to **Applications | Applications | Add Application** and select the application you want to integrate. In the **Overview** section, you see the application's capabilities:

Capabilities

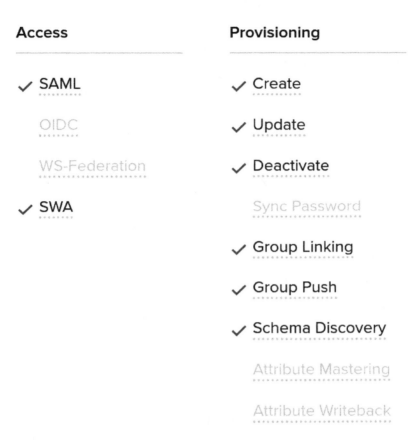

Access

✓ SAML

OIDC

WS-Federation

✓ SWA

Provisioning

✓ Create

✓ Update

✓ Deactivate

Sync Password

✓ Group Linking

✓ Group Push

✓ Schema Discovery

Attribute Mastering

Attribute Writeback

Figure 5.1 – Examples of the capabilities of an application

Using group rules allows you to automate the account assignment of users to applications.

If a user changes department, the *update* operation can deprovision a user from an application, if that application isn't assigned to the user's new department. That way, you stay updated on your security and can pass any audit coming your way.

As the last step, if a user is deactivated in Okta, they can also be deactivated in downstream applications, if they support the *deactivation* operation. This way, you can be certain that users have no access to data after they have left the organization.

So, let's first take a look at how we provision users.

Provisioning users

Setting up applications with provisioning capabilities can be pretty straightforward. We have looked at some of these features before in different chapters, but let's have a look at how the full provisioning process would look for an application, to get a gathered view. Once the app is added, as done in *Chapter 3, Single Sign-On for a Great End User Experience*, you go to the **Provisioning** tab and start the integration. Okta guides you through this and it can be different for each application. In general, Okta mainly uses a service account to gain access to the application and its resources. Once the integration is set up, the service account will be leveraged through SCIM or other means to manage the users. The side panel may have some or all of the options **To App**, **To Okta**, and **Integration**, which could look like this:

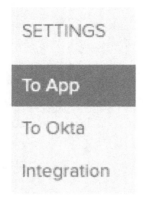

Figure 5.2 – Provisioning settings

In the **Integration** tab, you can see information on how Okta and the application connect to each other. As every application has a different requirement, it is beyond the scope of this book to go over all of them. These integrations usually use an API key, but also might require a service admin who can authorize certain scopes of the application. We go over APIs, authorization, and scopes in *Chapter 7, API Management*. Let's go over the **To App** and **To Okta** options now.

In the **To App** section, you can set up how Okta can manage different options for the users in the application. By simply enabling the options **Create Users**, **Update User Attributes**, **Deactivate Users**, and **Sync Password**, you enable Okta to start managing the identities in the application:

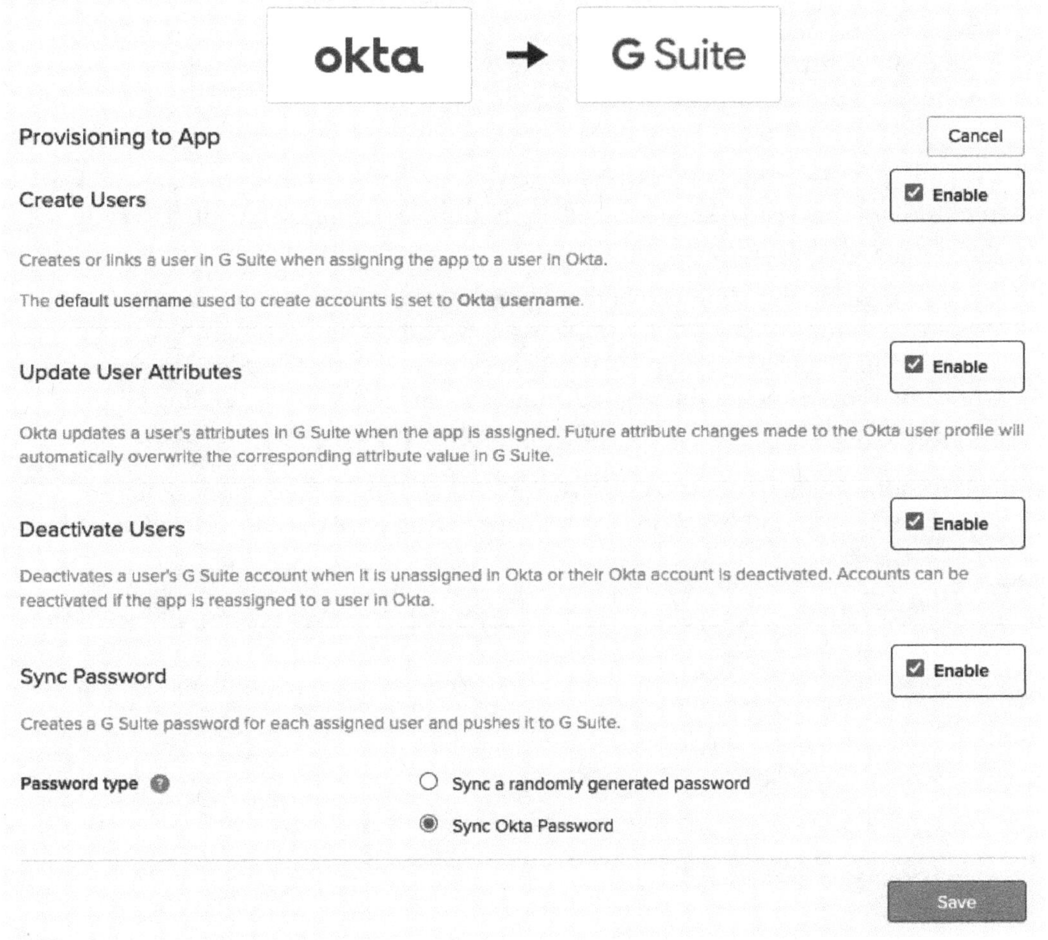

Figure 5.3 – To App settings

These options are not very hard to understand but can have an impact on how you want to manage your users with Okta:

- **Create Users**: This can be quite straightforward, but perhaps the application has different sources that create users and Okta only needs to manage the users after they have been created.

- **Update User Attributes**: This allows Okta to sync anything that changes on the user's profile through profile mapping into the user's profile in the integrated application.

- **Deactivate Users**: This makes sure the user's state is synced with the state in Okta. If that is not the desired state for that application, leave the **Deactivate Users** checkmark box unchecked.

- **Sync Password**: This allows Okta to update the password in the app by either syncing a random password or the Okta password into the app after the user's password in Okta has been updated. Unchecking it will of course lead to passwords not being synced and might be good enough if SSO is set up. Depending on the scenario and strategy, one or the other option will probably fit your needs.

Some applications might have extra options. For instance, the content management application Box allows some extra options to manage data once the user gets offboarded:

Figure 5.4 – Box options for content management after deactivation

These options are very specific to the application and aren't commonly used across all applications supporting provisioning.

In the **To Okta** settings, we can set up different elements with regards to importing data into Okta and how to handle that. Let's go over the different settings:

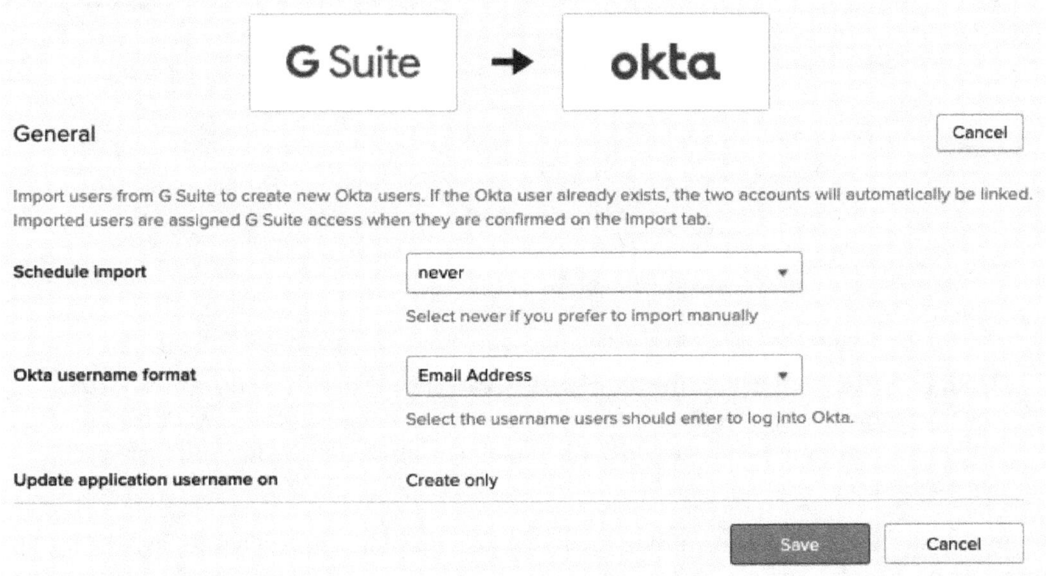

Figure 5.5 – General settings for provisioning toward Okta

Here's what these settings mean:

- **Schedule import**: After you click on **Edit**, you can choose in which periodic timeframe you want the integration to scan for new users. For every import it does, it will also check for groups and update that information too. A scheduled import can be done as often as every hour or as rarely as every 2 days. If you set it to **never**, it will only import manually, which you can do on the **Import** tab of the application.

- **Okta username format**: The imported users might need to have a username set and the next option allows you to choose which imported value is set as the Okta username.

  You can either go for **Email Address** or pick **Custom** and use Expression Language to create your own structure for the username based on the attributes available to you from the application and Okta. The setting looks like this:

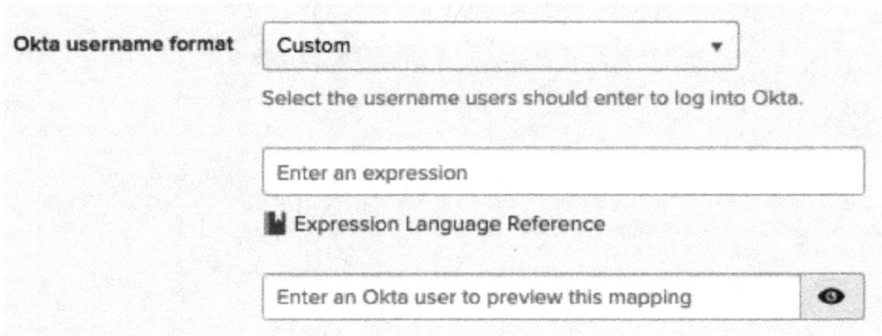

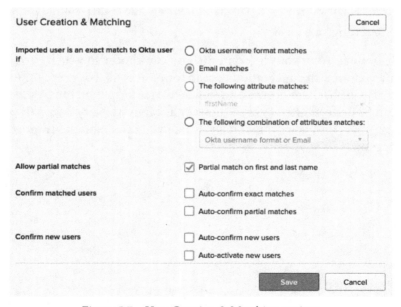

Figure 5.6 – Custom Username options for newly imported users

- **Update application username on**: Here you can choose to either create or update the username if that is needed in the application. Click **Save** and the periodic import and name convention will start to apply for all new users coming in from that specific application.

On the next section of settings on the same page, you can determine what to do with these imported users:

Figure 5.7 – User Creation & Matching settings

Just as we discussed in *Chapter 2*, *Working with Universal Directory*, these settings are similar in setup. In this **User Creation & Matching** section, you can set how imported users are checked against possible existing users in Okta and how Okta needs to confirm and activate these users.

Under the **Imported user is an exact match to Okta user if** setting, you can choose from the following options:

- **Okta username format matches**: This setting checks whether the username in the app matches an existing Okta username.

- **Email matches**: Selecting this option checks whether an email address matches the user's Okta email address.

- **The following attribute matches**: By choosing this option, you can select an attribute you want to match on, for example, `firstName`, or title, or `phoneNumber`.

- **The following combination of attributes matches**: This is similar to the previous option, but allows you to choose pre-set attribute combinations, for example, **Okta Username format or Email**, or **Email and Name**.

> **Important note**
> Be cautious with using attributes that might have values that are similar to other users. It can allow users to be overwritten or misused.

Any of these options makes sure Okta won't import the user as a new user if there is a match. Having multiple users with unconnected identities has consequences for the user experience. Think of importing a user from Google Workspace with user profile values that don't match with their equivalents in Slack. The user might be automatically activated by both import methods and all of sudden have two accounts in Okta. Preventing that is the main reason to match users.

The next option is to allow partial matches. By turning that on, Okta will also check on matches with the first and last name. It can be that usernames, email addresses, and other attributes are different. Depending on how the mapping is set up, this can have an impact on the user's login credentials. Be cautious with this option – it can unexpectedly change the user experience and have an impact on what IT needs to do to remedy the problems.

After this, Okta wants to know how to act if matches are found. The first selection is for whether users can be auto-confirmed if an exact match or partial match is found. By ticking any of those boxes, Okta will import the user and connect the identities. Active users will get access to the app through Okta, and the identity in the app will be managed based on what you set up in the **To App** tab.

Lastly, Okta would like to know what to do with newfound users. The two options are as follows:

- Auto-confirming will import the new user into Okta, but will not activate the imported users. You might have good reasons to do that at a different time or after managing the identity manually or with other services.

- Auto-activating will immediately activate the user and send an activation email to them. This is the fastest way to have new users come into Okta from another source.

You can of course also manually import users if required. By going to the **Import** tab, you will be presented with an **Import** button. Clicking on that will start an import job. Depending on the application, this can either go quickly or rather slowly. It depends on how the APIs are integrated.

In the following screenshot, you can see an empty **Import** tab:

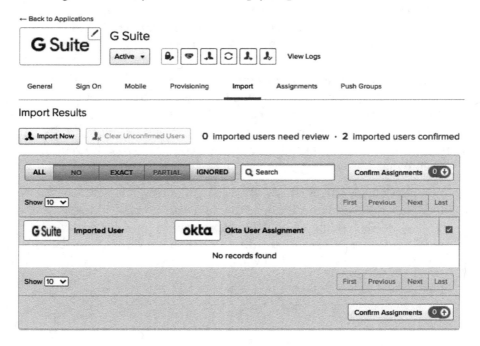

Figure 5.8 – Manually importing users from the Import tab

> **Important note**
> The **Import** tab is always available even if provisioning isn't set up. In that case, you can import a CSV and that will import the users into the application's **Import** tab.

Once you have run an import, users will start coming in and have different statuses.

If you have set up any auto-confirmations or auto-activations, users following your matches will be auto-confirmed and perhaps auto-activated. If not, you can do that from the **Import** window.

This is what an **Import** tab filled with newly imported users looks like:

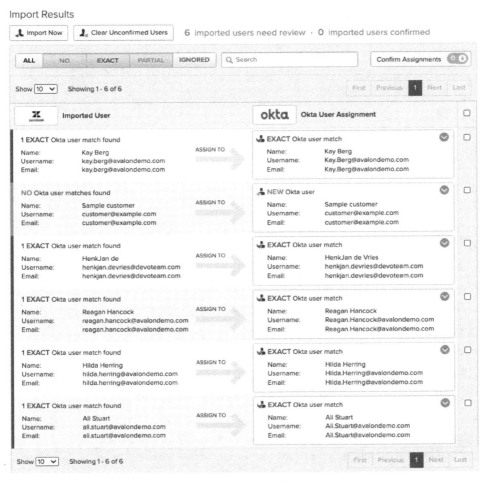

Figure 5.9 – Imported users

On the left, you will see the imported users with their application information, showing **Name**, **Username**, and **Email**.

On the right, you will see if Okta found a match based on any of the previously mentioned attributes.

On each of the imported users, you can choose what to do with them by clicking the small round arrow. This will show the different options:

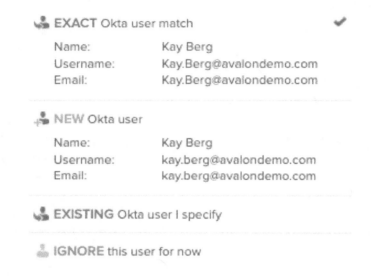

Figure 5.10 – Import options

In this case, Okta has found an exact match. Let's look at all the options:

- **EXACT**: An exact match is found by Okta with an existing Okta user based on the matching rules you defined in the **User Creation & Matching** section.

- **NEW**: Create a new Okta user with the information found from the application.

- **EXISTING**: Match the user that was found against an existing user that we search for and specify within the **Import** window.

- **IGNORE**: No action will be taken on the found user. It will be ignored and the user will be added to the filter **IGNORED** in the **Import** window.

Perhaps you want the user to have an alternative account in Okta. Then creating a new user is the best way to go. Matching the user against an Okta user we specify is often used if the user is partially matched or has different email or username attributes. Ignoring the user will not confirm or activate the user. This is often done for service accounts that are also imported or guest users that do not need to be added into Okta.

Once you have checked the matches Okta made and are ready, you can select the users you want to confirm by ticking the checkbox next to their names.

If you have a large import, you can change the page view to show more users, and ticking the checkbox at the top will tick all checkboxes on the page shown. If you go to the next page, you can repeat bulk selection for all the users you want to confirm.

The **Confirm assignments** button at the top and bottom of the page will show the number of users you have selected in any option. When you click on it, it will ask you if you also want to activate the users. Depending on your import strategy, this might be a welcome option, or perhaps you want to wait until the activation date, or need to do more on the user accounts before activating.

Here, we can see a **Confirm Imported User Assignments** window ready to import, but not activate, the users:

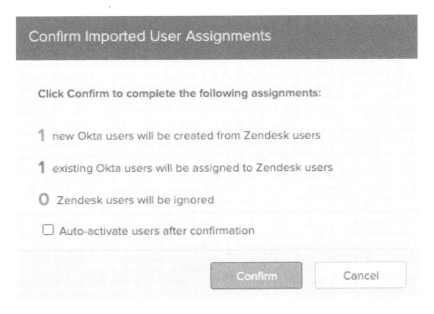

Figure 5.11 – Manual confirmation window

Once you have clicked **Confirm**, the selected users will disappear from the list. The ones you have ignored will be added to the **IGNORED** filter in the **Import** tab; the rest will be in your directory, ready to be managed from this point on.

In this case, we have set up an integration to be able to provision users to an application and import new users from it. This is a great way to manage and consolidate your users in the different applications you might have. But this can be made even more automated with an HR system to master users. Let's take a look at that.

Mastering users

An employee's journey within a company usually starts and ends with the Human Resource department. They are in charge of the hiring process and collect critical information about a new hire, such as contact information, the role they are going to fulfill, the department they are part of, the location they will be working at, and their start date. This is typically information that IT admins want to maintain a correct user directory and make sure employees have the right access at the right time. Using your HR system as a master can allow you to manage all this from top to bottom with integrations.

Some HR systems have an existing integration in the OIN, such as Workday, BambooHR, Namely, UltiPro, and SuccessFactors. These different systems have different capabilities. Some have deep integrations with possibilities such as group push, while some are more basic, with just attribute sync as a possibility.

If you are using an HR system without an available integration, there are still ways you can use it as a master: API calls or CSV mastering.

> **Important note**
> Using Okta's REST APIs, you can simulate typical integration actions using any program or scripting language that is capable of submitting web-based API requests and processing the results. Although that topic is outside the scope of this book, more information can be found at the Okta developer's site (`https://developer.okta.com/docs/reference/`).

If your HR system can export a CSV file, you can use that as a master in Okta. Let's look at how to set that up in Okta. Navigate to **Directory | Directory Integrations**, and click **Add Directory** and choose **Add CSV Directory**. In the **General** settings, for the initial setup, you only have to give your directory a name. Click **Done**. After that, you will do the rest of the setup.

The menu options look like this:

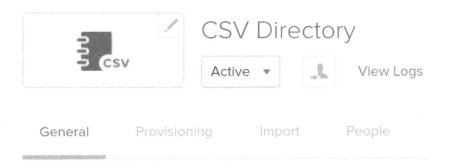

Figure 5.12 – Settings for a CSV directory

In the **General** tab you see as an option in your new directory, you only do basic settings, such as describing the directory. If you use different CSV directories for different types of users (such as one for employees, one for contractors, and one for partners), you can describe that here.

The **Provisioning** tab is where the magic happens. To process the data in the CSV file, you have a lightweight agent at your disposal. You can install this agent on a Linux or Windows server. These are the prerequisites:

- The **On-Premise Provisioning** (**OPP**) agent needs to be installed on Linux (CentOS or RHEL) or Microsoft Windows Server (x86/x64) and sits behind a firewall.
- The OPP agent version must be 1.03.00 or higher.
- The CSV file must have a .csv extension and be saved to a folder on-premises.
- Your CSV file must be in UTF-8 format.
- The OPP agent needs read permissions for the CSV file.
- All active users must be present for every CSV import.
- All required attributes must be present for every CSV import.
- All attributes and headers must be formatted properly.

These are the settings on the **Provisioning** tab under **Integration**:

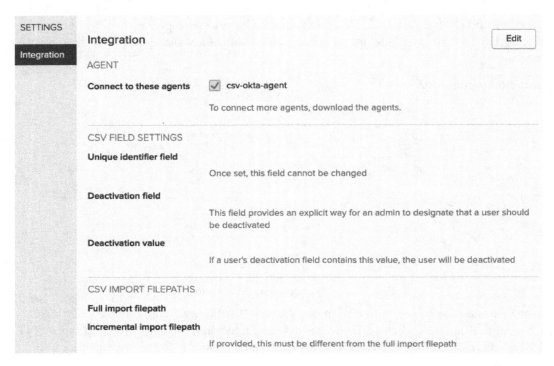

Figure 5.13 – Overview of the CSV directory Integration page

Here's what each of these settings is used for:

- **Connect to these agents**: This will show all running agents. The ticked boxes will be the selected agents that this integration will be used to sync with.

- **Unique identifier field**: The attribute from your CSV that will be used as a unique identifier. Remember that this should be the attribute name, not the display name, for example, userID.

- **Deactivation field**: The deactivation field in the CSV can be used to determine whether the user needs to be deactivated. By setting the field name here, Okta will check and act if the value is given for that user. Think of having a field named **Status**.

- **Deactivation value**: This setting has the value on which Okta must trigger a deactivation. For example, the value Deactivated.

- **Full import file path**: The full file path to the CSV file. For example, Windows: `C:\Users\Administrator\Desktop\csv\test.csv` or Linux: `/opt/OktaProvisioningAgent/csv/test.csv`.

- **Incremental import file path**: This is optional and can be used if you also have incremental updates. This file path needs to be different from the full import file path.

With that, we're done with the **Provisioning** tab. Next, are the **Import** and **People** tabs. They work similarly for CSV directories as for other directories, such as the AD integration we looked at in *Chapter 2, Working with Universal Directory*. The settings for **EXACT** and **PARTIAL** matches in **Import** are set as described previously in this chapter, in the *Provisioning users* section. The **People** tab shows imported users from this directory.

Now let's take a look at how an HR system might master your users, and how that is set up.

For HR systems with pre-built integrations in the OIN, there are different kinds of settings for each, which you are guided through by the setup. Let's look at how it works for BambooHR, a popular HR application. Start by navigating to **Applications | Applications** and click **Add Application**. Search for BambooHR and click to start the setup. In the **General** settings, you get to set up the following:

1. **Application label**: The name of the app seen by end users.

2. **Subdomain**: Enter your domain name, so if you usually log in with `http://acme.bamboohr.com/`, enter `acme`.

3. **Application visibility**: Checkboxes for whether the application is to be visible or not.

4. **Browser plugin auto-submit**: A selection to automatically log in users when they land on the login page.

For this specific application, you can select SWA or SAML 2.0. If you also want to set up SSO for your users, the best end user experience will be with SAML. Since we've been through how to set up applications for SSO in *Chapter 3, Single Sign-On for a Great End User Experience*, you can now just select SWA. What we want to achieve is to get to the **Provisioning** tab in the application setup.

> **Important note**
> You don't have to set up SSO for your end users within applications to be able to use the provisioning features.

After finishing up your setup of the application and going through the integration steps to allow provisioning to happen, you can now switch on your HR application as a master. Go to the **Provisioning** tab and select **To Okta**. Scroll down to **Profile & Lifecycle Mastering**. You have to enable the **Allow BambooHR to master Okta users** checkbox in this section. Click **Edit** to check it. When you do, you get some additional options:

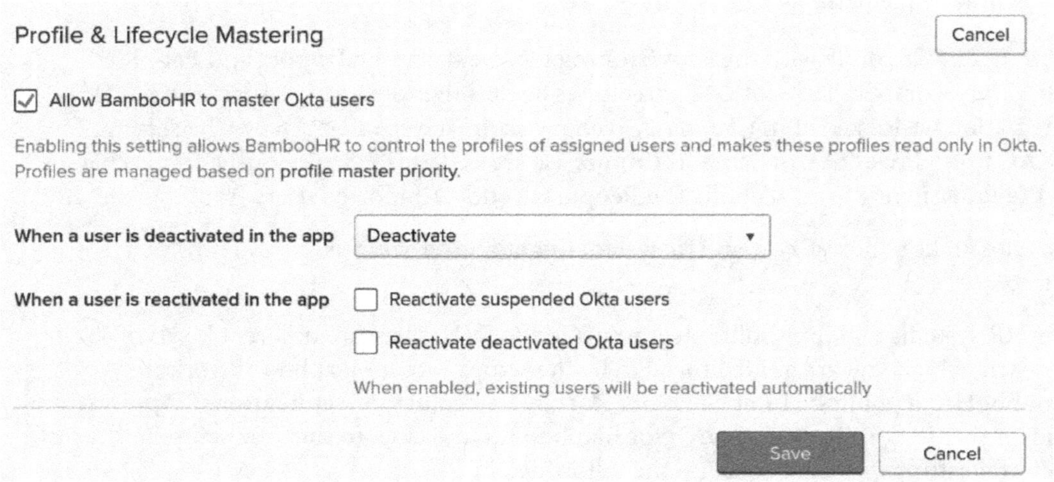

Figure 5.14 – Options for provisioning

For a typical provisioning setup, you would want the default setting set to **Deactivate**, meaning a user is deactivated in Okta when they are deactivated in BambooHR. You can also select the following options if the user is deactivated in the app:

- **Do nothing**: This will not change the account's status in Okta at all.

- **Suspend**: This will suspend the account in Okta, but not deactivate it, to prevent any other deactivations in other applications.

The next setting depends on what you choose for the first option. If you select to deactivate a user in Okta, you might also want to set it to activate them if they are activated again in BambooHR.

Now we need to import the users from BambooHR to connect their identities against any already existing accounts in Okta or import new users. Once you have done that, on the **Import** tab, you will see that all users that have been connected or imported will show a reference on their profile stating that they are mastered by BambooHR.

You will also see that you are no longer able to edit any attributes on the user directly, and it will state that the user is mastered by your HR.

We have talked about provisioning users and setting up mastering from different sources. Let's look at how we can go even deeper using Okta's options to further enrich user profiles.

Provisioning rich profiles

The capabilities in Okta to enrich user profiles within provisioning are big. One example of a feature that will help you is the **Okta Expression Language**. It is based on the **Spring Expression Language (SpEL)**, with which you can transform and query objects at runtime. With Expression Language, you can make changes to attributes and reference them before storing them on the Okta user, or before sending them to an application for authentication or provisioning. There is a lot of information on this topic, and going through all of it is out of the scope of this book. What we will do is look at the most commonly used categories and examples of them. If you have any other needs within your organization, you can find more information here: `https://developer.okta.com/docs/reference/okta-expression-language/`. To be able to look into these topics, we need some basic knowledge. All users have an Okta profile, independent of how the user is mastered. In addition to that, all users have an application user profile, for each application they are assigned to.

Before we look at exactly what we can do within Expression Language, we'll look into profile mapping. We've touched upon it in *Chapter 2, Working with Universal Directory*, for directories, but let's look more closely at it for applications. If you have a directory integrated or an application with provisioning capabilities, you can map attributes from them to the user stored in Okta. This is called **attribute mapping**. Let's look at what this looks like in an application like Google Workspace.

Keeping track of attributes with Attribute Mapping

Navigate to **Applications** and find your application, in this case, Google Workspace.
Click on the **Provisioning** tab. In the menu to the left, you can select whether you want
to set mapping to or from the application. You can do both. If you, for instance, select **To
Okta** and scroll down, you see the Okta attribute mapping at the end. You will see a list of
mapped attributes. This looks the same whether you pick **To Okta** or **To App**:

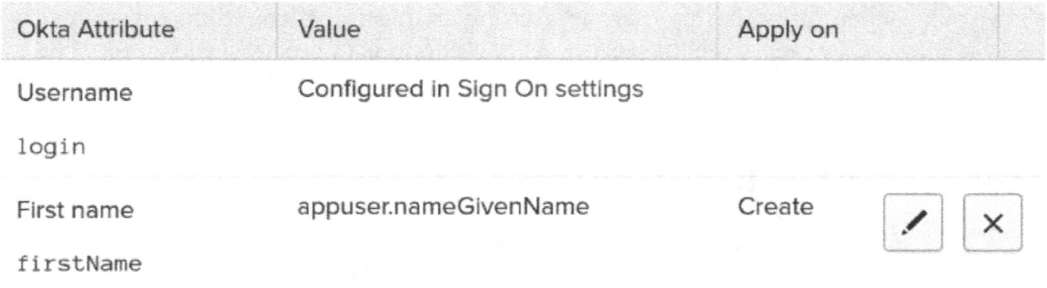

Okta Attribute	Value	Apply on	
Username login	Configured in Sign On settings		
First name firstName	appuser.nameGivenName	Create	✏ ✕

Figure 5.15 – Example of attribute mapping

In this example, we can see that **Username** is based on **Sign On Settings**, and that the
First name attribute for this application's user profile is picked up from the application. If
you want to make changes to this, you can click the pen icon to the right. By doing so, you
can select attribute values:

- **Same value for all users**
- **Expression**
- Map from *application*, for example, a Google Workspace profile

This last selection is what was used for our preceding example. By selecting this, you get
a list of the available attributes to match. You will also get to set when you want to apply
your mapping, on **Create** or **Create and Update**.

If we go back to the list of attributes, you can also click the button at the bottom to see all
Unmapped Attributes. For instance, from an application such as Workplace by Facebook,
we might want to get the ProfileURL attribute, and then push that attribute to a second
application.

You might also want to look into the **Profile Editor** section of your application, and for that, you have a convenient link. With the **Profile Editor**, you can, for instance, set that a specific attribute is mastered by a different master, such as an application with provisioning capabilities. Find that attribute in the **Profile Editor** list, then click the **i** icon to the right. If you select **Master** priority, you can set a different master for this specific attribute. You can set up your own custom attribute. For both of these, see *Chapter 2, Working with Universal Directory*. If you want to populate that attribute with parts of other attributes or reference another attribute, you will need to use Expression Language. So let's jump into that!

Attribute magic with Okta Expression Language

As mentioned earlier, there are different categories of Okta Expression Language operations. We will look into the following:

- Referencing user attributes
- Referencing application and organization attributes
- Functions

So where will these expressions be placed? For instance, if you create a new attribute, you will be able to map and populate it with expressions. Navigate to **Directory | Profile Editor** and select the application or directory where your new attribute will live. If we continue with the preceding example of Google Workspace, you will click **Mappings** next to **Google Workspace** in the list.

So, what can you enter there? Let's look at *referencing user attributes* first:

- If you are in an application mapping, such as Google Workspace, and you want to reference the Okta user, you use the following:

  user.$attribute where $attribute would be replaced with the actual attribute name, for example:

  user.firstName

- If you instead want to reference an attribute from an application user profile, you use the following:

  $appuser.$attribute

- And with an example where you might want to pull in an attribute from the Zendesk application user profile to the Google Workspace application user profile, you would use the following:

  Zendesk.firstName in the Google Workspace **Profile Editor** mapping.

In the same way, we can use *Reference Application and Organization* attributes:

- For instance, if you want to use an application's domain name, you can use the following:

  `$app.$attribute`, which would give:

  `zendesk_app.companySubDomain`

- To reference the Okta organization in an application mapping, you would use `org.$attribute` and would get the following, for instance:

  `Org.subdomain`

These two categories are quite straightforward and there are more kinds available. Refer to `https://developer.okta.com/docs/reference/okta-expression-language/` for more examples. A more intricate category is to transform attributes with functions. These would typically be used when you want to, for instance, remove one part of an attribute or combine two different attributes, to create a new one. There are many functions, but let's look at some of them. With `String`, you can change attributes in multiple ways:

- The first one is `String.join`.

  An example with this would be the following:

  `String.join("", "This", "is", "a", "test")` giving the output `Thisisatest`. If you instead want that with spaces, you can use `String.append`.

- A useful kind of string function is to get output from what is before or after a character. This could, for instance, be `String.substringBefore`.

  This is good to use with an `@` if you want to use the unique name from an email and remove the domain name:

  `String.substringBefore("john.doe@acme.com", "@")` would give the output `john.doe`.

- It's also possible to reference standards such as the numeric standards or country and state codes. `Iso3166Convert.toAlpha3(string)` could be used to transform a numeric country code into a text country code, for instance:

  `Iso3166Convert.toAlpha3("840")` turns `840` into USA according to ISO 3166. This can be useful if one application outputs it in one format and it's needed by another application in the other format.

These mappings will be used in the profile mapping dialog box. You select whether you want to do mapping from the application to Okta or the other way around. The mappings are clearly marked, with a yellow arrow indicating only attribute creation or a green one indicating that updates are allowed – see *Figure 5.16*. If you enter a new expression mapping, you can test it out, by searching for a user in the **Preview** box at the bottom. When you're done, you click **Save Mappings**:

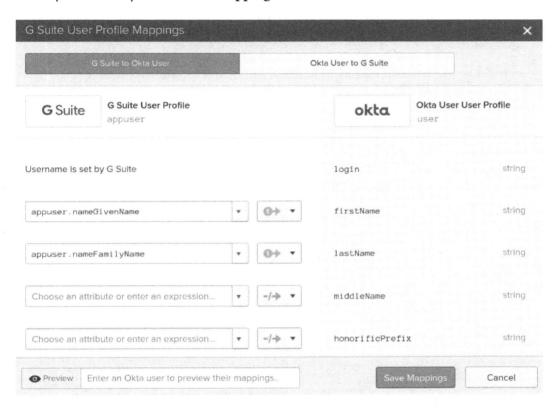

Figure 5.16 – Example of Expression Language mappings for an application

Now that you've saved your mappings, you're done with this part. There are many more examples of Expression Language at the link referenced earlier. Now let's move on to how you can do automation with and for your groups.

Setting up group rules

Group automation, or group rules, can be considered the best way to simplify administrators' work with Okta. Anything that requires setup and maintenance and is repetitive work can be automated with Okta's group rules.

Setting up group rules allows you to manage your workforce in bulk and allows you to manage the following:

- The user directory

- Application provisioning and single sign-on assignments

- Security policy assignments

- Directory and application group pushes

Because of the 360-degree view of a user in Okta, and its assigned groups, administrators can easily deliver quick setup, automation, remediation, and application management when using Okta groups. By allowing users to come in from different sources, and have their groups be added to Okta too, you can make sure the users are correctly assigned and managed by using Okta's group rules.

The strength lies in the simple options for the multitude of functions to be used in these group rules. Sometimes a simple assignment based on a profile attribute value can be enough to assign a user to a specific group or multiple groups:

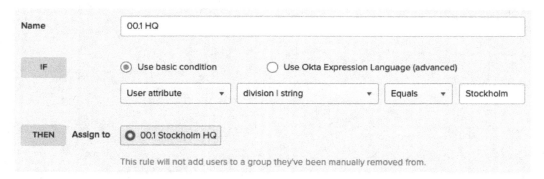

Figure 5.17 – Group assignment based on an attribute value

As shown here, a simple attribute value will assign the user to the selected group. This can be straightforward, and easy to use for organization structures using the department attribute to assign users to their corresponding department groups.

Sometimes it's because you want users to be added to a group based on another group assignment:

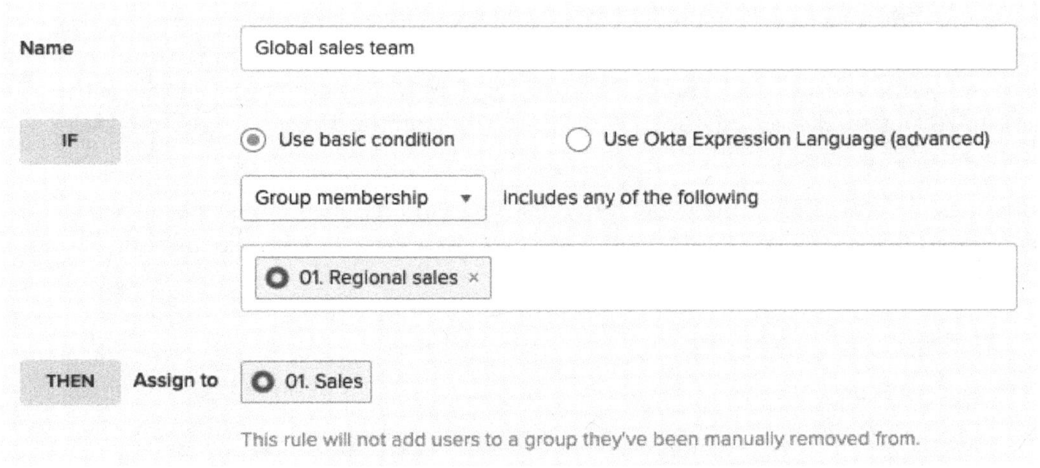

Name	Global sales team

IF — ● Use basic condition   ○ Use Okta Expression Language (advanced)

Group membership ▼ | includes any of the following

O 01. Regional sales ×

THEN   Assign to   **O** 01. Sales

This rule will not add users to a group they've been manually removed from.

Figure 5.18 – Group assignment based on another group assignment

Perhaps you have a granular setup and want to bring in users from other groups based on their assignments. So, in this case, we assign users to the generic **Sales** group if they are part of a more specific sales group.

Sometimes you might want to use application or directory groups to assign the user to other groups. Let's say an **Active Directory** (**AD**) group allows automation to assign other pushed AD groups to a user:

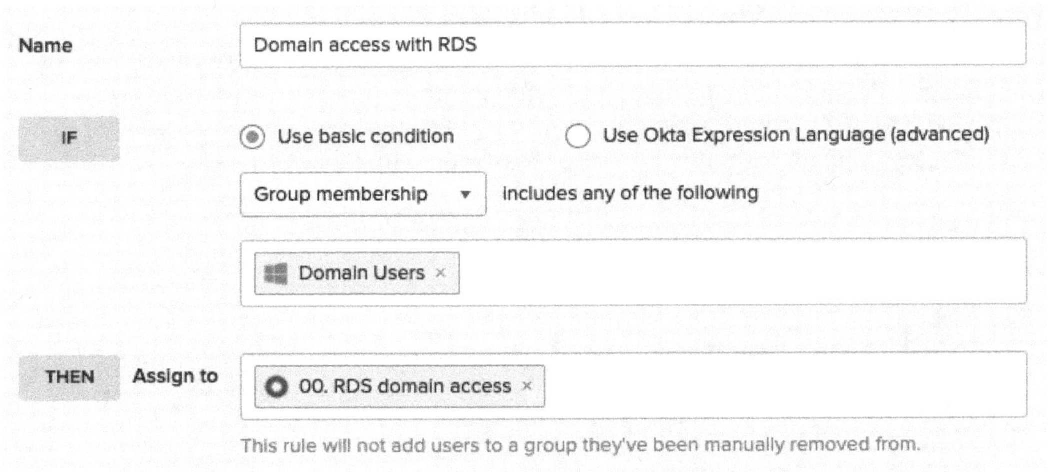

Name	Domain access with RDS

IF — ● Use basic condition   ○ Use Okta Expression Language (advanced)

Group membership ▼ | includes any of the following

Domain Users ×

THEN   Assign to   **O** 00. RDS domain access ×

This rule will not add users to a group they've been manually removed from.

Figure 5.19 – Group assignment rule based on AD group membership

Having the directory groups come into Okta allows you to see more of a user's connections. In this example, using *Figure 5.18*, we can use the group assignment within AD to assign them back to a **Remote Desktop Services** (**RDS**) group that can push the user into AD again, delivering one level of focus for IT on the directory structure from within Okta, while managing AD.

Sometimes the group assignment can be a bit stricter and requires more rule values before assigning. In that case, Okta allows you to use Okta Expression Language to set up larger and stricter rules:

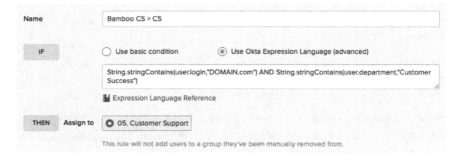

Figure 5.20 – Group assignment rule based on Okta's Expression Language

Using Okta's Expression Language, you can filter and funnel the users you are looking for before you assign them to the correct group. In this case, a specific domain and department value will assign the user to the **Customer Support** group.

It can also be that certain circumstances allow the user to be added to a group because of policy changes. Perhaps offboarding requires the user to move over to SMS during their grace period. Using a group to assign the user to a policy that needs them to enroll SMS and grant access to Okta with only SMS as a factor would look like this:

Name	Limited access during offboarding grace period
IF	◉ Use basic condition ○ Use Okta Expression Language (advanced)
	Group membership ▾ Includes any of the following
	◉ 90. Offboarding - grace period ✕
THEN Assign to	◉ 98.2 MFA SMS
	This rule will not add users to a group they've been manually removed from.

Figure 5.21 – Group assignment to a group for policy enrollment

While you might allow offboarded users to keep access to certain applications, you want to make sure they are accessing your systems in a secure manner. Perhaps they now need to use their own device and have problems with installing apps. Enrolling them into SMS might be less secure, but still better than no security at all.

Let's say you allow users to have specific access to licenses that are group managed. Sometimes it's wise to have these options as profile attributes and use them to assign the user to the license with the help of a group:

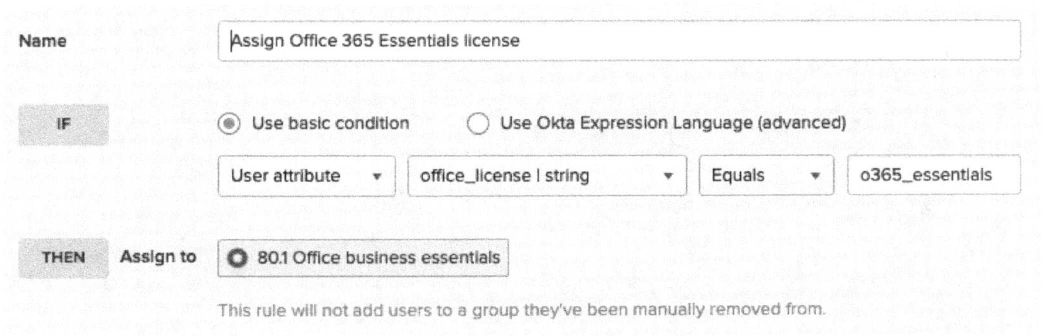

Name	Assign Office 365 Essentials license

IF	⦿ Use basic condition ◯ Use Okta Expression Language (advanced)
	User attribute ▾ office_license	string ▾ Equals ▾ o365_essentials

THEN	Assign to	◉ 80.1 Office business essentials

This rule will not add users to a group they've been manually removed from.

Figure 5.22 – Group assignment rule for license management

Adding the different types of profile attributes can help you further automate this process. Sometimes it requires input from HR; sometimes IT needs to do it. In this case, a drop-down choice field on the user profile allows the user to be assigned to the Office Business Essentials group, which will provision the user into Office365 with that specific license.

All these and many more rules can easily be set up in the Okta **Push Groups** section. There might be situations where you need to be more efficient or you simply like your work to be coded. In that case, Okta allows all of this and more to be managed by its APIs where you can use the same functionality to create, update, (de)activate, or delete any or all of these rules.

> **Important note**
> As the options are very broad, and the documentation on APIs is very extensive, it won't be possible to go into detail on this topic. To find out more about group rule APIs, please visit Okta's extensive developer API resource site: https://developer.okta.com/docs/reference/api/groups/#group-rule-operations.

Whenever the value changes for the user (for example, the user moves from the Sales to the Marketing team), and the rules pick up the change, the user will get reassigned to the marketing group and unassigned from the sales group. This allows lean management and no need to add custom management to unassign users. Okta will be able to understand the impact and change accordingly.

On a user's profile, it is clear in what way groups are assigned to the user, by the descriptive text. Any group assigned with rules is shown with a clickable link to the rule itself:

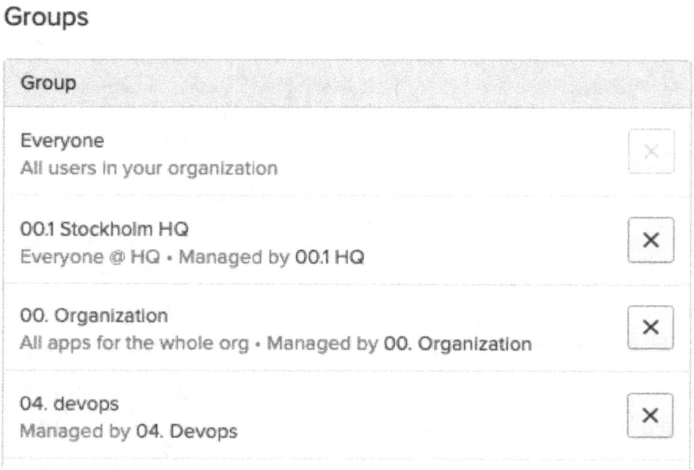

Groups

Group	
Everyone All users in your organization	×
00.1 Stockholm HQ Everyone @ HQ · Managed by 00.1 HQ	×
00. Organization All apps for the whole org · Managed by 00. Organization	×
04. devops Managed by 04. Devops	×

Figure 5.23 – Group rules shown in the Groups section of a user's profile

As we discussed earlier, in *Chapter 3, Single Sign-On for a Great End User Experience*, usually there is an order to how policies are presented. In the case of group rules, this doesn't apply. These do not need to be, and technically cannot be, differently ordered to allow them to work properly.

Group rules can act upon changes made by other group rules. Meaning that one group rule can trigger other group rules because of group (re-)assignment. These cascading rules can have performance issues and it's considered best practice to try to combine them together in one rule if the situation allows that.

It can happen that a user gets assigned to a group based on the condition of the rule, even if they shouldn't be, because of logic that isn't configurable in the rules. In that case, you can exclude a user's assignment through a couple of methods:

- Exclude the user in the rule
- Remove the user from the group

That exclusion could look like this:

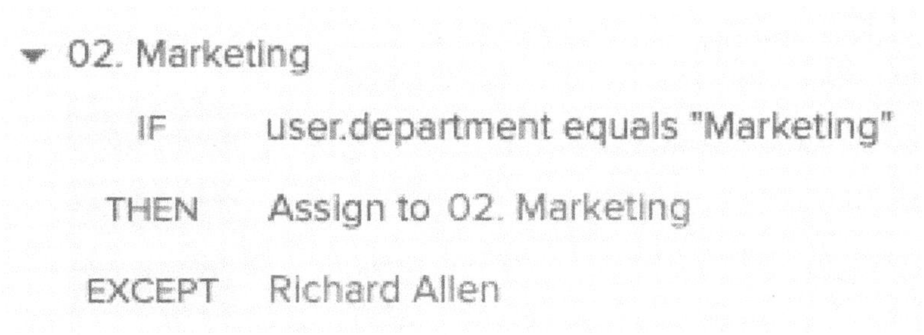

▼ 02. Marketing

    IF   user.department equals "Marketing"

    THEN   Assign to 02. Marketing

    EXCEPT Richard Allen

Figure 5.24 – Group rule with an excluded user

These actions make sure the users aren't assigned to the group. If the user needs to be re-assigned to the group after being excluded by a rule, you can remove the user from the **EXCEPT** list in the rule. Re-activating the rule will re-evaluate the user and add them back to the group based on the group rule.

Sometimes group rules can have uncalculated results that can have a worse outcome than you would have predicted. Especially in the case where groups are used for provisioning, it's wise to keep in mind what certain changes can do to application assignment.

Group rules truly help automate most of your tasks, allowing user creation, management, and application assignment. They are also used for policy management and therefore can have multiple tasks to do. And while the setup is fairly simple, they can have a positive influence on any IT employee's daily routine, but can also have a large impact and need to be handled with caution and thoroughness.

In the next section, we will go over how users can request access to applications that might not be captured within automation rules so their management is more manual.

Setting up self-service options

Users have their personal dashboards to see and manage their applications. For applications integrated with SAML or OIDC, they would be automatically signed in when clicking on any of them. For SWA applications, where admins have set that end users will enter their own credentials, they will be prompted to do so the first time they click on an icon. After they are logged in, Okta will ask whether the login was successful. If the answer is yes, the credentials will be stored. If not, the end user will be able to try again.

The end users can re-arrange their applications by simply clicking and dragging. To find applications quickly, you can arrange applications in different tabs or simply use the search bar at the top of the page.

With the Add Applications feature for end users, they are able to add private applications, or corporate-owned applications if this is enabled. Navigate to **Applications | Self Service** in the admin console. In the topmost section, you can see the available options for requestable applications, and your current selections enabled:

- **Allow users to add org-managed apps**
- **Allow users to add personal apps**
- **Allow users to email "Technical Contact" to request an app**

Below, you can see what applications you have configured for users to request.

If you have org-managed applications that you don't want to provision for all users from the start, but would like to offer them if users need the application, you can turn on the feature to allow users to add them.

By going to **Applications | Self Service**, you can select to turn on the feature **Allow users to add org-managed apps**:

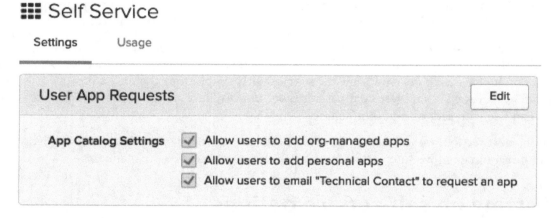

Figure 5.25 – Options to enable users to request an application

To enable an application to be self-assigned by a user, navigate to **Application | Application** and select the app you want to configure. In the **Assignments** tab, you'll find **Self-service** to the right. Click **Edit** and change **Allow users to request app** to **Yes**. If you want to set an approval flow, you can also change **Approval** to **Required**. If left on the default setting, **Not Required**, the application can be assigned by the user without any approval being needed:

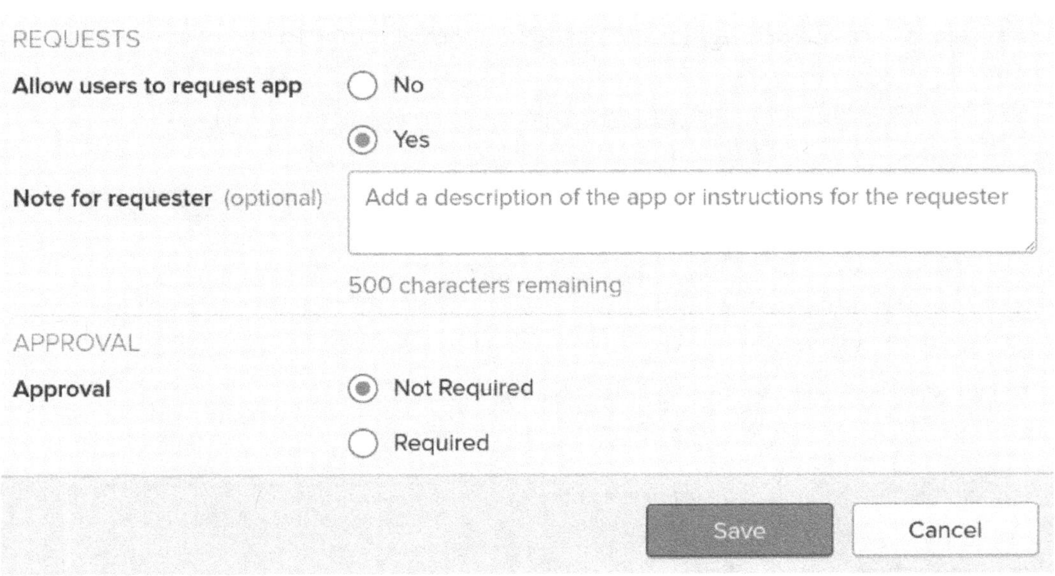

REQUESTS

Allow users to request app   ○ No

◉ Yes

Note for requester (optional)   Add a description of the app or instructions for the requester

500 characters remaining

APPROVAL

Approval   ◉ Not Required

○ Required

[Save]   [Cancel]

Figure 5.26 – Options to enable users to request an application

You can assign the approval of the request to one or multiple users, or to one or more groups. For groups, one single group can't contain more than 100 members. Everyone in the group gets a notification of the request but only one has to approve it. By assigning it to more than one, you can create a chain of approval. This chain of approval is limited to 10 layers and approvers can only be part of the chain once. Approvers will be given entitlements: **Hidden**, **Read**, **Write**. These are used to set what approvers can do on the requester's account. You should always aim for the least privilege approach, but some applications require attributes for provisioning. If so, set an approver to have **Write** access. If you want to change the order of approvers, you can easily just drag and drop the users or groups. If the application doesn't support automatic provisioning, you can use the last step of an approval chain as the provisioning. Make sure the last approver is an administrator, who can provision the account and give access.

The last step is to set the settings for notifications as well as a time frame for approvers:

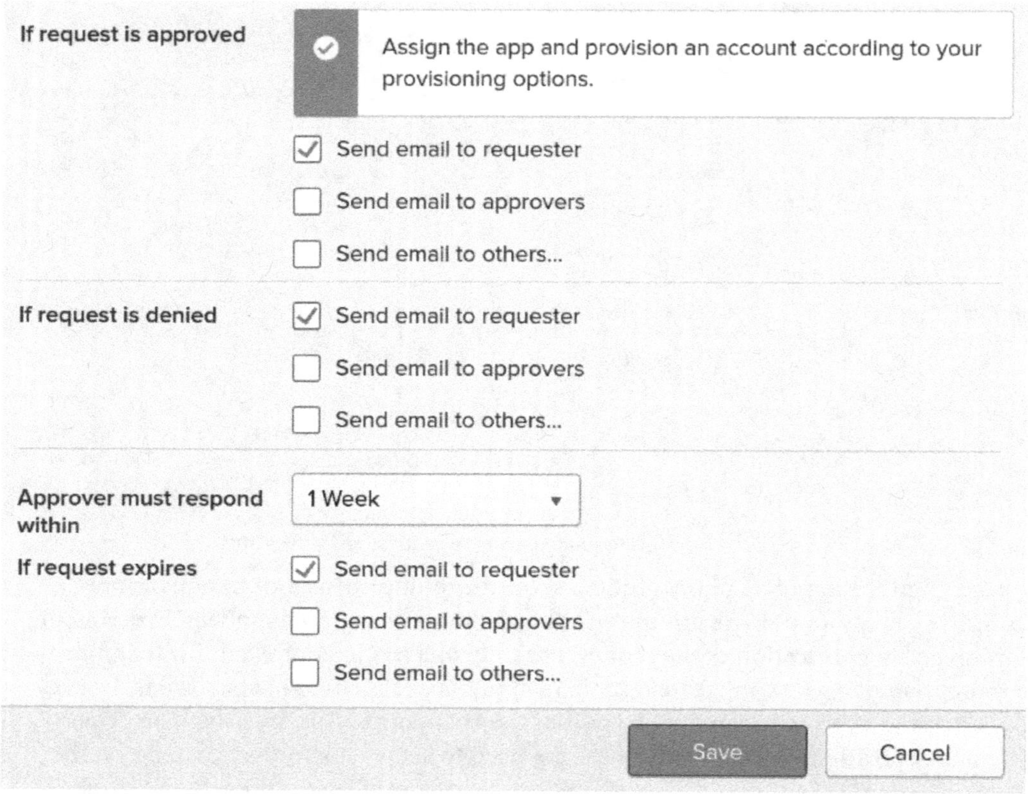

Figure 5.27 – Options for notifications in the approval flow

If you didn't check the box to allow users to request applications at the beginning, you will be prompted to do so when clicking **Save**. Otherwise, you are now done!

Let's move on to different abilities for workflows.

Using workflow capabilities

The workflow capabilities within Okta expand across three areas: **Inline Hooks**, **Event Hooks**, and **Automation**. These areas have different functionalities and different options they can fulfill.

Inline Hooks

With Inline Hooks, you can call your own custom code with help from Okta's REST API. The outbound calls are triggered by events in your Okta process flows. Your custom code will be a web service with an internet accessible endpoint. The service isn't hosted in Okta; it's hosted by you. Inline Hooks use synchronous calls, which means that the process that triggered the hook/outbound call is paused until it receives an answer from your service.

So how are these hooks added? Let's look at that.

> **Tip**
> Only super administrators can view and configure Inline Hooks.

Navigate to **Workflow | Inline Hooks**. Click **Add Inline Hook** and then select what kind you want to use:

- **SAML**: Lets you modify assertions sent to SAML applications
- **Token**: Lets you modify tokens issued by your own authorization servers
- **Password Import**: Lets you import the passwords of users logging in

To configure your new hook, you will need to enter the following information:

- **Name**: A name that describes the function of the hook
- **URL**: A URL pointed at the endpoint to call in your web service
- **Authentication field**: The authorization header name
- **Authentication secret**: The field name's corresponding value string
- **Custom header fields**: Optional field name/value pairs to send with the request

After saving, you need to pair the endpoint with the right Okta process flow. How to do this depends on the kind of inline hook you have set up (**SAML**, **Token**, or **Password Import**). If you click on any of the types of hooks in the list in Okta, you will receive information on how to connect your specific type of hook, to enable it.

> **Important note**
> Check out this help center section of Okta to understand how to further implement Inline Hooks for your business needs: `https://developer.`
> `okta.com/docs/concepts/inline-hooks/#currently-`
> `supported-types`.

Event Hooks

Event Hooks are like webhooks. They send Okta events that are interesting to other systems, via `HTTP POST`, when they occur. Possible use cases for this kind of functionality could be the following:

- Sending a notification in a Slack channel when something suspicious occurs with a user

- Adding a customer to all systems in your marketing stack, after they sign up for your service

Exactly as with Inline Hooks, you need a web service with an open endpoint. When a specific event occurs in your Okta org, an `HTTP POST` is sent to this endpoint. As opposed to Inline Hooks, Event Hooks are asynchronous calls, and the process is not paused while it waits for the response from your web service. The setup however is exactly the same. By navigating to **Workflow | Event Hooks** and clicking **Create Event Hook**, you get to enter information in the same fields as for Inline Hooks.

Automation

Automation is a section that allows simple actions to trigger on different conditions.

Any new automation starts with a *time-based element* and will look at *one or more groups*. Additionally, you can add the following triggers to the automation: **User Inactivity in Okta** and **User password expiration in Okta**. These conditions combined in any way can set off different actions in the automation. You can add an action to *send an email to the user*, and/or *change the user's life cycle state* to suspended, deactivated, or deleted. An automation setup can look as follows:

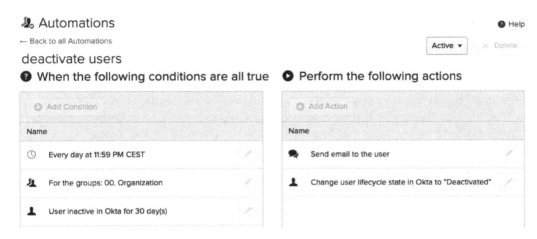

Figure 5.28 – Automation flow to deactivate a user after 30 days of inactivity

In this automation, we have set up a deactivation flow if the user has been inactive for 30 days. The automation runs every day at 11:59 P.M. and it checks the entire organization group as the potential user population. If it finds a user meeting these conditions, an email is sent to the user and the user's state is set to deactivated. You can preview and change the email that is sent while setting up the automation.

After saving the different triggers and actions and naming the automation, it can be activated and will be running in the background.

Depending on the size of your Okta org, it can take up to 24 hours before the automation starts evaluating. These small automations can help automate simple tasks. If you want to do much more with Okta, please read the following section on Okta Workflows, Okta's advanced workflow engine built to automate every step of your IT business.

Using Okta Workflows

Okta Workflows is a GUI-driven no-code automation tool Okta released in 2019. This large pool of functionality allows Okta to be capable of managing different aspects of the user life cycle more granularly. This differs quite extensively versus the simpler automations we talked about in the previous section. Workflows allows you to incorporate dozens of applications, and your own functionalities as part of a workflow.

> **Important note**
>
> Workflows is part of the **Advanced Life Cycle Management** (**ALCM**) product from Okta and requires additional licensing. Not every Okta org will have these features.

Workflows can do a lot. Let's look at a few use cases:

- *The provisioning and deprovisioning of app accounts*: Okta Workflows can automatically detect and act on newly added accounts. These newly joined employees with their Okta account will be assigned to the required applications, be granted the necessary entitlements, and even receive folder shares based on who they are and what their role is. Additionally, a message can be sent to their manager to make sure they are welcomed correctly. On the other hand, Okta Workflows can suspend accounts, transfer over any digital assets to the required accounts or users, grant a grace period to allow manual work on the suspended user, and eventually deactivate the user within all and any connected applications.

- *Using logic and timing to sequence actions*: Using Workflows grants the opportunity to get work done in advance. Using options such as creating deactivated accounts in applications allows you to make sure work can be done upfront. Once onboarding time is around the corner, Workflows will activate the account within Okta and activate application accounts as well. When a user leaves the company, they can still have access to payroll for personal administrative reasons and, after a year, close the account entirely.

- *Conflict resolving capabilities*: Workflows can have logic built in to detect and resolve conflicts when it comes to user accounts; for instance, creating unique usernames for applications such as Slack, to make sure deactivated existing accounts aren't reactivated for a new user.

- *Using notifications for all types of events*: Using communication tools can help bring information to the correct people. Making sure managers are notified on Slack that a new employee will start, or sending emails to IT to notify them about factor problems are all functionalities you can leverage with Okta Workflows.

- *Expanding Log and APIs*: With the use of exports and CSV files, Okta can send details periodically, but also send details of events to third-party systems to make sure all details surrounding users, applications, and systems are up to date and directly accessible for the right people.

For Okta to truly get a grip on all aspects of the user's identity within the different applications, new integrations need to be set up. This means Okta doesn't use the integrations already in Okta, but needs to redo the integrations again in the Workflows interface. Currently, Okta only allows pre-built integrations to be set up.

Your first Workflows contact

First, you need to have access to the Workflows app itself. When it's turned on for your Okta org, you can access the **Workflows console** under the **Workflow Settings** menu:

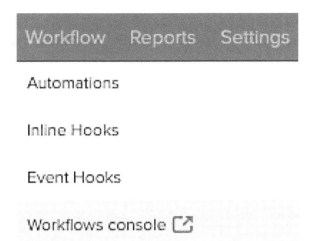

Figure 5.29 – Workflows menu section

This feature will appear for any admin who is an organization administrator or super administrator.

When you access the Workflows console, no integration has been set up. In your Okta integrations, a preset OIDC app has been created to set up the environment.

To start, you follow the settings windows to integrate Workflows with Okta:

1. In the admin console, go to **Applications | Applications**.

2. Select **Okta Workflows OAuth**, and then open the **Sign On** tab.

3. Open a second browser tab and in the admin console, go to **Workflow | Workflows console**.

4. In **Workflows console**, click **New Connection**.

5. In the **Connection Nickname** field, enter the display name that you want to appear in your connector list.

6. In the **Domain field**, enter your Okta org's domain, without `https://` and `-admin`, if applicable. For example, if the URL is `https://organization-admin.okta.com`, your domain is `organization.okta.com`.

7. In the admin console, copy the client ID from the Okta Workflows OAuth app. Return to the **Workflows console**, and paste it in the **Client ID** field of the **Connection** window.

8. In the admin console, copy the client secret from the Okta Workflows OAuth app. Return to the **Workflows console** and paste it in the **Client Secret** field of the **Connection** window.

9. In the **Workflows console**, click **Create**.

Done! You have added your Okta org as an integration in Workflows.

To integrate other compatible applications with Workflows, Okta provides step-by-step instructions that you can follow. Detailed explanations of these integrations are beyond the scope of this book and can be found within the Workflows interface.

Now you can trigger on events, and do actions in Okta and any other integration you have set up. Let's look more deeply into these events and actions that workflows use.

Okta Workflows automation flows

To be sure you understand all the elements within Workflows, we need to be clear on the different naming within the Workflows product:

- **Workflows**: The Okta product used to automate business logic.
- **Flows**: Flows are the workflows that are built to do the heavy work with integrations.
- **Flowcards**: Flowcards are the steps in a workflow. These steps are visualized from left to right on the **Flow** page.
- **Event**: The Event is the trigger from where a **Flow** starts. There can only be one Event in a Flow.
- **Actions**: Actions are Flowcards that do something in the Flow, such as sending commands to the Flowcard integration.
- **Functions**: Functions are cards that allow you to change how the flow interacts with moving data.

A complete Flow with Flowcards could look as follows:

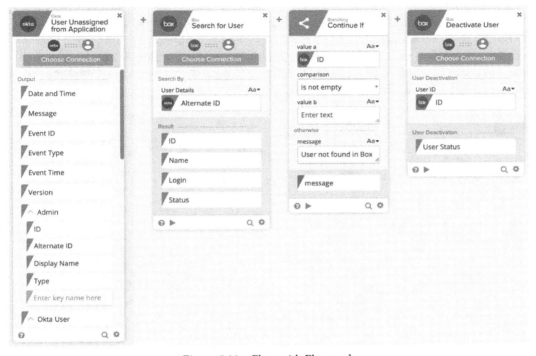

Figure 5.30 – Flow with Flowcards

Here you can see a sample flow. The first Flowcard is the trigger card. This Flowcard allows the entire Flow to trigger. The second Flowcard is an action Flowcard, and it searches for the user in Okta based on the triggered event. The third is a functions Flowcard determining whether the Flow is allowed to continue if the condition is met. In this example, it uses a **Continue If** function. And the last Flowcard is another action Flowcard, sending an action into the connected app.

The data moving between the different Flowcards allows the Flow to handle, determine, and use the data in any way you see fit.

Flowcards have input fields and output fields. Input fields are mapped against other fields in previous Flowcards. Output fields generate what you think is needed for that Flowcard. This can be created by the event, action, or function you used. Flows allow a drag and drop mechanism. By simply dragging any field into another Flowcard's input field, you have mapped the data from these two fields. Fields can be used multiple times, and can be used to connect to different input field on other Flowcards. This makes it super easy to reuse data from one specific Flowcard in any other:

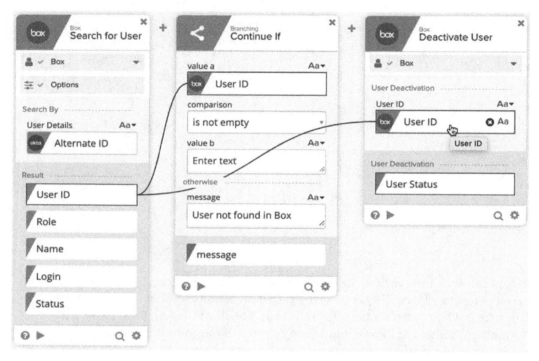

Figure 5.31 – Mapping data from one field to multiple others

Additionally, you can add note Flowcards to the Flow to expand more on what the actions are doing and to make sure everyone else understands the Flow in its entirety.

Platform features

Okta Workflows comes with some additional features that help you expand the possibilities even more:

- **Tables** are datastores within your Flows. They can generate data during Flow executions, store data for reporting, or create constants tables to be reused in different flows for recalling information. All of this is stored within the Okta Workflows interface and available without re-authorizing the user's session.

  Tables can be exported and saved as a .csv file, to be sent (with a Flow) to whom it may concern. For example, sending security a monthly report on bad login attempts, or showing offboarding statistics to department heads and HR. All of this can be done with the help of tables.

  Tables can also be accessed within a Flow to get the information needed and add it as context, or used as information that needs to be transformed, or you can simply delete the info in a table. By adding a functions card for the table, you can do whatever you like with the data in it.

- **API endpoints** are other types of triggers that can kickstart a Flow. Using a third-party system with the right security access can start a Flow with data sent along. Let's say your HR system doesn't have any integration out of the box with Okta but does have API capabilities. With some simple scripting, you can use the Okta Workflows API endpoints to have new users created, updated, or even deactivated. Based on the content sent along within the POST call, you can allow a Flow to use the start date to wait on the action for creation or have the deactivation be prescheduled and run once the date is met.

  By changing the exposure in the Flow settings, endpoints of the workflow can become more open to the public. In that case, you can allow other services to trigger on, and perhaps give information back on data from various applications, or allow services to register new users into your Okta system. This can also be done by third parties that you do not control but would like to give automated access to your systems.

- History is available per Flow and is stored for up to 30 days. This allows you as an admin to check if everything went right, or fix issues if the Flow didn't behave as expected. As flows can have sensitive data in them, allowing the storage of history requires an opt in. You can do this within the Flow by checking the **Save all data** checkbox in the **Save** dialog box or clicking on the **Enable Save Data** link in the right pane of the **Flow History** page. You can disable this any time you want. This might be relevant when **Personally Identifiable Information (PII)** is moving within your Flow and you need to debug when creating the Flow. Once you have determined it's working as expected, turning off the Flow history can be a good step to take.

Okta has a lot of different use cases and tutorials to help you start your first Workflows experience. It is recommended to read through `learn.workflows.okta.com` and check out their growing library of examples and flows they talk you through.

Summary

In this chapter, we have pieced together things we've learned in previous chapters, and with that looked at how a complete user provisioning life cycle can work. We've looked at how using your HR system as a master brings extra power to your IT resources and reduces friction between HR and IT. We have gone through how you can work with mapping from different applications and directories, as well as an introduction to referencing and changing attributes with Expression Language. Further, we have looked at the capabilities within group automations, specifically for provisioning flows. Lastly, we have dived into how you can use different kinds of hooks to automate processes to and from Okta, as well as using Okta's new advanced features for Workflows. With this knowledge, you will be able to start your provisioning setup with ease. Secondly, you have gained knowledge about how to use Okta's automation to help your IT operations. Lastly, understanding the basics of Workflows will help you to create automation that can replace manual processes.

In the next chapter, we will look into how to customize the Okta experience for your end users.

6
Customizing Your Okta GUI

So far, we have focused a lot on the administrator panel and all the features that make Okta a leader in its field, but none of Okta's capabilities would matter if the user experience wasn't good. We will now look a little more at the user experience and what we as admins can do to change it. To start, we will look at the different features end users have. After that, we'll go into how we can customize the user dashboard, with a logo and colors. We will go through what different administrator settings there are to configure the dashboard. While looking at the admin settings, we will also see how to modify what is sent from Okta, such as emails and SMS messages. Lastly, we will investigate how you can customize the login page and how to manage and host a custom login widget on your own login page. The following topics are covered in this chapter:

- Understanding the basics of end user functionality and customization
- The user dashboard and Okta plugin settings
- Custom domain setup and custom page creation

Understanding the basics of end user functionality and customization

Before we can change any settings for end users to optimize the experience, we must understand what their interface looks like and what we can change. As mentioned before, when an end user logs in to the dashboard, they see all available applications. By default, they have a tab called **Work**, where they can add their own tabs and organize their applications.

On the end user dashboard, users can modify how apps are shown, add their own applications, and manage any credentials within the apps that are set up as **Secure Web Authentication** (**SWA**) applications.

> **Important note**
> Okta is currently switching over to a new look and feel for the dashboard. We will be referencing the new dashboard layout; we'll occasionally reference the old dashboard where necessary.

Let's go over the different sections of the dashboard:

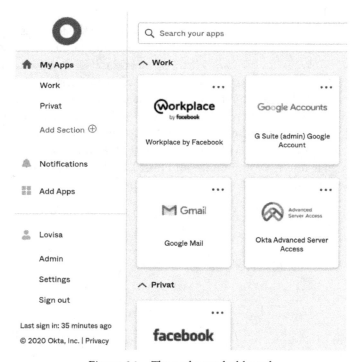

Figure 6.1 – The end user dashboard

The left column is where users can find the different sections they have created and quick links to the **App catalog** and **Notifications** sections. At the bottom, admins can access the **Admin** center; all users will have access to the settings and an option for signing out is available.

In the search bar at the top, users can easily search for an application. You also have **Settings** and **Sign Out**. On the old dashboard, they appear when you click your name next to the search bar. This is what the old menu looks like:

Figure 6.2 – The old end user menu

If you are using the new end user's dashboard, the menu will look like this:

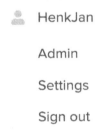

HenkJan

Admin

Settings

Sign out

Figure 6.3 – The new end user menu in the sidebar

In the **Settings** menu, end users will find a lot of information. These are the sections:

- **Personal Information**
- **Security Image**
- **Extra Verification**
- **Display Language**
- **Change Password**
- **Forgotten Password Question**
- **Forgot Password Text Message**

In the first section, users can modify their personal information and review any information that you as an administrator are showing them. If they click **Edit**, they can change the fields that are open to them. At certain times, users might be required to re-authenticate to change any settings. This is a security feature you can change in the admin console under **Settings | Customization: Reauthentication Settings**. It can only be set to 5 or 15 minutes.

Next, users are able to change their security image, if needed. This is only visible if **Security Image** is enabled in the admin console:

Figure 6.4 – Security image options

In *Chapter 4, Increasing Security with Adaptive Multifactor Authentication*, we learned how to update your MFA enrollments, which is covered in the following part of the settings page:

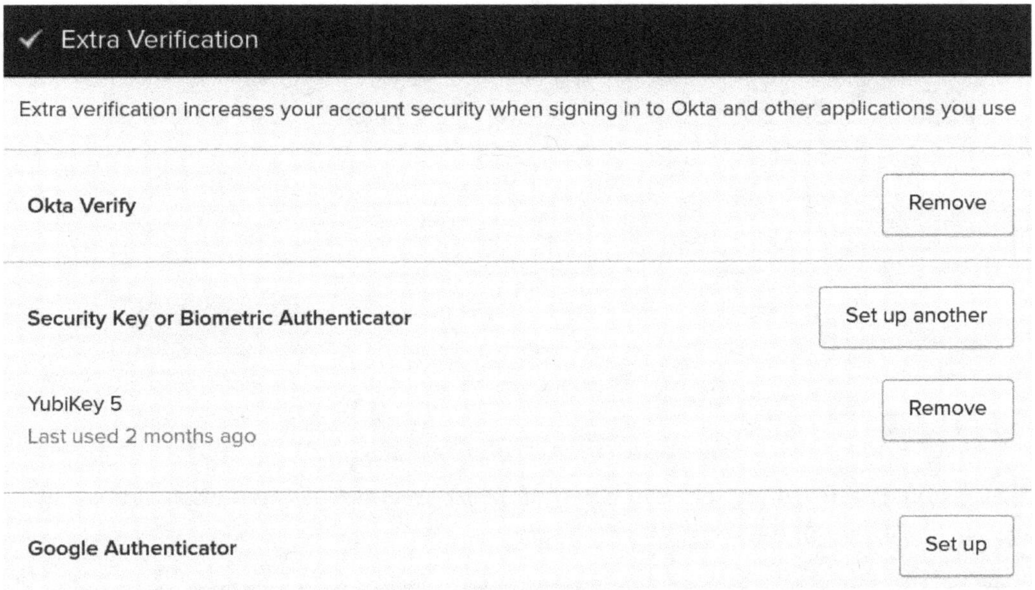

Figure 6.5 – Multifactor configuration settings

Depending on how your policies are set up, this section will show only the available factors the user can enroll into that are applicable to them. If and when you set up additional factor enrollment policies that use groups the user is part of, more factors will be added here.

In the next section, the end user can update the display language. Currently, Okta supports 27 different languages – to see a list of supported languages, refer to `https://help.okta.com/en/prod/Content/Topics/Reference/ref-supported-languages.htm`:

Figure 6.6 – Display language settings

In the **Change Password** section, end users can proactively update their password according to the policy you have set:

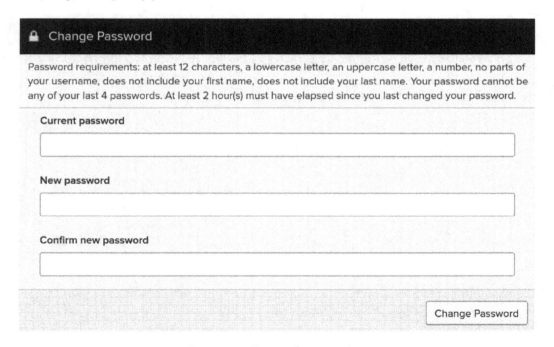

Figure 6.7 – Password reset section

After that, end users can update the security question they have set. Both the question and the answer can be updated by clicking **Edit**:

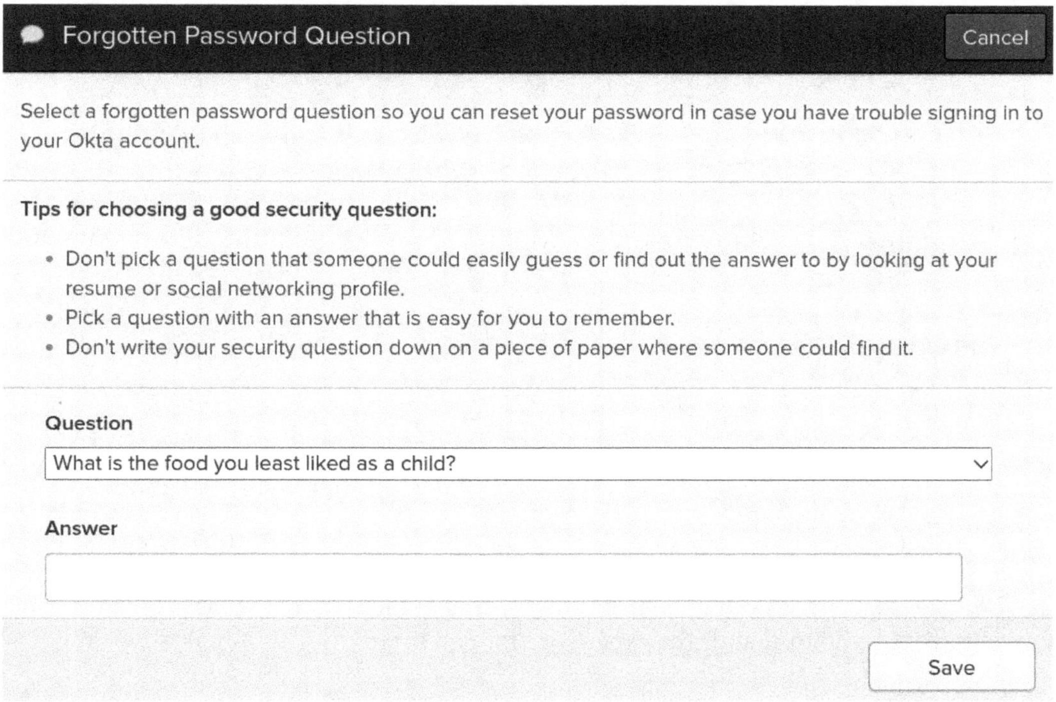

Figure 6.8 – Security question section

In the last section, the end user is able to update what phone number a recovery text can be sent to when users use self-service reset options:

Figure 6.9 – Recovery number reset options

Okay, that's all that end users can do from their side; let's look at what we as administrators can do to change the experience for end users.

Visual end user settings

A great way for you as an admin to make your users feel comfortable in Okta is to work with the visual settings. Let's see how that works.

> **Important note**
> As of the end of 2019, Okta has started offering a new modern dashboard, where certain visuals have changed. This might change even more as the modern dashboard evolves over time.

In the admin panel, navigate to **Settings | Appearance**. To change what Okta looks like to your end users, you can start with **Application Theme** to the right:

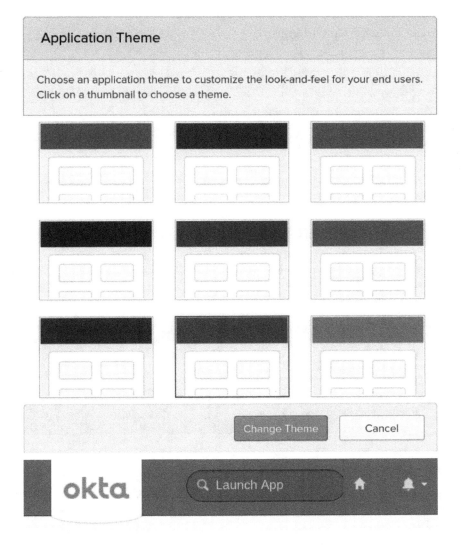

Figure 6.10 – Theme selection and the result

By selecting a different color than the default from the previewed mini dashboards, and then clicking **Change Theme**, your selection will be applied. This only applies to the old dashboard.

To make it even better, you can upload your organization's logo to the dashboard. Go to the bottom right and click **Upload logo**:

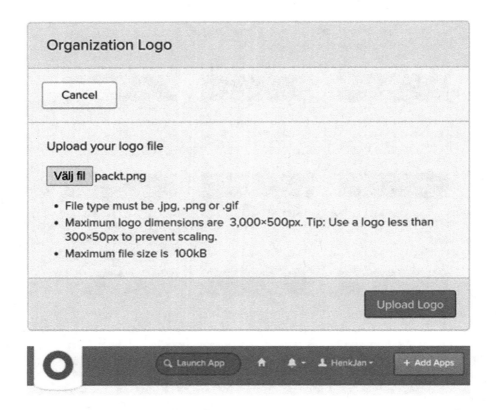

Figure 6.11 – The settings for replacing the Okta logo with your own

By selecting your own logo and clicking **Save**, you will replace the Okta logo at the top-left corner of the dashboard. The logo must fulfill these conditions:

- It must be a .jpg, .png, or .gif file.
- The logo dimensions can be a maximum of 3,000 × 500 px.
- The file size must be less than 100 kB.

There's more you can do with this logo. In the top-most section to the left on the **Feature settings** page, you can customize **Display Options**:

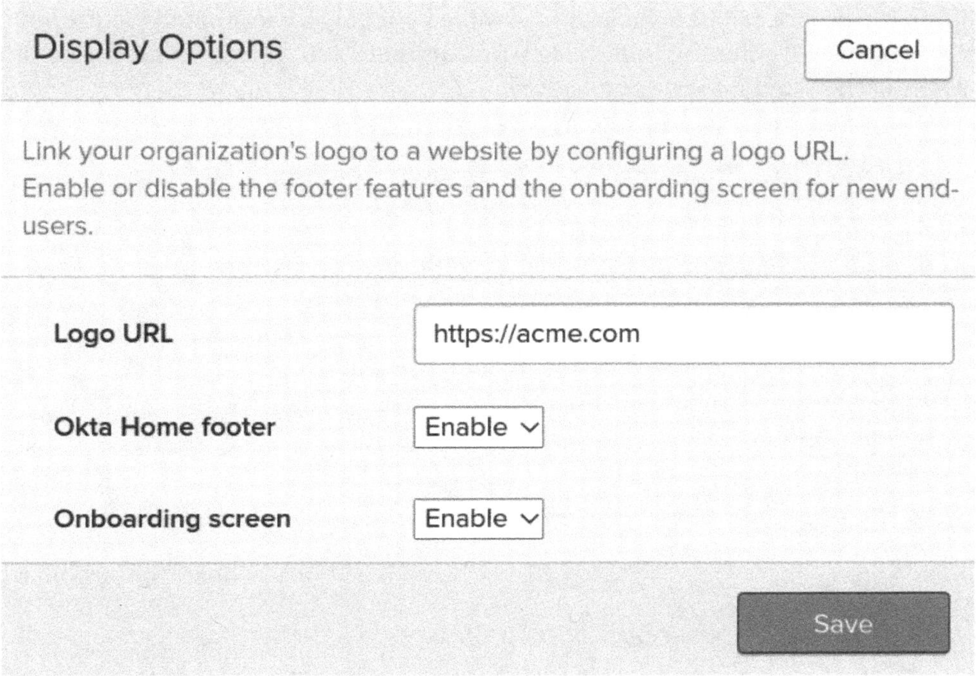

Display Options   Cancel

Link your organization's logo to a website by configuring a logo URL.
Enable or disable the footer features and the onboarding screen for new end-users.

Logo URL	https://acme.com
Okta Home footer	Enable ∨
Onboarding screen	Enable ∨

Save

Figure 6.12 – Options for Display Options

This is what you can do:

- **Logo URL**: After uploading a logo, you can add a URL that leads to your desired website when you click it.

- **Okta Home footer**: With this footer, users get links to Okta's website and their help site.

- **Onboarding screen**: With this setting enabled, your end users get a pop-up message when they activate their account:

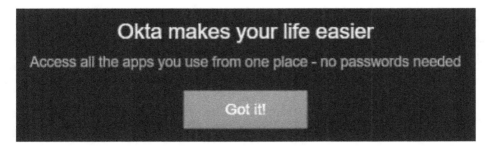

Figure 6.13 – Popup for new users

The sign-in experience can be enhanced even more by setting a background picture for your sign-in screen. By clicking **Edit** in **Sign-In Configuration**, you get to select a picture to set as the background for your sign-in page:

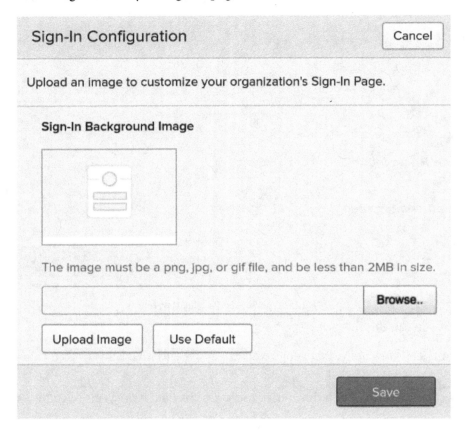

Figure 6.14 – Simple sign-in configuration

The chosen picture needs to follow these restrictions:

- It must be a .jpg, .png, or .gif file.
- The file size must be less than 2 MB.

By navigating to **Settings | Customization**, you can make some more changes to the sign-in page:

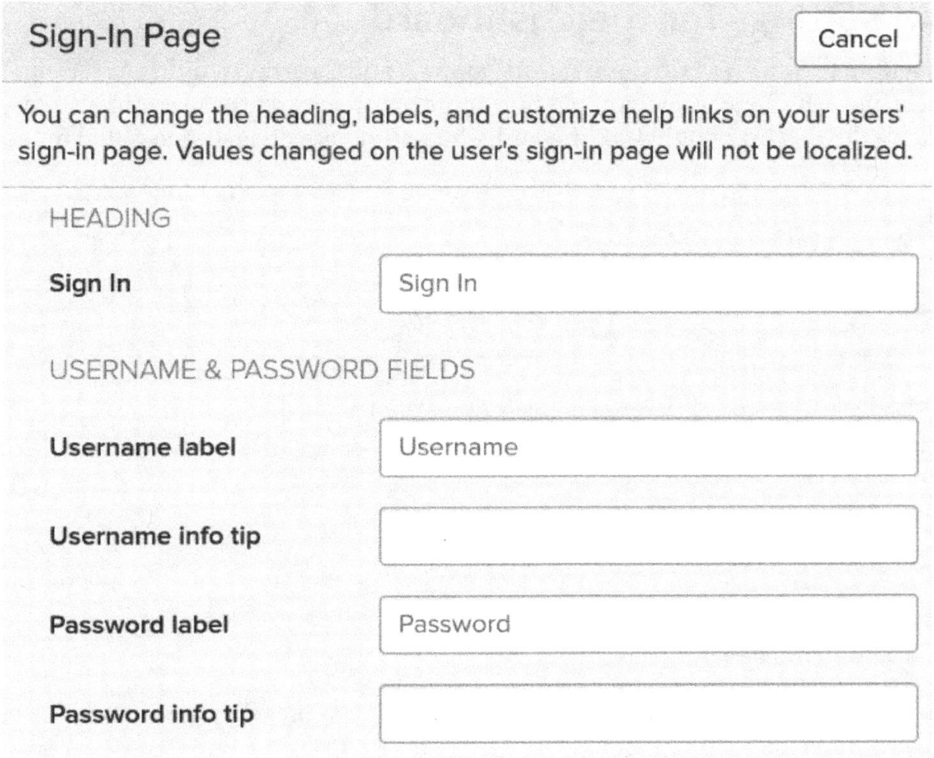

Figure 6.15 – Some of the options for the sign-in page

There are multiple options, including labels for logging in. There is also a big section on customizing help links and their labels. If you want to add a link to your own Okta help site, this is where you would add it.

In the next section, we will look at what settings you as an administrator can set for the end user's experience after login.

The end user dashboard and Okta plugin settings

Now that we have looked at what settings we can configure for the login experience, let's see what we can do for the experience inside Okta.

Admin settings for the dashboard

If you navigate to **Settings | Customization**, you will find an array of different settings that you can use. It's here where you can find some of the settings the user can also see when they go to **Settings** on their dashboard. The settings are divided into different tabs:

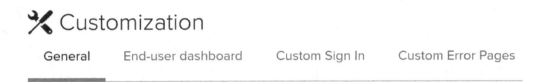

Figure 6.16 – Categories of customization

The categories are as follows:

- **General**
- **End-user dashboard**
- **Custom Sign In**
- **Custom Error Pages**

In this section, we will look at the first two; let's start with **General**.

In the **User Account** section, you can manage settings for how users can change their personal information and/or password information. If this information is managed by another application, you can write a message that will be shown to your end users on their settings page:

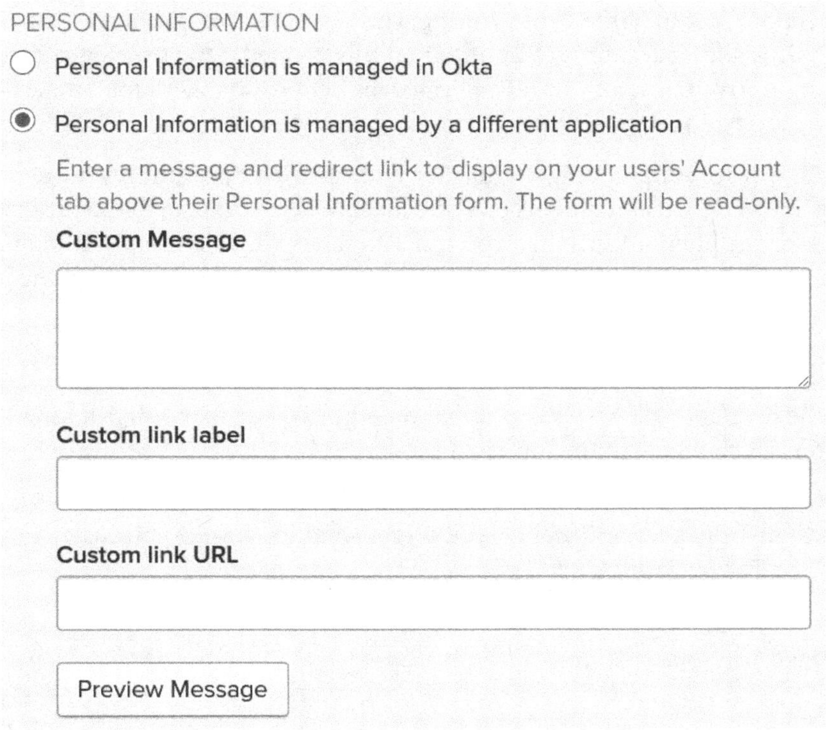

PERSONAL INFORMATION

○ Personal Information is managed in Okta

◉ Personal Information is managed by a different application

Enter a message and redirect link to display on your users' Account
tab above their Personal Information form. The form will be read-only.

Custom Message

Custom link label

Custom link URL

Preview Message

Figure 6.17 – Options for personal information

You can write a message to your end users about which application they should navigate
to to update their information and supply a URL there. This could, for instance, be an HR
system. The same goes for password management.

Under **Optional User Account Field**, you can enable or disable the end users' ability to
update their **Secondary email** and **Security image** settings.

Regarding **Okta User Communications**, Okta can contact your end users to get
information on their experience with Okta. If you don't want this, you can opt out of this
communication for your tenant here.

The section on the custom URL domain will be handled in the next section in this chapter.

Moving forward in the available settings, with **Deprovisioning workflow**, you can enable
or disable deprovisioning tasks generated by life cycle management actions on user
accounts.

In the next section, **Just in Time Provisioning**, you can enable or disable just-in-time provisioning. This allows accounts to be automatically created if the user signs in for the first time using **Active Directory (AD)** delegated authentication, Desktop Single Sign On, or inbound **Security Assertion Markup Language (SAML)**.

After that, you will see some setting options for **Okta Browser plugin**. If your end users are not allowed to install plugins on their machines, you can enable centralized management for the plugin. With that, you can also select which groups you want to enable it for. The last configuration is to enable a warning if end users are logging in to an Okta organization other than your own.

If you need to embed Okta in an iFrame, you can do so in the next section.

If you want the default display language to be something other than English for all of your end users, you can change it in the top-right section.

If you want to use a sign-out page other than Okta's default, you can add the URL in the section after **Sign-In page**. For instance, you might want to redirect your users to your website after signing out from Okta:

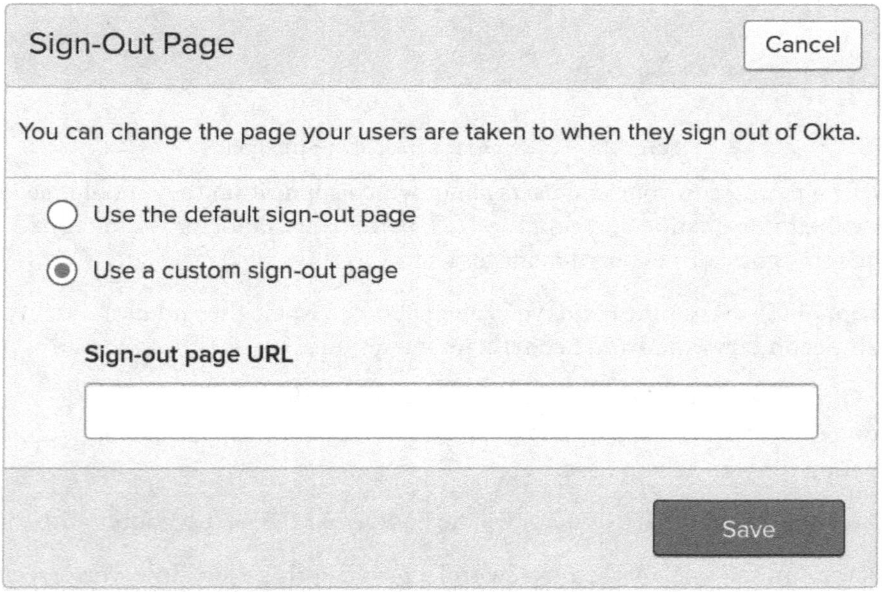

Figure 6.18 – Enter your own URL for the sign-out page

In the next section, you can disable the animation Okta displays while redirecting users to applications, so that users see a blank page instead. This can be useful if you have users with bad bandwidth.

If a user tries to access an application they are not assigned to, they will get an error message. If you want to redirect them to another URL instead of that, you can do so in the **Application Access Error Page** section.

When end users sign in to their dashboard, they get a section at the top with their most recently used applications:

Figure 6.19 – Section with recently used applications

If you want to disable this, do so in the last section of the **General Customization** settings page.

We have now walked through everything in the **General** tab – let's move on to the next tab, **End-user dashboard**, where you can manage company-wide settings for how the dashboard works:

Figure 6.20 – Configuration of the dashboard

Using the plus sign, you can create a new tab to assign to all or only new users. After creating another tab, you can also click and drag applications to that tab. You can add up to four more tabs. The **Work** tab can be renamed by hovering over it and clicking the pencil icon.

> **Important note**
>
> If you choose to save your changes for all users, existing users will get a notification about the changes upon their next sign in. Once applied, the user is free to rearrange their tabs and icons however they wish. The forced change will not reverse their settings.

All changes will overwrite any pre-existing dashboards done by individual users. This can be disruptive if used wrongly, but it's helpful for new starters. As it cannot be set up to manage different departments or teams, make sure to keep your company-wide settings for tabs on a basic level, making it easy for end users to update it to fit their own needs afterwards.

To be able to use the last two tabs, you need to set up a custom URL domain. We will look at how that works and what we can do with it in the next section. First, we will see what kinds of settings we can configure for the Okta browser plugin.

Okta plugin settings

The Okta plugin is a dashboard built into a browser extension. It allows you to navigate to any of your apps with ease without having to go back to your Okta page:

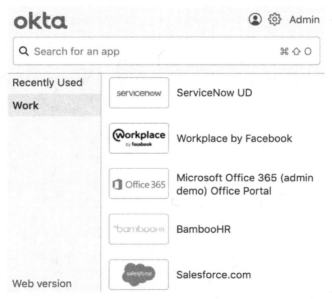

Figure 6.21 – The Okta plugin (new plugin layout)

One additional option is the account selector, for if you have more than one Okta session running with different tenants:

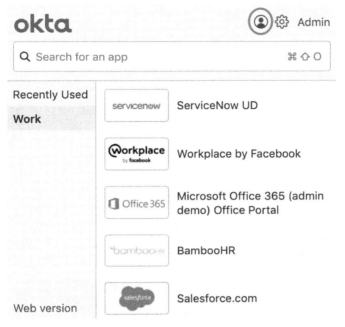

Figure 6.22 – The Okta plugin tenant selector

Specific settings for the plugin can be seen in the following screenshot:

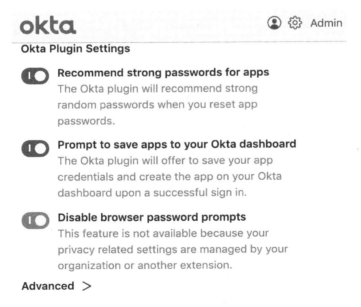

Figure 6.23 – The Okta plugin settings

These are the settings you can manage:

- You can have the plugin prompt for strong passwords when it detects a password reset happening on a known application.

- The plugin will ask to save new apps for end users if it's allowed to store new applications. This will pop up when the user logs in to a new application that Okta detects and determines to be a new app.

- You can prevent browser keychains from saving Okta login details, thereby ensuring that your secured and stored passwords for apps in Okta aren't leaked into unmanaged browser keychains.

For troubleshooting or investigation, you can click on **Advanced** in the Okta plugin and have the plugin write logs to the developer console of the browser. Use the local JavaScript instead of the most recent version packaged in the plugin and reset the plugin entirely, deleting any issues there might be with cookies and cache stored in the browser:

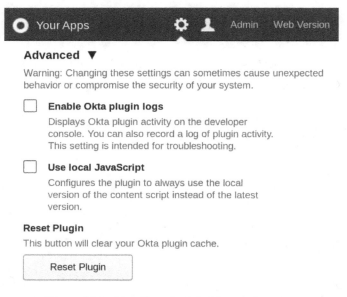

Figure 6.24 – The Okta plugin's Advanced section

Lastly, if you are an admin, the plugin will also show an option to go directly to the Okta admin dashboard (based on the chosen account in the plugin) and skip some steps by doing so:

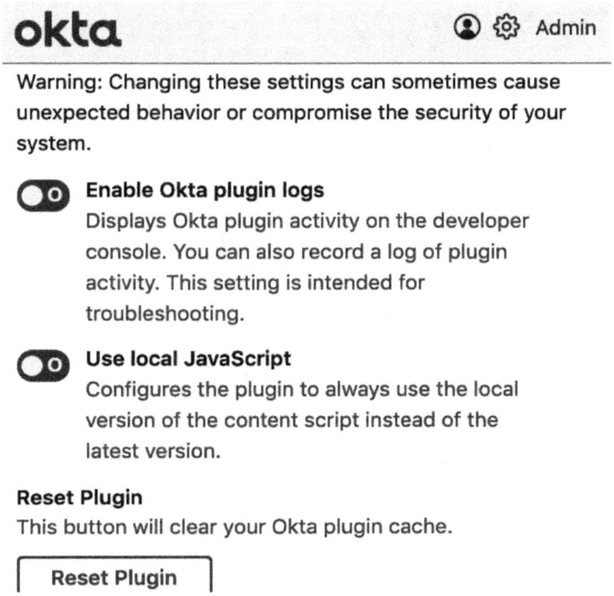

okta   Admin

Warning: Changing these settings can sometimes cause unexpected behavior or compromise the security of your system.

Enable Okta plugin logs
Displays Okta plugin activity on the developer console. You can also record a log of plugin activity. This setting is intended for troubleshooting.

Use local JavaScript
Configures the plugin to always use the local version of the content script instead of the latest version.

Reset Plugin
This button will clear your Okta plugin cache.

 Reset Plugin

Figure 6.25 – The Okta plugin admin button (highlighted)

The plugin is available for different browsers. Using the most recent version of the browser and plugin will give the best experience and the highest availability. It is recommended to make sure that users update, so they are able to use any new features that the browser or Okta provide. Find out more information about the continuous development of the plugin here: `https://help.okta.com/en/prod/Content/Topics/Apps/Apps_Browser_Plugin.htm`.

Custom domain setup and custom page creation

There can be different reasons that you might want a custom Okta domain. In this section, we will look into how that is done and how we can use it.

Customizing the sign-in page

You can set a custom URL domain for your Okta tenant. This can be useful if you don't want the end users to know that you are using Okta for application access. For instance, this can be interesting if you want to host an Okta login widget on your intranet. We will look into this later in this section. This custom URL needs to be set up on an Okta subdomain, and your main domain will remain as is. These are the steps to set up the custom URL:

1. In the first step, you need a domain you own (as well as a subdomain, like login. example.com) and you will need to be able to prove that you own it.

2. After that, you will have to update DNS records. You will receive information about the host and data from the setup wizard, which is then to be used in your domain registrar. Wait for the DNS registrar to update, then go back to Okta to verify it.

3. After that, you need to enter your TLS certificate, private key, and possible certificate chain. You will paste the PEM-encoded certificate and public key in the assigned fields. Remember to use the Begin and End lines for each of them.

4. The last step is to add an alias from your custom domain to the Okta subdomain by creating a CNAME record for your custom domain name. You do this in your domain registrar.

> **Important note**
>
> When you set up a custom domain, users are not rerouted from your main domain. You will have to tell users to start using the new custom domain name. If you have SAML or **Web Services Federation** (**WS-Fed**) applications, you might have to update them with the new domain if you want them to see the custom domain.

Now that we have a custom URL domain, we can go back to **Settings | Customization**, and look at the two remaining tabs. Using the **Custom Sign in** tab, you can change the look of the sign-in page with HTML code, directly in the editor in Okta. After making your changes, you can easily see them with the **Preview** button. When you are done with your changes, you hit **Save** and **Publish**. If you want to reset to the defaults, click the **Reset to Default** button. Apart from the HTML editor, you can also find the feature to change the labels and links on the default login page. If you use the login widget, you can find what version is used here. We will go into the details of that soon.

> **Important note**
> The custom URL domain needs to be set up to be able to have an Okta-hosted custom sign-in page.

But first, let's see what we can do in terms of custom error pages. Just like the custom sign-in page, you need a custom URL domain set up to be able to configure this. You also get an HTML editor to make changes and preview them in the same place:

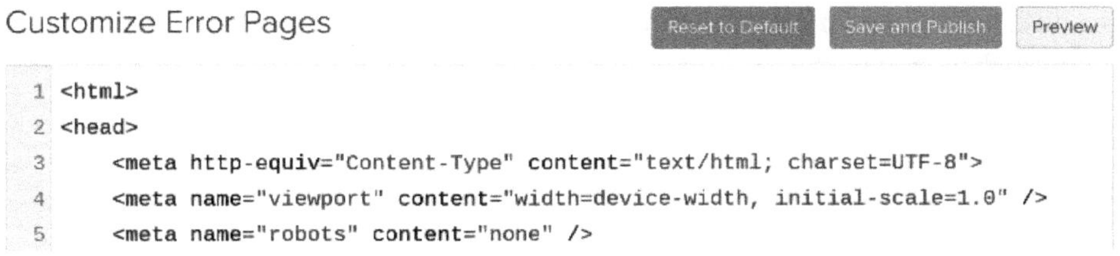

Customize Error Pages   Reset to Default   Save and Publish   Preview

```
1  <html>
2  <head>
3      <meta http-equiv="Content-Type" content="text/html; charset=UTF-8">
4      <meta name="viewport" content="width=device-width, initial-scale=1.0" />
5      <meta name="robots" content="none" />
```

Figure 6.26 – HTML editor for custom error page

If you're wondering when an error page is used, it's when a critical error occurs or an application is misconfigured.

If you want to take the sign-in customization to the next level, you can also self-host an Okta widget. In this scenario, you can host the login on, for instance, your intranet, and make it easy for your end users to log in from a page that they recognize.

To get this working, you need to install the widget.

There are a lot of code snippets available; you can visit this link for more information: `https://developer.okta.com/code/javascript/okta_sign-in_widget/`.

To install the widget, there are two options:

- Linking out to the Okta CDN
- Local installation via npm

If you want to use the CDN, use this code in your HTML:

```
<!-- Latest CDN production Javascript and CSS -->
<script src='https://global.oktacdn.com/okta-signin-
widget/4.1.4/js/okta-sign-in.min.js'
      type='text/javascript'></script><link href='https://
global.oktacdn.com/okta-signin-widget/4.1.4/css/okta-sign-in.
min.css'
      type='text/css' rel='stylesheet'/>
```

If you want to use npm, use this:

```
# Run this command in your project root folder.npm install @
okta/okta-signin-widget -save
```

For more information and the latest data, refer to the preceding link.

After that, you will have to enable **Cross-Origin Resource Sharing** (**CORS**) which we will look in detail in *Chapter 7, API Management*. Since the widget needs to make cross-origin requests, you need to add your application's URL to the trusted origins of your Okta tenant. This is how you do that:

1. Navigate to **Security | API | Trusted Origins**.

2. Click **Add Origin** and in the field, enter a name for the organization origin.

3. For the origin URL, enter the base URL for the website you want to allow cross-origin requests from.

4. CORS needs to be selected as the **Type** option.

When you're done, click **Save**.

If you want to read more about CORS and Okta, you can visit this URL: https://developer.okta.com/docs/guides/enable-cors/overview/.

After enabling CORS, you can start using the widget. Use this code to initialize the widget:

```
<
div id = 'widget-container' > < /div> <
script >
    var signIn = new OktaSignIn({
        baseUrl: 'https://${yourOktaDomain}'
    });
signIn.renderEl({
        el: '#widget-container'
        },
        function success(res) {
            if (res.status === 'SUCCESS') {
                console.log('Do something with this
sessionToken', res.session.token);
            } else { // The user can be in another
authentication state that requires further action.
                // For more information about these states,
```

```
see:
                    //    https://github.com/okta/okta-signin-
widget#rendereloptions-success-error}
            }
        ); <
        /script>
```

The preceding link specifies different use cases and what code to use for them. For instance, if you want to use the widget to let your end users log in to the default dashboard, you would use this:

```
function success(res) {  if (res.status === 'SUCCESS') {
res.session.setCookieAndRedirect('https://${yourOktaDomain}/
app/UserHome');   }}
```

Now you know all the basics to host your own login widget. The last thing in the custom settings for end users is customizing the notifications that can be sent to them.

Custom notification templates

The last part of configuring customizations for your end users is changing how standard emails and text messages look. Start by navigating to **Settings** | **Emails & SMS**. There is one tab for emails and one for SMS – let's start with emails.

First off, you can start by setting the email address of the sender. By default, it's noreply@okta.com, but if you would rather have the address of your IT support, for instance, you can set it by clicking the email address. This will open up a new window where you can set up your own email address.

> **Important note**
>
> This setting requires you to change DNS records and potentially add **Sender Policy Framework** (**SPF**) records. As these records differ according to the domain provider and within the systems allowed to use your domain to email from, we recommend following this guide from Okta to understand the requirements to make these changes: https://help.okta.com/en/prod/Content/Topics/Settings/Settings_Configure_A_Custom_Email_Domain.htm.

Under the tabs to the left, you get a list of the different default emails being sent by Okta. You can click them to preview them. By clicking **Edit**, you can update the content or appearance of the email, for any language:

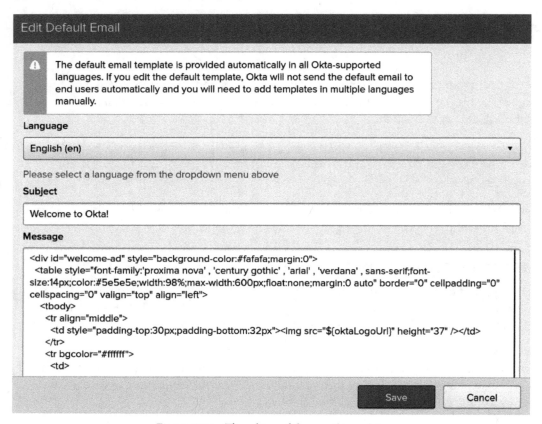

Figure 6.27 – The editor of the email template

If you edit a template, the translated versions will not be automatically updated. You will see a list of the versions of the specific email when you select an email in the list to the left:

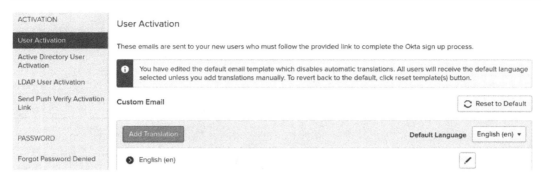

Figure 6.28 – The functionality to add alternative translations for email templates

It works the same for SMS, but there is only one notification to edit. You can make changes to the message that end users receive for their MFA SMS verification code – just remember to keep the message under 159 characters. To update the message, click the pencil icon under **Action**. Just as with email notifications, you can create your message in different languages.

Summary

In this chapter, we have focused on end users and their experience with Okta. We have explored the default experience for end users, but also the different ways in which we can change that experience. We've looked at how we can make the sign-in page match your company profile. After that experience for end users, we've also looked at how we can configure the dashboard and the settings end users can set themselves. For using Okta, we've looked at the Okta browser plugin and the settings we can manage for end users. For when these settings are not enough, we've also looked at how to configure a custom URL domain and the different things we can do with that, including setting up a self-hosting login widget. Lastly, we've updated the notifications templates.

In the next chapter, we will go into the advanced parts of Okta and look at API access management.

Section 2: Extending Okta

In this second part, we will deep dive into the more advanced features of Okta: API access management, advanced server access, and Access Gateway.

This part of the book comprises the following chapters:

- *Chapter 7, API Management*
- *Chapter 8, Managing Access with Advanced Server Access*
- *Chapter 9, Leveraging Access Gateway for Your On-Premises Applications*

7
API Management

Up to this point in this book, we've looked at Okta's fundamental functionality. When we've looked at giving users access, it's been to applications. In this chapter, we're taking a step into more advanced features, such as the **Application Programming Interface (API)** management of Okta and access to APIs of external applications. This can be both for an organization or Okta's APIs, as well as access to self-developed OpenID Connect applications. This is not a feature that every organization needs, but it's a feature that gives that little extra to the organization that needs it.

In this chapter, we will look at the following:

- API terminology
- Managing Okta with APIs
- API Access Management fundamentals
- API Access Management administration

API terminology

There is some terminology that we need to go through, to be able to understand all aspects of API management and API access management:

- **API product**: An application with a group of API endpoints. These endpoints can have different needs and use cases, but listen to the same authorization server to understand what a user or service can and cannot do. It also is the service that a user logs into using OpenID Connect with an ID token.

- **API**: These are the endpoints where data is available and interchangeable between systems depending on the request and resource and access grant.

- **Authorization server**: An authorization server is at its core an OAuth 2.0 minting machine, utilizing Okta's scopes, claims, and access policies. You can create authorization servers in Okta, typically one server per API product. The server is typically used for one use case rather than one endpoint.

- **Scopes**: Scopes are operations performed on your API endpoints. They are built into the application, and access is requested from the authorization server with the setup claims and policies.

- **Claims**: Claims are statements used to authorize the user's request to do something within the application. Claims are usually not added to the ID token, as that is used to authenticate. Claims are added to the access token created by the authorization server based on the scope and policies. Claims can be generic or custom based on the API endpoints. Think of these examples for the standard claims: email, name, or role. For your custom claims, it could be that you want specific details such as custom profile information or group assignments added to either type of token.

- **Tokens**: ID and access tokens are used differently. ID tokens carry information about the user and are used to log in and access a system using OpenID Connect. Access tokens are dynamic and utilized to gain access to resources based on granted scopes within the access token.

- **Payload**: The information is sent along with the API call to the receiving server with additional information regarding the required actions.

Let's get an understanding of what we can do with APIs and Okta.

Managing Okta with APIs

The use of APIs has been increasing and has become a large part of any organization's footprint. Within all departments, APIs are used to share, transfer, move, read, change, delete, and adjust data from any system to any system.

We might have to start by looking at what an API is and why Okta's functionality in this area is needed. Back in the early days, a web program was hosted on a web server and the browser only displayed its content through HTML sent from the server. These days, you might have apps on your smartphone or single-page apps, both that run code on your device or on the client. These apps connect with a backend service, usually exposed through an API. Simply put, you can say that services and applications that handle smaller tasks and connect and interact with each other through APIs are called microservices. As this newer model of applications becomes more and more common, finding a way of managing these APIs becomes more critical. The opportunity for applications to utilize outside information from other applications is beneficial to the application builder, because they don't have to gather, store, and manage that information themselves. Using API integrations allows applications to receive or pull in data that is required for their service, but have the user be in charge of what is and isn't allowed. As mentioned in previous chapters, Okta was built with an API-first strategy. This means most admin-related interface actions are also configurable using Okta's ever-growing API catalog.

Having access to Okta's APIs allows other systems to manage Okta, read information within your Okta org, and change or update information.

> **Important note**
> Take a look here to find out more about Okta's API catalog: `https://developer.okta.com/docs/reference/`.

Let's take a look at how we can use Okta's own APIs.

Using Okta's own APIs

Using Okta's APIs allows you to orchestrate a lot of possible manual work in Okta in a more managed and automated way. You can also simply do a specific call to Okta to make sure the action is done. Sometimes, a repetitive task can become quite tedious in the administrator interface, and using Okta's APIs can help to resolve that.

Preparing to use Okta APIs

Various code languages can be used to work with APIs in Okta, such as Python or PHP. If you're not familiar with any coding language, you can utilize the **Postman** software to show examples of how to send API calls to Okta, since it's low code and available to anyone. Postman is a software development tool and is used to test API calls. How to work with it and install it is further explained at `www.postman.com`.

> **Important note**
>
> Okta delivers all their available APIs in convenient Postman collections, which are quick and easy to import into Postman. You can find the collections here: `https://developer.okta.com/docs/reference/postman-collections/`.

You can go to the collections page on Okta's developer site and import all available collections to use.

As there are many different languages that can be used to work with Okta's APIs, we can't go through everything here. The examples in this chapter are done using `curl`.

Next, we need to have an understanding of how we are able to use the APIs. Okta's API endpoint requires a token to authorize the action you want to do.

Tokens

To authenticate requests to the Okta API, API tokens are used. Only administrators can issue tokens. These tokens are based on the privileges that the administrator has.

> **Tip**
>
> Use service accounts to generate tokens so that permissions for tokens don't unexpectedly change.

The validity of a token is 30 days, and the time is renewed when it's used for an API request. If a token is not used in 30 days, it can't be used again. If the admin account that created the token is deactivated, the token is also revoked. If the account is reactivated, so is the token.

You find your organization's API tokens by going to the **Security | API | Tokens** menu. On the page is a list of all your tokens. You see the name of the tokens and in front of them a color marker to indicate the status. By hovering over the colored dot, you can read information about the status. The possible statuses are as follows:

- **Green**: The token was used in the last 3 days.
- **Gray**: The token has not been used for 3 days, but it's not within 7 days of expiring.
- **Red**: The token is within 7 days of expiring.
- **Yellow**: The token is suspicious.

Normally, a suspicious token is not associated with a known agent. You can investigate it by clicking on it, to see provisioning for the associated agent. For instance, the AD agent used to integrate with an AD directory will have its own token to manage Okta's Universal Directory and all the users and groups in it.

To create a new token, click the **Create Token** button. On the first page of the setup, you will only have to give your token a name. Remember that if you want to create more tokens for different tasks, name them properly, to be able to see which is which. On the next page of the setup, you will receive the token value.

> **Important note**
> Copy the token value directly when the token is created. After that point, the value will be hashed and you can never see it again.

After you've copied the value, you can use it in the designated service you want to connect with Okta. Click **Ok, got it!**.

If you have many tokens, you can filter them by type in the menu to the left. To revoke a token, you simply click the trashcan icon next to the token name.

Now that we have created a token, let's look at how to use it and actually send a call to Okta's APIs.

Examples of tasks with Okta's APIs

To be able to work with Okta's APIs, a basic understanding of the usage of these APIs is good to have. Let's do that by illustrating some examples.

A company admin needs to quickly add some groups and wants to use the Okta APIs for that. By using the API, the admin can create the groups without ever touching the browser interface.

The admin can state the name and description, which will be reflected in the Okta console groups overview. After sending this API request, Okta will respond with an answer. If all is correct, the group will be created.

The call the admin uses could be similar to this:

```
curl -v -X POST \-H "Accept: application/json" \-H "Content-
Type: application/json" \-H "Authorization: SSWS ${api_token}"
\-d '{
  "profile": {
    "name": "West Coast Users",
    "description": "All Users West of The Rockies"
```

```
            }
        }'
  "https://${yourOktaDomain}/api/v1/groups"
```

While the first part is required to make sure the API call is accepted and correct using -H as the statement for the headers, the second part simply states the actual creation of the group with the accompanying details.

> **Important note**
> To understand the basic usage and get an overview of all the elements that are required to use Okta's APIs, go to
> https://developer.okta.com/docs/reference/api-overview/.

A response will be sent back and it will state what is done. The first half of the response will include the ID that is created for the group, together with additional standard information that Okta sends along. The response will also show the group's profile, including the name and description:

```
{
  "id": "00g1emaKYZTWRYYRRTSK",
  "created": "2015-02-06T10:11:28.000Z",
  "lastUpdated": "2015-10-05T19:16:43.000Z",
  "lastMembershipUpdated": "2015-11-28T19:15:32.000Z",
  "objectClass": [ "okta:user_group" ],
  "type": "OKTA_GROUP",
  "profile": {
    "name": "West Coast Users",
    "description": "All Users West of The Rockies"
  },
```

In the second half of the response, Okta sends along several relevant links that can be used for additional calls or actions that the admin might want to make on the freshly created group after creation:

```
"_links": {
  "logo": [ {
    "name": "medium",
```

```
          "href": "https://${yourOktaDomain}/img/logos/groups/
oktamedium.png",
          "type": "image/png"
      },
      {
    "name": "large",
        "href": "https://${yourOktaDomain}/img/logos/groups/okta-
large.png",
          "type": "image/png"
      }
    ],
    "users": {
      "href": "https://${yourOktaDomain}/api/v1/
groups/00g1emaKYZTWRYYRRTSK/users"
    },
    "apps": {
      "href": "https://${yourOktaDomain}/api/v1/
groups/00g1emaKYZTWRYYRRTSK/apps"
    }
    }
}
```

The responses from Okta can be different depending on the request or API, but it gives information back that can be relevant for the next API calls or delivers an understanding of what the current situation is.

So, let's continue and create a new user with the basic details and add them to the previously created group. The API call for that would be like this:

```
curl -v -X POST \-H "Accept: application/json" \-H "Content-
Type: application/json" \-H "Authorization: SSWS ${api_
token}" \-d '{
  "profile": {
    "firstName": "Isaac",
    "lastName": "Brock",
    "email": "isaac.brock@example.com",
    "login": "isaac.brock@example.com"
  },
  "groupIds": ["00g1emaKYZTWRYYRRTSK"]
```

```
    }'
https://${yourOktaDomain}/api/v1/users?activate=true
```

What we did here is start again with the same required elements, including accompanying headers. Then, we create a user with a profile, adding their minimum required profile values. Secondly, we assign the user to the previously created group. Lastly, we activate the user using the activation URL.

The response we get shows information about the user being created:

```
{
  "id": "00ub0oNGTSWTBKOLGLNR",
  "status": "STAGED",
  "created": "2013-07-02T21:36:25.344Z",
  "activated": null,
  "statusChanged": null,
  "lastLogin": null,
  "lastUpdated": "2013-07-02T21:36:25.344Z",
  "passwordChanged": null,
  "profile": {
    "firstName": "Isaac",
    "lastName": "Brock",
    "email": "isaac.brock@example.com",
    "login": "isaac.brock@example.com",
    "mobilePhone": "555-415-1337"
  },
  "credentials": {
    "provider": {
      "type": "OKTA",
      "name": "OKTA"
    }
  },
}
```

The second half of the response lists links to use on the user. These are quite self-explanatory:

```
"_links": {
        "schema": {
            "href": "${yourOktaDomain}/api/v1/meta/schemas/
user/oscuxbnkcNLVXoum3356"
        },
        "activate": {
            "href": "${yourOktaDomain}/api/v1/
users/00u5tiakg9PsvboKz357/lifecycle/activate",
            "method": "POST"
        },
        "self": {
            "href": "${yourOktaDomain}/api/v1/
users/00u5tiakg9PsvboKz357"
        },
        "type": {
            "href": "${yourOktaDomain}/api/v1/meta/types/user/
otyuxbnkcNLVXoum3356"
        }
    }
}
```

By incorporating these APIs, you can make specific work processes less repetitive and more automated.

> **Important note**
> Okta has a well-documented repository on all their publicly available APIs on their developer site. Please visit `https://developer.okta.com/docs/reference/` for more examples.

So, let's take a look at how we can start using the APIs by creating a token.

Trusted origins

If you are thinking of creating an alternative interface to manage and handle Okta's APIs, you need to make sure you configure your trusted origins. Or, if you want to implement Okta's own login widget on a custom login page, **Cross-Origin Resource Sharing** (**CORS**) is required too. Check out Okta's reference page about their custom sign-in widget here: `https://developer.okta.com/code/javascript/okta_ sign-in_widget/`.

CORS allows AJAX calls to be done from different domains than where the scripts are loaded. Web browsers don't allow these actions according to the *same-origin security policies* (`https://developer.mozilla.org/en-US/docs/Web/Security/ Same-origin_policy`). The same-origin security policies make sure services and sites don't get access to or use cookies that another website might have stored, thereby stopping any malicious activity. But there are legitimate reasons, because these rules apply to the combination of protocol, domain, and port used. So, you might have a website at `https://myshop.com` and use `https://api.myshop.com` as a way to interact with your APIs. These two would not be able to communicate based on the same-origin security policies.

This is unless CORS definitions are set up and allow the browser and the server to interact with each other through a cross-origin request. By using CORS, you can allow your own web page with a self-hosted Okta sign-in widget to interact with Okta.

Let's see how we can set CORS up.

When doing cross-origin web requests and redirects, they all need to be whitelisted. You do this by adding a trusted origin, which is a combination of the URI scheme, hostname, and port number of a page. Click the **Trusted Origins** tab under **Security | API | Trusted Origins**:

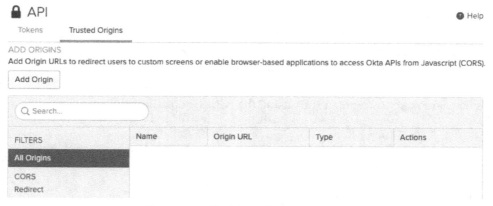

Figure 7.1 – The Trusted Origins menu

After that, you need to click **Add Origin**:

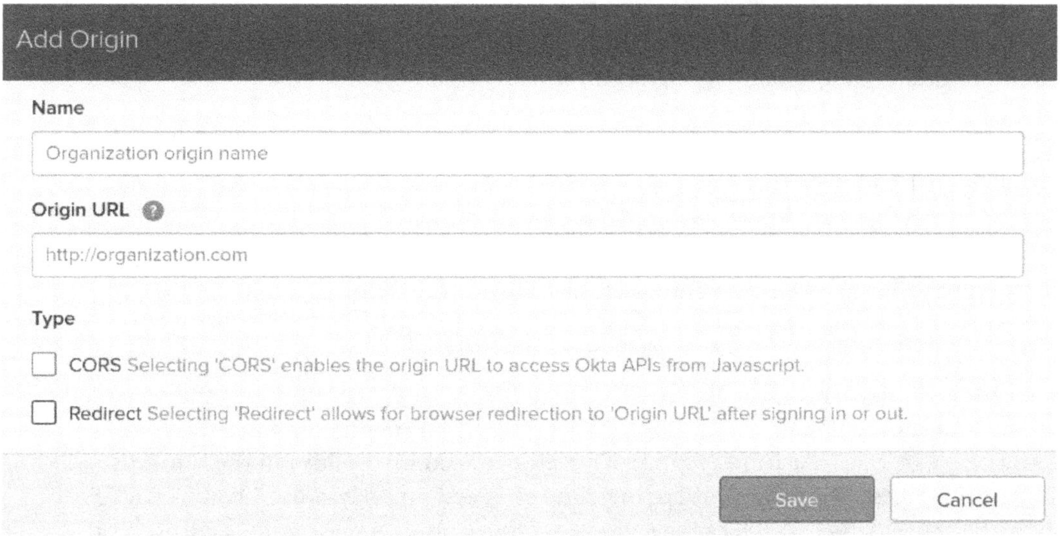

Figure 7.2 – Settings for a trusted origin

Add this information to create a trusted origin:

1.   Give the trusted origin a name.

2.   Enter the URL for Okta API access or custom page redirect.

3.   Select whether to give access for **CORS** or **Redirect**.

What's the difference between CORS and redirects? Let's have a look:

- **CORS**: XMLHttpRequest is sent from JavaScript on your website to the Okta API using an Okta session cookie.

- **Redirect**: After signing in or out, the redirect allows your browser to redirect you to this trusted website.

After clicking **Save**, you're done!

For more information on using your CORS setup in your own environments, we recommend going to https://developer.mozilla.org/en-US/docs/Web/ HTTP/CORS and checking out how to implement it.

Rate limits

There are rate limits on how many API calls can be done within a certain amount of time. This is to protect Okta's service for all customers and is usual for **Software as a Service (SaaS)** providers. Rates are divided into three sections:

- Org-wide rate limits
- Concurrent rate limits
- Okta-generated email message rate limits

All different calls and their rate limits can be found at the following link:

`https://developer.okta.com/docs/reference/rate-limits/`

So, we took a quick dive into Okta's APIs; there is a lot to say about them, and we can't include all the details in this book. We highly recommend going to `https://developer.okta.com` and creating a developer account. Follow all the tutorials and best practices they provide there to get up to speed on how to use Okta in the best way with Okta's APIs. Now, let's take a look at Okta's other API product, API Access Management.

API Access Management fundamentals

Using APIs is beneficial because they are automatable and can be programmed to do just what is needed. In many cases, APIs are used by users to help their work be more automated and remove repetitive tasks. By connecting the APIs from different applications, users can all of a sudden see their data in different places, interact with it, and manipulate it where and how they want and like.

On the other side, developers and IT teams might invest in creating custom services and or applications to make their life, or that of their colleagues, better. Creating these applications usually entails adding APIs to open up data streams to collect and bring it all together.

Lastly, if your organization's business model is to build services or web products, chances are they'll be using APIs to connect to other applications, partners, systems, and so on.

All of these APIs require different needs, approaches, and management.

According to Okta (`https://www.okta.com/resources/whitepaper/api-security-from-concepts-to-components/`), you can divide API security into five levels of API management.

Level 1 – no security

We might have to start by looking at what an API is and why Okta's functionality in this area is needed. Just serving up some data and it not being secure is the wrong starting point, but it's usually where services are born. An internal developer is asked to create something that gathers information from different sources for the sales team to look at. That might transform into a tool that needs to be shared with partners, which then evolves into a publicly available resource. Initially, developers might rely on the fact that the APIs are private, but when the application becomes publicly-facing, without a doubt you can expect that there will be ways to access those private APIs. Okta calls this method the *no security* method. Hidden APIs within applications might seem a logical way to hold off attackers, but unfortunately, once it's public, it's easy pickings for bad parties to find a weakness and get access to your inner parts.

Level 2 – using API keys

API keys are becoming a more common way to secure access and are used to allow development based on access rights. By having the developers create API keys with their own permissions, it allows them to do their work in a way that won't disrupt what they need to accomplish and it is secured within the permission set that the key was created in. This is definitely better than no security at all, Level 1, but still has some problems.

So, why isn't this the highest security level? It can be the case that the key is also used for public-facing permissions and users might, unfortunately, have more access granted than needed. The key in itself might seem secure, but if these are used, and perhaps even used across multiple services, it can become a large plane of entry points with possible over-permissioned accesses based on that single key.

Reusing keys across multiple applications can also bring issues in regard to rotating or renewing them, as they might have been used in too many different systems. This can make changes almost impossible. If these keys then fall into the wrong hands because of team members leaving, sending over the keys publicly via copy-paste, it can become a large problem. Having a policy to only use a key for a single use case is wise, but with the possibility of developers doing it wrong, an organization can never be sure that security is at the highest standard.

Level 3 – OAuth 2.0

With OAuth 2.0 tokens, you are capable of granting granular access and usage rights for users developing APIs. OAuth 2.0 tokens are used to set the level of access that the token users are allowed to have. The token also has an expiration time or date. This means that a simple read request on a logging system might only need read rights for the token, and a long expiration time. A service capable of updating and deleting information from your CRM system might need much more granular writing rights and a much shorter expiration time to make sure over-usage is prevented.

The benefits of using scopes are that the token only has those rights it's been set up with, and don't carry all the permissions of the administrator who created the token. This makes sure that no over-access is given away. Secondly, the token expires. This means the attacker has a limited amount of time to access the system and extract data. After expiration, the attacker will not be able to gain access again without compromising the users' authentication too.

Level 4 – API gateways

API access gateways are great tools to connect any API to all other APIs available within the organization. API gateways help to support different layers in the organization. IT architects have more control over who has access to what in any degree and manner. Developers are capable of easily connecting different microservices together, leaving the API management up to the gateway. Gateways offer great insight into policy enforcement, logging, and auditing. You can say that your gateway is a hub for your APIs. Instead of connecting every API to each other, you handle them through your hub. This makes the connections in your architecture less entangled like spaghetti and more well-thought-out and arranged like a spider's web.

In many cases, API gateway vendors offer tools to create and sometimes rotate API keys. A more limited amount also have OAuth 2.0 capabilities using simple user profiles. This way, developers can use their keys and be sure that these are securely managed and rotated when needed. Also, users are using profile access scopes to access the services they need, when they need to, in the best way possible.

But API gateways are external services with their own user directories and management. They don't have the full view of the user's situation based on context and access within the organization.

> **Important note**
> Okta has some great information on using API gateways. Check out their digital book on the subject here: `https://developer.okta.com/books/api-security/gateways/`.

Level 5 – API gateways and API Access Management

This is where Okta comes in. Together with API gateways, Okta can securely manage users, authenticate, and authorize them based on the full context of the user at that given moment.

In the gateway, we either trust or don't trust the users. Connecting Okta, we can add more granularity to that and make sure the users can do as much as they need within the boundaries of policies and access rights.

Of course, not every company has an API gateway. Using Okta's API Access Management allows you to connect your applications using OAuth 2.0 and **OpenID Connect** (**OIDC**), making sure you are capable of using your own Okta universal directory, as described in *Chapter 2, Working with Universal Directory*. Additionally, you can use contextual factors such as zones and groups to make sure that access is granted. All of these features are managed from within Okta, without the need for a gateway.

This service is beneficial for different things:

- You can create an Okta-hosted, custom authorization server. With a server, you can manage sets of API endpoints, for many client apps, for many different roles.
- You can configure your own scopes and claims, and map them to your user profiles.
- With OAuth, tokens are passed instead of credentials.
- Your APIs are protected with the latest standards.
- As for other kinds of access within Okta, you can manage access to APIs with rules.

> **Important note**
> There are many best practices for working with Okta API Access Management. To read them all, reference `https://developer.okta.com/docs/concepts/api-access-management/`.

Now that we've understood the value of Okta's API Access Management, let's learn how to use it and set it up for an application.

API Access Management administration

So, let's go into the Okta administrator panel to set up some of the features that were examined in the last section. Navigate to **Security | API**. Here, we see that we have three tabs we can work with:

- **Authentication Servers**
- **Tokens**
- **Trusted Origins**

This is what it looks like in the admin panel:

Figure 7.3 – Available tabs for API management

As we already spoke about **Tokens** and **Trusted Origins** earlier in this chapter, we will now only focus on **Authorization Servers**. If you don't have the API Access Management product enabled, you will only see this menu for the default org authorization server, explained next.

Authorization server

To start off, we need to look at why you might need an authorization server. An authorization server is basically something to create and solidify (or **mint**, as it's normally called) Oauth 2.0 or OpenID Connect tokens. You can use it for authentication for your OpenID Connect applications or grant access to specific API endpoints with the help of scopes, as well as to provide authorization to your web services. Putting it simply, when using OpenID Connect or OAuth 2.0, the authorization server authenticates a user and issues an ID or access token. Every server has its own issuer URI and signing key for tokens. This makes for secure boundaries.

There are two different kinds of servers available: org and custom authorization servers. The **Org Authorization** server comes by default with every Okta tenant. This authorization server is used to allow **Single Sign-On (SSO)** into Okta and get API access tokens for Okta's APIs. It's used to do SSO with Okta or to receive an access token to Okta's APIs. The server can't be customized; it's only for Okta to consume or validate tokens. The access tokens from this server can't be used by your own applications.

For the **Org Authorization** server, clients can use the following endpoints for metadata-related information of your Okta tenant, programmatically:

```
OpenID: https://${yourOktaOrg}/.well-known/openid-configuration
OAuth: https://${yourOktaOrg}/.well-known/oauth-authorization-server
```

The **Custom Authorization** server is what you create and use to secure your APIs. You can create multiple servers, with different scopes, claims, and access policies. Okta provides one default **Custom Authorization** server, pre-configured, including a basic access policy and rule.

So, how do we set this up? In the **Authorization Servers tab**, click **Add Authorization Server**. You will then get to fill in the following information:

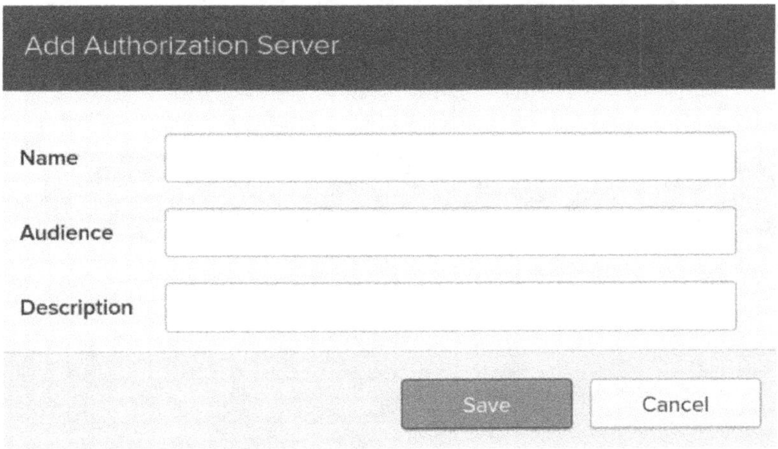

Figure 7.4 – First configuration for a new authorization server

Fill in the information:

- **Name**: Give your server a descriptive name.
- **Audience**: This is the URI for the OAuth resource that consumes the token.
- **Description**: Optionally, you can give the server a description.

When you click **Save**, you will create the server and get more options for setup:

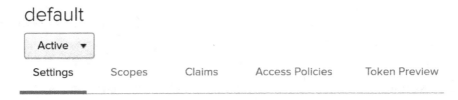

Figure 7.5 – Available menus in a server

If we look closer at the **Settings** menu, you will see the configurations we just made while creating the server. You also see that you can set whether **Signing Key Rotation** should be **Automatic** or **Manual**. This is set to **Automatic** as default; **Manual** should only be used if a client is unable to automatically poll the server to update the list of signing keys. We will go into more detail on key rotation at the end of the chapter.

The next tab on your newly created server is **Scopes**. To create a new scope, click **Add Scope**:

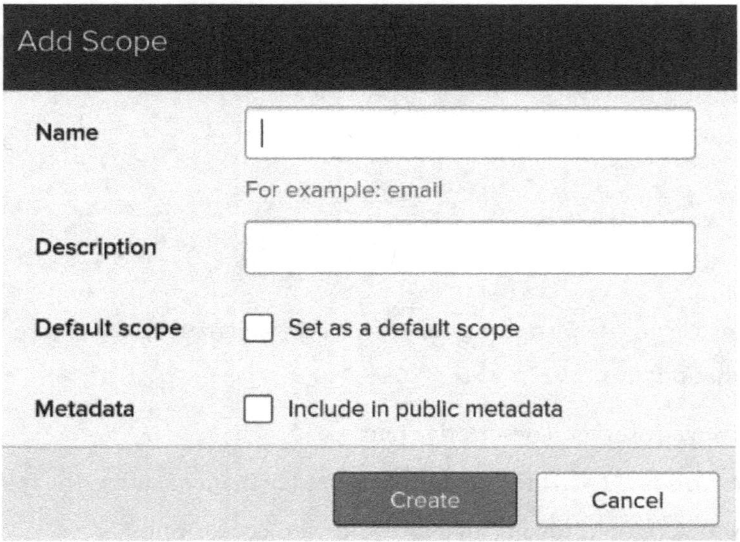

Figure 7.6 – Settings to add a scope

Enter the details for the following fields:

- **Name**: Give the scope a name – for instance, `email`.

- **Description**: Give a description of what the scope will be used for.

- **Default scope**: Check this box if you want Okta to authorize requests to applications that don't have specified scopes. If so, for a request that passed the access policy, Okta returns all the default scope in the access tokens.

- **Metadata**: Check this box if you want the scope to be publicly discoverable.

Click **Create** to finish the scope configuration. On the main page, you will see a full list of all your scopes.

Next up is **Claims**. Claims are divided into two categories: **ID tokens** and **access requests**. To create a new claim, click **Add Claim**:

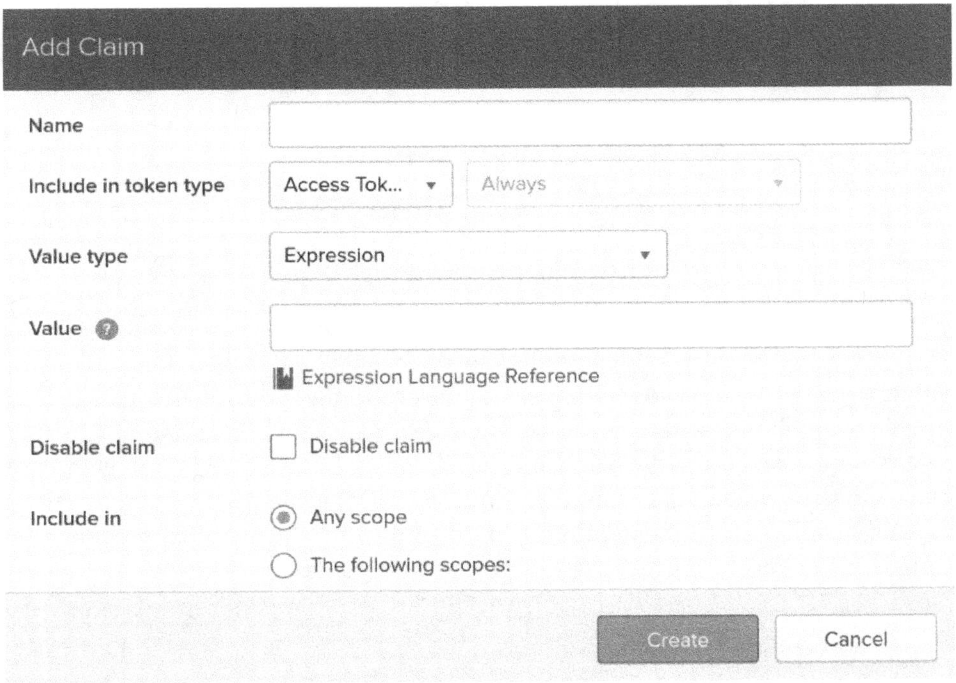

Figure 7.7 – Setup of claims

Let's go through this setup:

- **Name**: Give this claim a descriptive name.

- **Include in token type**: Choose between **ID Token** and **Access Token**, depending on your use case. If you choose **ID Token**, you also get to choose when the authorization server is to provide a claim in the token; if you choose **Access Token**, the field is set to **Always**:

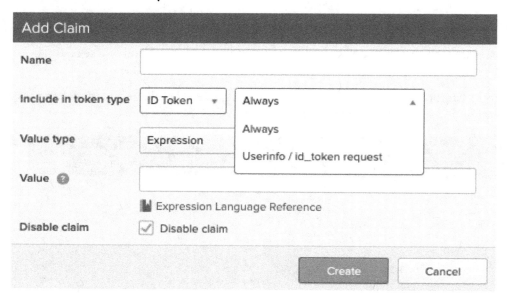

Figure 7.8 – Token type menu when ID Token is chosen

- **Value type**: In this drop-down menu, you select whether you will define the claim with a group filter or with expression language. If you select **Expression**, you get to enter your expression in the field value below. If you select **Groups**, you get to filter groups in the field below. For example, you can select just the sales team by selecting the sales team group, or be even more granular and use the Okta Expression Language to filter the correct users or groups for this claim:

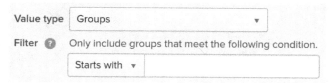

Figure 7.9 – If you select Groups instead of Expression, the field below it changes

Moving on in the setup, we have two more options:

- **Disable claim**: If you want the claim to be disabled for a while – for instance, for testing or debugging.

- **Include in**: Select whether you want the claim to be for every scope, or select the scopes you want it to be valid for.

Click **Create** to finalize the setup of your new claim. If you have many claims set up, you can filter them by type in the menu to the left. By using the pen and trash can icon to the right of each claim, you can edit or delete your claim.

Next up, we have access policies. These let different services access your server and its scopes and claims. Move to the **Access Policy** tab and click **Add Policy**:

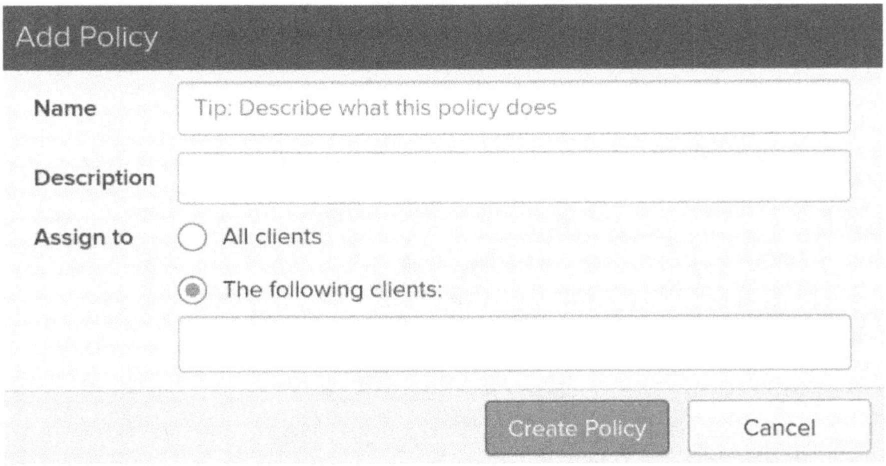

Figure 7.10 – Setup of a new access policy

The setup is fairly straightforward:

- **Name**: Give the policy a descriptive name.

- **Description**: You can add a description, which is especially important if you have several that do similar things.

- **Assign to**: If you want your policy to apply to all clients, leave the option set to **All clients**. If you want to select clients, change to **The following clients:**, and enter the clients whom this policy is aimed at.

After that, click **Create Policy** and you are done. On the screen, you see a list of all your access policies, similar to what it looks like for policies for passwords, and other policy sections. In the list to the left, you can drag and drop your policies, to prioritize them. For each policy, you can select whether you want to **Deactivate**, **Edit**, or **Delete** it. Also, as for other policies within Okta, you have to create at least one rule. Let's look at that now. Click **Add Rule**:

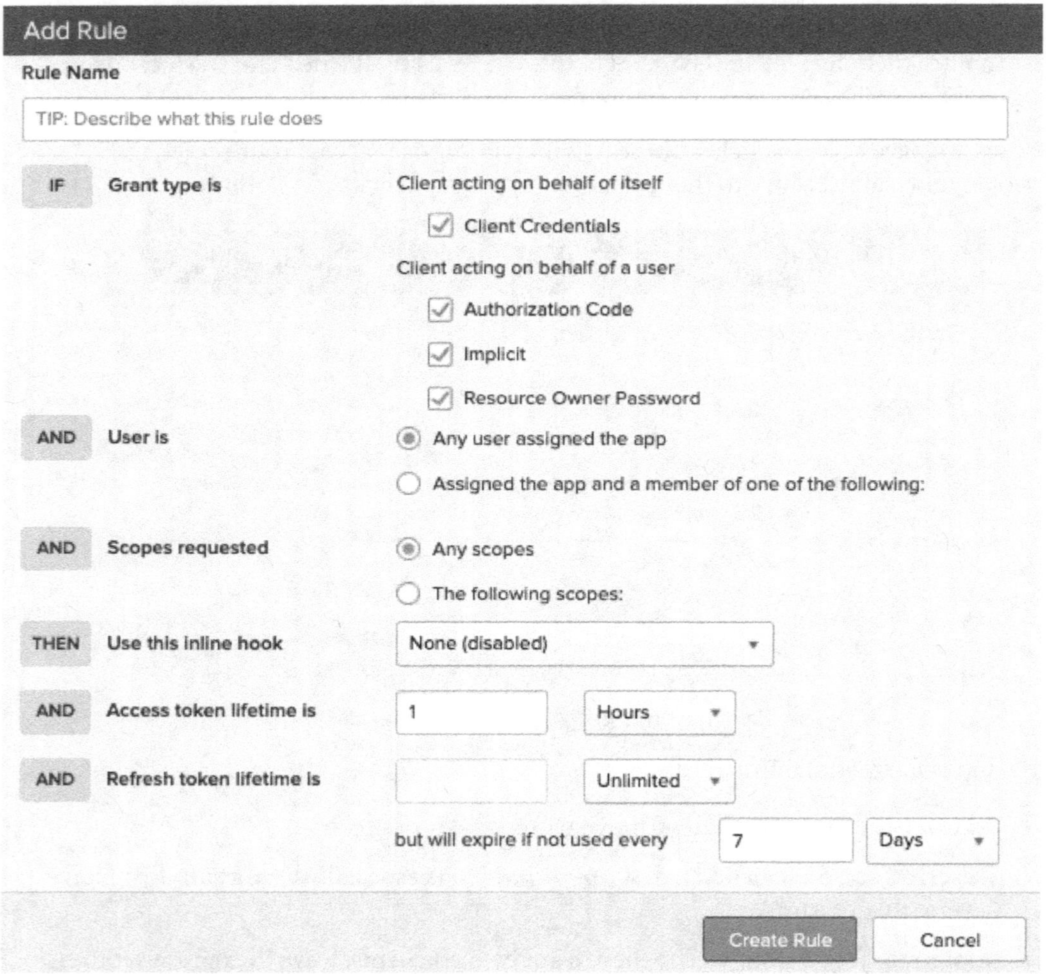

Figure 7.11 – Configuration of an access policy rule

So, let's dive into it:

- **Rule Name**: Select a descriptive name.

Under the **IF** option, we have the following:

- **Grant type is**: You can choose whether the client is acting as itself or as a user. It's possible to select both, but if it's as a user, select any or all of the methods.

Under the **AND** options, we have the following:

- **User is**: You get this option if you selected **Client acting on behalf of a user** in the **IF** statement. You will be able to select any of the users assigned to the app.

- **Scopes requested**: Select the scopes that are granted if the user meets the conditions stated.

Under the **THEN** options, we have the following:

- **Use this inline hook**: If you have inline hooks set up, you will be able to call upon them here. If not, the only option is **None**.

- **Access token lifetime is**: Decide what lifetime a token has, before it's revoked.

Under the **AND** option, we have the following:

- **Refresh token lifetime is**: The default is set to **Unlimited**, but you can select **Minutes**, **Hours**, or **Days**, and set a number. You also get to select after how long it will expire if it's not used within its lifetime.

That is all; you have now created a rule. If you add multiple rules, you sort them, just as with the policies. When a client request comes in, it starts from the top and when it matches to one policy and/or rule, it doesn't move further down. Also, as with policies, you can select whether the rule should be active or not, edit it, and delete it.

Now, we have set up our authorization server, allowing an outside application or service delegate authentication to Okta, and letting Okta manage the claims and scopes for that app. Let's look at key rotation.

Key rotation

Key rotation is used to replace an existing signing key with a new cryptographic key. It is considered best practice in the industry to rotate these keys periodically. Okta automatically rotates keys four times a year.

> **Important note**
> This standard rotation can be changed by Okta without notice.

Authorization servers can be set to manually rotate keys instead of automatically. As the rotation of keys is considered best practice, it is wise to investigate whether a change to manual is truly needed. Manual rotation requires admins to go into the admin console and click on **Rotate Signing Keys**. If you go to your authorization server, in the **Settings** tab at the top, you will find the button to do so. This button will only appear if you first set the authorization server to manual rotation:

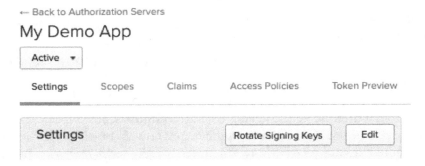

Figure 7.12 – The manual Rotate Signing Keys button

At the bottom of the **Settings** tab, you will see the **Previous**, **Current**, and **Next** keys:

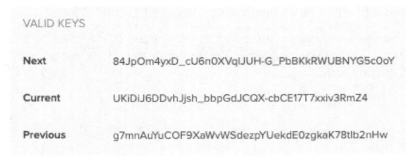

Figure 7.13 – Rotated signing keys

These actions can also be done using Okta's APIs. This allows the developer to rotate if necessary, simply using code, instead of having the IT team and or security do this for them and passing the new key along.

> **Tip**
>
> More information on how to use Okta's APIs to get and rotate the signing keys can be found here:
>
> ```
> https://developer.okta.com/docs/reference/api/
> authorization-servers/#get-authorization-server-
> keys
> ```

Summary

This chapter probably got your head spinning with abbreviations and links. But what we have tried to do is give a brief but full overview of what you can do with Okta's own APIs, understanding how to use them and what possibilities you have. You learned how to do some administrator tasks, such as adding a user, without using the administrator console, which can make some tasks less repetitive. We provided extra reference links to outside sources to get into more detail where needed. On the other side, we went through Okta's own API Access Management product to get a clear view of how to use Okta as your API access system and how to set it up. You learned the important things to think about if you have APIs that need protecting, thus giving your organization a chance to increase its security using Okta. In the next chapter, we will investigate and uncover the possibilities of using Okta's Advanced Server Access product and how you can benefit from it.

8
Managing Access with Advanced Server Access

Okta's **Advanced Server Access (ASA)** is a fairly new product, launched in 2019. With ASA, you can extend Okta's core products to your server fleet. With Universal Directory, you get a single source of truth for your server accounts. With Lifecycle Management, you can automate the provisioning of these accounts. With Single Sign-On, you can create simple and reliable authentication for your workflows. Lastly, you can fully utilize the contextual **Multi-Factor Authentication (MFA)** controls for your server accounts. In this chapter, we will go through why a product such as ASA is needed, as well as what you need to do to set up and manage ASA.

To understand this fully, in this chapter we'll look at the following:

- ASA – a high-level overview
- Setting up ASA
- Managing your ASA environment
- Automation

ASA – a high-level overview

Throughout the book, we have only spoken about managing applications. With ASA, Okta expands their touch plane by securing access to the server infrastructure. By doing so, the road to zero trust becomes a reality for more parts of your business than just users, applications, and devices. Also, as cloud adoption becomes an increasingly important DevOps job, making sure automation is the driver of it all is where Okta fits in.

Managing servers in your organization as part of your own infrastructure, or as part of your business model, means that your developers need to have access. This access is normally given using privileged accounts, either using the **Command-Line Interface (CLI)** with **Secure Shell (SSH)** or with privileged accounts accessing the server with **Remote Desktop Protocol (RDP)**. These accounts are granted access based on the role of the accessing user, but over-privileged access can quickly become a problem. Commonly, you will see that besides possible individual user privileges, access to more critical tasks is given using shared admin credentials. These, of course, have more access rights, but also allow a lot more access to the entire infrastructure. Security can be at risk at that point. Implementing a zero-trust strategy will help you and your team shift from network-related security to the application side.

Security nowadays is mainly managed by the user, not the **Infrastructure-as-a-Service (IaaS)** vendor. As these services become more and more difficult, you have to make sure that you meet all the compliancy regulations for your services. Making a mistake can lead to immense problems. On the other hand, having your DevOps engineers manage dozens, perhaps even hundreds, of servers and microservices requires a lot of access. All these admin and user credentials require some sort of oversight, and when your fleet of systems grows, so will your user credential stack. Managing this can become a giant on its own in work and time. As said before, overprivileging accounts is more common than not. Developers might be given the same access to a range of servers, while they might require different rights in each of them. Auditing all of this becomes a large problem. Using cloud services allows the fast adoption and expansion of different systems for different needs. Access management becomes increasingly harder to manage with this expansion, especially when automation comes into play. What if the admin leaves – how are you certain that they actually have no access to systems anymore? Lastly, while we always want to make end users happy, developers are even more important. They *will* find ways to make life easier, and that usually entails bypassing security if needed. So, we have to make sure both security and productivity go up; otherwise, it's doomed to fail.

So, what's behind this ASA? Let's take a look at some practical elements.

Users that log in using their local SSH tools will find that they need to store a **Rivest–Shamir–Adleman (RSA) public-key crypto system** key for authentication. The key can be used for different privileged roles for that user. The main concerns are that these RSA keys are static and hosted locally. This can comprise a range of security issues:

- It has no awareness of the user.
- It doesn't take context into consideration.
- It trusts the entity it's on, regardless of what is done with it.
- No possibility to provision or deprovision users while scaling the fleet.

ASA can help on these fronts, as it is an identity-first management system for servers. It will work across cloud and on-premises environments. The unique outstanding element in this strategy is the use of an *ephemeral credential mechanism*. These dynamic credentials are created on demand for the user, based on context and with the required task access. It allows you to make sure that your users can only access that server when and how they need to with just the right set of privileges to fulfill the job. This makes sure we can enhance our setup, by doing the following:

- Increasing access security, by not giving out the keys to the castle.
- Setting rules for access and tokens, so we don't have to have credentials valid for a long time.
- Having better, and possibly automated, scalability.
- Having dynamic access from Okta, rather than statics keys being stored on local machines.
- Getting complete syslogs on who accesses what, and when, increasing auditing capabilities.

These ephemeral credentials are tightly created and expire in minutes, leaving no room to share, phish, or otherwise lose the credential all together. By using Okta's Identity Cloud, it's using and backed by all the context Okta delivers to make sure policies are enforced. Adding additional MFA can add more security while still keeping access simple.

While this is quite revolutionary, other vendors might have similar features in place. What makes Okta so unique is having the ability to combine all contexts and truly set the identity of the user in the center of it all. This will allow a zero-trust approach to become reality and make life more secure, more productive, and easier to manage.

So, how does this work?

Working with ASA is a two-way system. You need to have access to servers from your system, and the servers need to be accessible to the assigned users.

Every server that needs to be accessed needs to enroll into ASA. This is done by using an enrollment token to securely add the server to ASA. On each server after enrollment, a lightweight agent called `sftd` runs and manages the local user and group accounts and any given entitlements, and captures all login events for ASA's system logs. It also makes sure it regularly communicates with Okta to make sure any updates are instantly mirrored in the servers, as it works locally with regular files such as `/etc/sudoers` and `/etc/passwd`.

On the user side, a small client is installed to allow communication between the user and Okta. The client agent also comes with CLI commands to help and ease usage. It will integrate with local SSH tools.

The user logs in using the CLI and gets redirected to Okta for authentication. Policies and MFA will apply, all the while looking at the context of the user and possibly the enrolled device context too.

Once authentication is granted, the CLI interface can show which servers the user has access to. By using `$ sft list-servers`, the accessible servers are listed. Accessing these servers requires no extra or new commands. By simply using `$ SSH {server name}`, the client application will create a short-lived **Certificate Authority** (**CA**) token with the right scopes, and grant access immediately. If the user hadn't logged in first with Okta, the command would have kickstarted an authentication process through the primary browser after the SSH command.

The authentication is bound to the machine and user, creating a secure and strong session that limits access from other systems and devices. Based on the role and group, the user has access to the machines that are part of the project the user is assigned to.

A project is a collection of different resources with their own configuration. They are further set up with additional access controls and policies. At least one project is needed in ASA.

This authentication will not use RSA keys, thus there isn't any SSH folder and there are no authorized key files present on the machine. The authentication is limited to the access and scope of the ephemeral certificate minted during authentication by the client. This allows you to have auditable trails traceable back to the user, because of the group assignments, permissions, and **Super User Do** (**SUDO**) entitlements that are set and managed by Okta.

Collections of servers are managed in ASA by projects. Projects contain the groups to which users are assigned, the tasks users are allowed to do, and details and events of the past. Users and groups are managed by Okta; make sure the correct users are assigned to the correct projects, for instance, using rules. These assigned groups and users are locally provisioned to the project's servers. Granting extra admin rights in the project will add SUDO privileges to the provisioned users on the Linux servers.

Sometimes, users might need to do specific actions on servers, but you do not want to give them full admin access. By assigning entitlements to groups, users are allowed to run commands, without having the full rights to the server.

Let's say your support team needs to be able to restart Apache on servers. Before, they were granted access with SUDO entitlements because the management of the team was too cumbersome and affected by changes. Now, using ASA, the users individually and as a group can have specific entitlements. The support group assigned to the project with the accessible servers allows them to do the following:

- Access the server they need access to
- Be provisioned to the servers with those entitlements
- Have enough rights to run the commands

With this, we can enforce least-privilege access for users, making sure the zero-trust approach is upheld.

So, now that we know what ASA is and why it's needed, let's have a look at how to set it up.

Setting up ASA

There are a few different steps needed to start using ASA:

1. Install ASA in Okta.
2. Enroll servers and install the agent.
3. Connect your team's servers.
4. Configure your servers.

Let's go through them in order, starting with installing ASA.

Installing ASA

ASA is its own product, and to be able to use it in your organization, you need to purchase it separately.

To start using ASA, you need to install the product in your Okta tenant. The product is available as an application, so you will start as you would when adding any application:

1. Go to **Applications | Applications**.

2. Click the button for **Add Application**.

3. Search for Okta Advanced Server Access, click on it, and then click **Add**.

In the following general setup, you get to fill in an Application Label and **Application Visibility**:

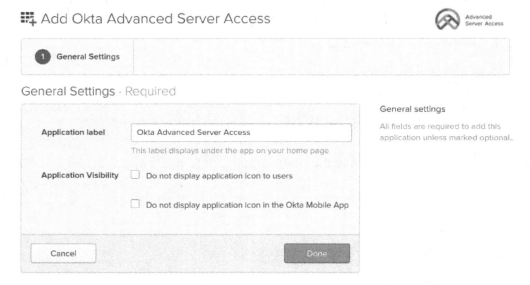

Figure 8.1 – General settings of the Okta ASA application

By clicking **Done**, you finalize the installation, and it's time for the settings.

> **Important note**
> You have to start by assigning the application to yourself.

To assign the application, do the following:

1. Go to the **Assignment** tab, click **Assign**, and select **Assign to people**.

2. Search for your own name, then click **Assign**.

3. You then get to select whether you want the username to stay as your Okta username, or whether you want to change it to something else.

4. Click **Save and go back**, then **Done**.

Now it's time to navigate to the ASA home page, `https://app.scaleft.com/`. Open this link in a new tab; you will need both this and your Okta tenant. To set up ASA on the website, do the following:

1. Select **Create a new team**.

2. Select a team name. This could be your company name. If you are just testing ASA, add `PoC` or `trial` to your name, to make sure you don't misuse a team name.

After this, you will see a section with the information you will need in Okta. Go back to your Okta tenant tab and select **Sign on** for your ASA application. Click **Edit** and scroll down to **ADVANCED SIGN-ON SETTINGS**:

ADVANCED SIGN-ON SETTINGS

These fields may be required for a Okta Advanced Server Access proprietary sign-on option or general setting.

Base URL

Enter your Base URL. Refer to the Setup Instructions above to obtain this value.

Audience Restriction

Enter your Audience Restriction. Refer to the Setup Instructions above to obtain this value.

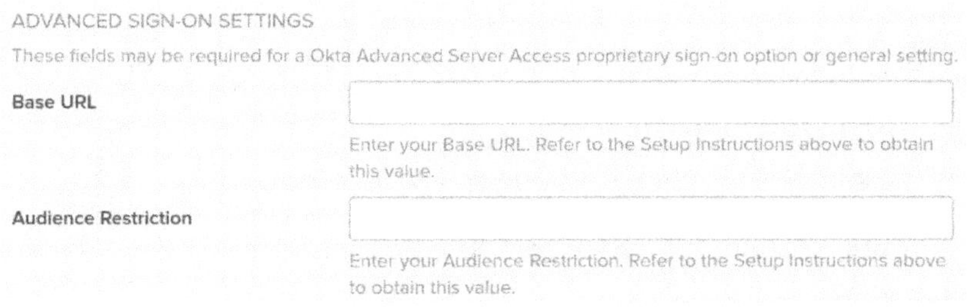

Figure 8.2 – Information needed from the ASA website

Copy and paste the **Base URL** and **Audience Restriction** values from the ASA website, then click **Save**.

Scrolling up to the SAML 2.0 settings, click the blue **Identity Provider metadata link**:

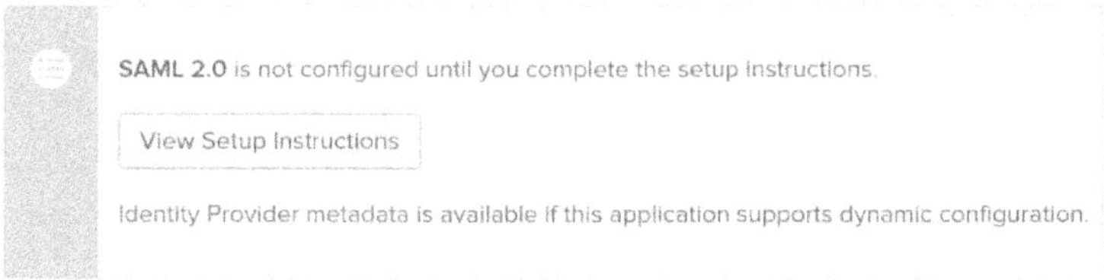

SAML 2.0 is not configured until you complete the setup instructions.

View Setup Instructions

Identity Provider metadata is available if this application supports dynamic configuration.

Figure 8.3 – Link for metadata

Clicking this link will open a new tab with information. Copy the URL of this tab. Go back to the ASA website:

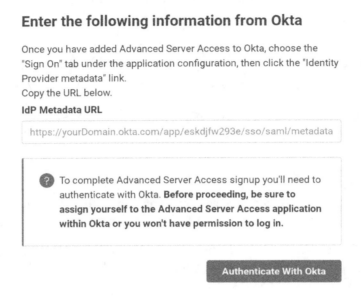

Enter the following information from Okta

Once you have added Advanced Server Access to Okta, choose the "Sign On" tab under the application configuration, then click the "Identity Provider metadata" link.
Copy the URL below.

IdP Metadata URL

https://yourDomain.okta.com/app/eskdjfw293e/sso/saml/metadata

To complete Advanced Server Access signup you'll need to authenticate with Okta. **Before proceeding, be sure to assign yourself to the Advanced Server Access application within Okta or you won't have permission to log in.**

Authenticate With Okta

Figure 8.4 – Setup on the ASA website

Do the following:

1. Paste the URL in **IdP Metadata URL**.

2. To verify the connection, click **Authenticate With Okta**.

When your verification is done, you have completed the installation! Now, we will look at how you enroll a server.

Enrolling a server

For ASA to interact with a server, an agent must be installed on the server, and the server must be enrolled in a project on the ASA website. The agent is working with the project to manage the server. With just default settings, the agent manages user accounts on the server, and client certificate authentication for SSH or RDP is enabled.

To enroll servers, you use an enrollment token. So, what is an enrollment token? It's a Base64-encoded object containing metadata that the agent uses to configure itself. To create an enrollment token, we need a project, so let's start with that. In the dashboard on the ASA website, click **Projects | Create Project**, where you have to enter the following information:

- **Project Name**: Give your project a name, preferably something so that you understand what server it's referring to.

- If you require preauthorization for users, check the **Require Preauthorization** box. With this, ASA will issue credentials to users who have been authorized previously. This is optional and requires a specific window of time for a user to be granted access to servers within the project.

- **On Demand User Time to Live (TTL)**: Here, you get to choose whether you want to create users on the server when the server is enrolled, or on demand when the user tries to access the server. For the first use case, leave this option as **Disabled**; otherwise, select the time stating how long the account will live before being removed from the server.

> **Important note**
> If you want to use on-demand account creation, the agent must be accessible on port 4421 of the network hop.

Now that you have your project, let's create the enrollment token. In the project you just created, go to the **Enrollment** tab. Scroll down and click **Create Enrollment Token**:

- **Description**: Give it a description based on what it will be used for. For instance, for a trial, you can name it `ASA trial token`.

You will get a notification that your token was successfully created. Copy the token. If you have a configuration management system, you can use it to store the token; otherwise, write it to a file on the server. Depending on the server type, your token can have different paths:

- For Linux: `/var/lib/sftd/enrollment.token`

- For Windows: `C:\windows\system32\config\systemprofile\AppData\Local\scaleft\enrollment.token`

Now, it's time to install the agent on your server. The installation process is the same for any server type, but the naming and code differ. The steps are as follows:

1. Add a repository.

2. Add the signing keys to your keychain, or configure trust for the signing key.

3. Install the server tool package, including the agent.

These steps are initiated by code and are unique per server type. For all the code snippets that you will need, go to `https://help.okta.com/en/prod/Content/Topics/ Adv_Server_Access/docs/install-agent.htm`.

For a Windows server, the process is even easier:

1. Start by downloading the ASA server tools. These are also found at the preceding link.

2. Double-click the download to install the **Microsoft Windows Installer (MSI)**, a Windows installer package file type.

That's it! Let's check whether the servers are enrolled. On the ASA website, go to your project and click on the **Servers** tab. Your server will appear on the tab if it was enrolled successfully. Let's move on to looking at the ASA client.

ASA client

To make calls using code, you can use the ASA client. By enrolling a client in your team, the client can perform actions on your behalf. The client can be installed on the following platforms:

*   macOS Sierra 10.12 through Catalina 10.15

*   Fedora

*   Ubuntu 16.04 and 18.04

*   Debian testing

*   Windows 8 and 10

The installation is similar; you download a client package and then run the installation. For each type of platform, reference this link for the downloadable package: `https:// help.okta.com/en/prod/Content/Topics/Adv_Server_Access/docs/ sft.htm`.

After you have clicked through the installation, it's time to enroll the client to a team. In the client, run the command in the client terminal:

```
sft enroll
```

The command opens a web page where you get to select what team to connect the client to. After you select the one you want to use for this client, click **Approve**. The command window in the client will let you know whether the enrollment was a success. If the enrollment was successful, you can see the client on the ASA website. In the menu to the left, click **Clients**, and see your client there.

So, what can we do with the client? There is a lot, and we won't go into everything here. Use commands to get help, see versions, use a specific account or team, and so on. Commands are in the following form:

```
sft [global options] command [command options] [arguments...]
```

These are the global options you can use in any command:

- Display help: `-h,  --help`
- Display version: `-v,  --version`
- Provide an alternative config file path: `--config-file`
- Use a specified account: `--account`
- Use a specified team: `--team`
- Use a specified instance of the ASA platform: `--instance`

An example of a command option is to use `sft config` to configure your client. The client comes with a default configuration set to supply the best security measure you might need. If you still want to set your own settings, there is a full array of commands for this. You can find commands for the client at `https://help.okta.com/en/prod/Content/Topics/Adv_Server_Access/docs/client.htm`.

We have gone through the setup of servers, clients, and enrollment. Let's take a look at how we can manage users, groups, and projects.

Managing your ASA environment

There are many different things within ASA that you can manage. Similar to what we mentioned earlier, you can also manage groups, users, and so on in ASA. So, we will not go into that again here. Instead, we will look at how you manage projects, which is an ASA-specific feature.

Managing projects

As you might remember, we created a project in the preceding section, to be able to create the enrollment token. If you want to secure anything in ASA, you will need a token. The project is used to connect a set of resources with a set of configurations. You can compare it to a domain in AD. The project will let you manage different kinds of servers or web applications. So, after you have created your project, as you did to create the enrollment token for a server, you want to add groups to it. Before we can do that, we have to create the group. When you have integrated ASA with Okta using **System for Cross-Domain Identity Management** (**SCIM**), you can sync your groups and users from Okta, making your administration much easier. To set that up, follow the provisioning integration process from *Chapter 5*, *Automating Using Life cycle Management*, or reference this link: `https://help.okta.com/en/prod/Content/Topics/Adv_Server_Access/docs/setup/configure-scim.htm`.

In ASA, we work with groups and team roles. Each group can be assigned a team role. Team roles can be the following:

- **Admins**: With this team role, users are able to manage other users, groups, and project resources.
- **Billing**: With this team role, users are able to get billing information and make payments.
- **Reporting**: With this role, users get read-only access, for reporting purposes.

So, after you have synced your groups to ASA, we can edit the usage and details even more. When you go to the groups list through the left menu, you will see all the groups. By default, you have two groups: **everyone** and **owners**. The group owners have the **Admin** team role and as the default, the person that created the ASA team belongs to this group. Any additional groups pushed from Okta will be listed here as well. To edit any settings, click on the group name to edit.

Under the **Actions** button, you can edit the group's team attributes. For example, you can edit the Unix GID (group number) if there is a specific need to have the group be numbered differently, or the Unix name and Windows group name.

In the following example, we have pushed the **04. devops** group to ASA. While the naming of the group is consistent in ASA, it has been transformed to **sft_devops** for Unix and Windows. In this case, it only used the last part of the name after the last *space* to create the naming for Unix and Windows. Additionally, it added the `sft_` prefix to it:

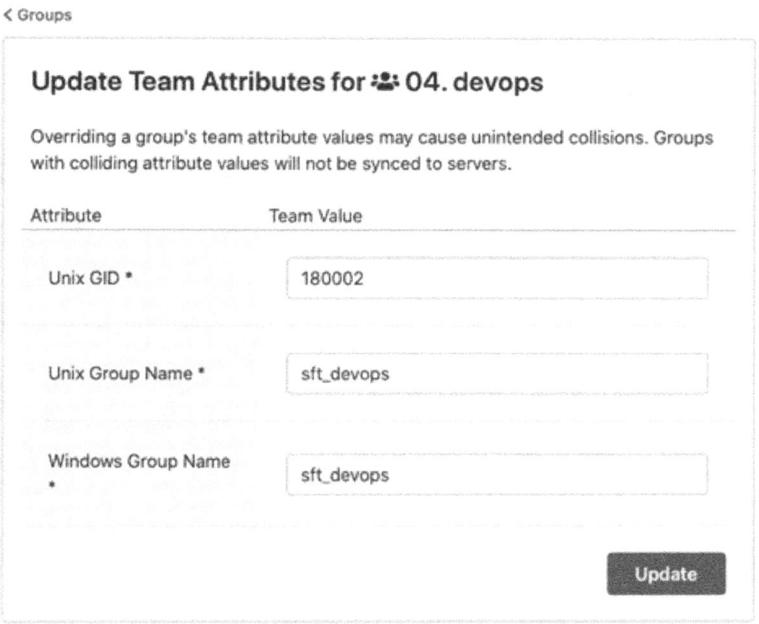

< Groups

Update Team Attributes for 🔊 04. devops

Overriding a group's team attribute values may cause unintended collisions. Groups with colliding attribute values will not be synced to servers.

Attribute	Team Value
Unix GID *	180002
Unix Group Name *	sft_devops
Windows Group Name *	sft_devops

Update

Figure 8.5 – Team attributes of a group in ASA

If you change any settings, don't forget to click **Update** to save your changes.

Back in the group's details overview, you can also assign a team role to your group. You can assign more than one team role to the group if that is needed.

Don't forget to click on **Update Roles** to save your changes.

Now that you have your groups, you probably want users to be added to them. As we explained in *Chapter 2, Working with Universal Directory*, you can push groups to applications. Users in those groups will be synced if they are also provisioned into the application under the **Assignments** tab in the application. The same goes for ASA. You need to assign users. Then, you can push these users into groups by using the **Push Group** function from Okta to ASA.

Just like the groups on the left-side menu, you can also click on users.

This will list the users provisioned into ASA. Users aren't editable, and will only show information on their profile that is relevant to ASA. No additional user information from Okta is synced, just the following:

- First name
- Last name

- Full name
- Email

It will appear as in the following screenshot:

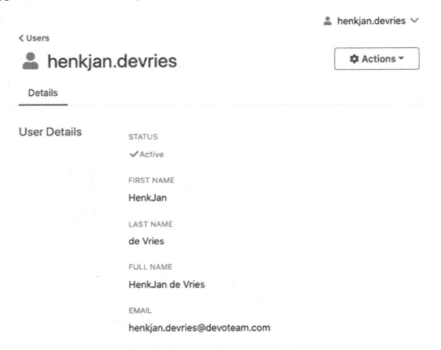

Figure 8.6 – User details in ASA

Additionally, ASA-created attributes are shown in the user overview too. These are not editable:

Figure 8.7 – User attributes in ASA

Lastly, on the user page, you will see the groups that the user is assigned to:

NAME	TEAM ROLES	FEDERATION
⚙ 👥 04. devops		✕
⚙ 👥 everyone		✕
⚙ 👥 owners	Admin	✕

User Groups   find by name...

Figure 8.8 – User-assigned groups in ASA

So, we understand how the synchronization of groups and users happens. Let's now go back to adding groups to the project:

1. Go to **Projects** in the left-side menu.
2. Select the project you want to add a group to.
3. Click the **Groups** tab in that project.

These are the different tabs in a project:

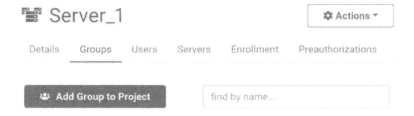

Figure 8.9 – Tab selections in a project

Here's what you need to do:

1. Click the **Add Group to Project** button.
2. Select what group to assign to this project in the group drop-down list.
3. By selecting **User** or **Admin** in the **Server Accounts Permission** section, you decide whether the accounts that are temporarily created will have user-level or administrative rights.
4. If you want your groups to be synchronized to the server(s) associated with this group and project, click the **Sync group to servers** checkbox.

The dialog box for adding the group to your project looks like this:

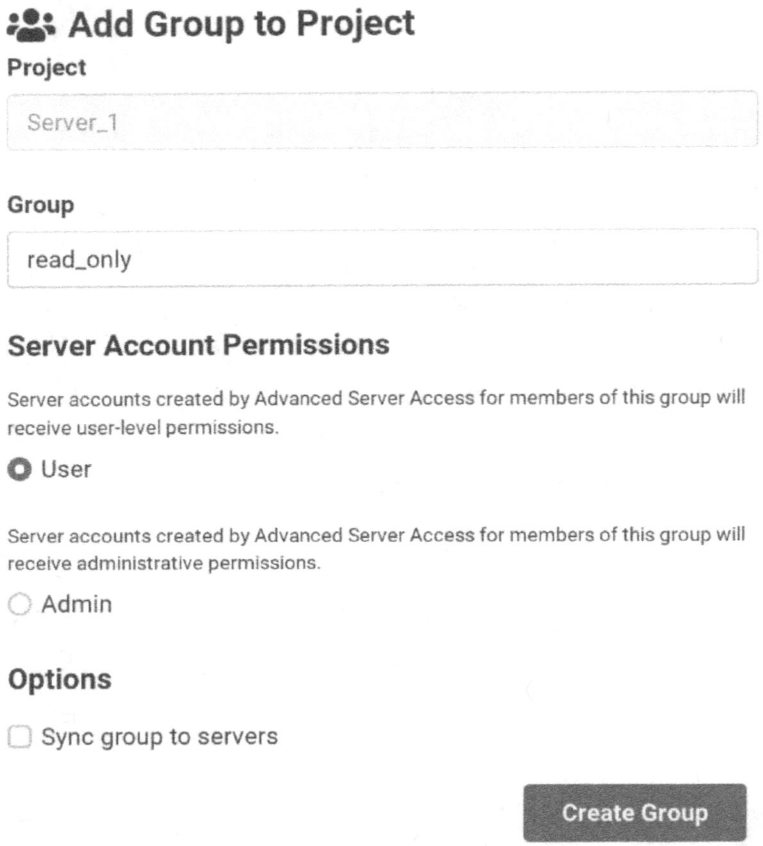

👥 Add Group to Project

Project

> Server_1

Group

> read_only

Server Account Permissions

Server accounts created by Advanced Server Access for members of this group will receive user-level permissions.

🔘 User

Server accounts created by Advanced Server Access for members of this group will receive administrative permissions.

⭕ Admin

Options

☐ Sync group to servers

Create Group

Figure 8.10 – Settings for adding a group to a project

That's it – you're done.

> **Important note**
> If you give admin-level permission on a Linux server, that means giving SUDO entitlements. If you give admin-level permissions on a Windows server, that means giving administrator permissions.

On a project, we can also create preauthorization for users. Let's look at this:

1. Go to the project you want to add preauthorization to.

2. On the **Preauthorization** tab, click the **Create Preauthorization** button.

3. Select a user you want to preauthorize.

4. Select an expiry date for this preauthorization in the **Expires at** field, then set a time.

5. Click **Submit**.

These are the different kinds of management we can adopt for projects in ASA. Now, let's look at how we can use ASA together with external tools to create automation in our daily lives.

Automation

Automating the enrollment of servers in ASA is eventually the best way to scale your infrastructure. This allows the quick management of all the servers across the board, along with the needed access per group and user. To make this happen, your infrastructure automation tools require a solution to allow your identity management to scale along with the infrastructure.

Using tools such as Hashicorp's Terraform (https://www.terraform.io) gives your admins options to create baked-in solutions that are run as soon as new servers are spun up. This allows enrollment automation to happen based on the common usage and access grants that are needed for those servers.

> **Important note**
> Okta also has a certified Terraform provider. To understand more and implement it, please visit https://registry.terraform.io/providers/oktadeveloper/okta/latest/docs.

Perhaps you have a service that requires its own server for each customer. Customers can sign up for free and you need to be able to create that server automatically. But you also want to make sure your admins can access that without having to manually get in or use shared credentials to gain access. By having the enrollment happen along with the creation, the server will automatically be enrolled based on the variables you added to the enrollment script. This will make sure the customer-specific server is added to the right project and group of admins. Perhaps the customers start paying for the services and upgrade their server to a more supported one. This might require your servers to move over from one group to another and have different groups of support and admin users being able to access that server. That can then be done automatically, based on rules.

As there are quite a few scenarios with different tools and infrastructure vendors, we recommend taking a look here to discover how you can implement ASA within your own cloud server fleet using infrastructure automation tools:

```
https://help.okta.com/en/prod/Content/Topics/Adv_Server_
Access/docs/cloud-deployment.htm
```

Summary

ASA is a great way to extend your identity-centric management to your servers and infrastructure. It allows your DevOps engineers to be busy with what they need to do without securing, updating, and managing static keys and credentials. This chapter gave insight into usage, but also showed steps on how to set up, install, and enroll servers. We also discussed how users can install their client to access their provisioned servers. We explained how project management can be done within ASA and we lightly touched on adding ASA as part of infrastructure automation using tools such as Hashicorp's Terraform.

In the last chapter, we will talk about the last product in Okta's IT products range: **Okta Access Gateway (OAG)**. With OAG, you can modernize your on-premises application landscape by incorporating them into your Okta setup and start shrinking your legacy web access management systems.

9

Leveraging Access Gateway for Your On-Premises Applications

In this last chapter of the book, we will go through another unique Okta product, called Okta Access Gateway. For many organizations, legacy **on-premises (on-prem)** applications are a problem when organizations want to modernize IT. To have a unified identity platform such as Okta, giving end users access with **Single Sign-On (SSO)**, the optimal case would be to include all applications. With Okta Access Gateway, that's possible. This feature is not for all organizations, and many Okta administrators will not have to work with this. When hosting Access Gateway within your organization, the technical skills required are higher than for other Okta features. But even so, it's good to have a high-level knowledge of this functionality. Here, you will gain more knowledge about what Access Gateway is and an overview of how to deploy it. You will learn how to deploy a sample application to your environment, and then you will get some insight into how to manage it.

In this chapter, we will look at the following topics:

- Access Gateway overview
- How to deploy Access Gateway
- Implementing a header-based application
- Administering Okta Access Gateway

Access Gateway overview

Using only cloud applications is not possible for many organizations out there. Instead, these organizations are looking at having a hybrid cloud solution for many years to come. For IT admins, this creates a problem. After deploying Okta and having one platform for identity, you don't want to manage identity in other places as well. With Access Gateway, you can utilize Okta's products, such as SSO and **Multi-Factor Authentication** (**MFA**), to applications that use header-based or URL-based authorization or Kerberos.

Even though there are all sorts of vendors out there that can help you access your legacy on-prem systems and software, it usually requires a lot of hardware, maintenance, and upkeep. Redundancy, management, updating, and patching all have their own issues and configurations that require timing, downtime, and fallbacks.

Even then, access probably is done using a VPN or other remote access capabilities to make sure that the users can truly access the required on-prem systems. These **Web Access Management** (**WAM**) solutions can quickly add up and become expensive overnight, as well as really hard to retire. Implementation can take a long time, and it might become so custom-made to your organization's requirements that any standard updates might be outside of your regular routines and require a lot of extra effort to keep it all running.

And don't forget all your testing and to factor in other environments before any change can go to production. This can force you to quickly have to add a lot of servers, just to be able to deploy new updates.

To sum it all up: WAM architecture relies on multiple server components and a vast network setup, including firewalls, load balancers, and network segmentation – into **demilitarized zones** (**DMZes**), intranet, and data network zones.

Okta's Access Gateway can solve this by reducing all these fronts, delivering a unified end users experience, less overhead in hardware, and a true cloud-first strategy. Having Okta's Access Gateway in the middle, you can have your product safely behind Okta's SSO and MFA, while delivering secure access.

Usually, an organization has a WAM solution running as the middleware to it all. Think of systems such as Oracle Access Manager, CA SiteMinder, Tivoli Access Manager/IBM Access, ADFS, and many more. Most of these systems are integrated into the on-prem apps.

To understand how the on-prem app actually works and whether it's capable of migrating to Okta, it's good to understand what Access Gateway supports as integration:

- Header-based authentication
- Agent-based authentication
- Java application servers
- SAML to **Commercial Off-The-Shelf (COTS)** and SaaS apps
- **Enterprise Resource Planning (ERP)**-based apps (E-Business Suite, PeopleSoft)

If the integration between the WAM and your app is using WAM proprietary SDKs, Okta possibly won't be able to integrate with it, if the custom integration was created using proprietary code. Only by changing the code of the app to more current-day and open-standard integrations (for example, SAML or OIDC) will Okta be able to integrate with it directly.

Perhaps you are in a situation where that is simply not possible. Then, Okta is most likely able to integrate with your WAM solution directly and deliver that unified sign-on process.

> **Important note**
> For most of the WAM solutions, you can find set-up instructions on how to add an identity provider at the vendor site.

It is in your best interest to have less reliance on self-managed hardware and large infrastructure setups to provide access to your critical systems. Adding Access Gateway and switching over to Okta can be quite a challenge, but rewarding once you have done it. If you want to migrate from a WAM to Okta Access Gateway, you can find Okta's guide on how to do that here: `https://www.okta.com/resources/whitepaper/wam-modernization-and-migration-guide/`.

Let's take a look at how to set up Okta Access Gateway and how to set up an app.

How to deploy Access Gateway

Deploying Okta Access Gateway isn't that hard, but does come with some requirements. You might need to integrate with your on-prem directory, AD, or LDAP. You need to understand which apps are currently integrated with your WAM and whether they are compatible with Okta. You need to have a strategy and process ready and be able to roll back, so don't go and take down the entire server center at once. Even though Okta can do a lot, good testing and setup is required.

The first step of deploying Access Gateway is to make sure you have gone through the list of prerequisites:

- **Underlying hardware**: Access Gateway was architected around using the SSE4.2 extension to the x64 instruction set, so the server you run Access Gateway on must support at least that instruction set. If you don't know what this is, you can read more here: `https://en.wikipedia.org/wiki/SSE4`.

- Access Gateway can run on Amazon Web Services, Oracle Cloud Infrastructure, Oracle VirtualBox, Microsoft Azure, VMware vSphere, or VMware workstations. On these, there is a lot of different supported technology that can work for you. For a complete list, see `https://help.okta.com/en/prod/Content/Topics/Access-Gateway/support-matrix.htm`.

- **Okta org**: Your Okta org will have to be used as an identity provider, so you will need a super admin account to configure that. This requires a service account for the Access Gateway instance, an API token from Okta (with super administrator rights), and configuration in Access Gateway to make your Okta org the identity provider.

- **Firewall and access requirements**: Access Gateway needs access to various ports and protocols. The full list is available here: `https://help.okta.com/en/prod/Content/Topics/Access-Gateway/deploy-pre-install-reqs.htm`.

- **Load balancer**: If your instance of Access Gateway is running in a high-availability configuration, you need a load balancer. Balancing should be done through a hash of the source port and IP address, and you should use **Source Network Address Translation (SNAT)** or **Dynamic Network Address Translation (DNAT)**. To understand more about consistent hashing with load balancing, please check out this wiki page: `https://en.wikipedia.org/wiki/Consistent_hashing`.

The next step is to select a hosting environment to install Access Gateway on. Okta delivers Access Gateway completely packaged as a **Virtual Machine (VM)**, so you can roll it out completely, without too much setup and too many dependencies.

When the requirement is there to have high availability, additional Okta Access Gateway nodes can be added to handle the request. An admin node is appointed for the distribution and management of the setup. Newly added Access Gateway nodes are provisioned through the admin node. These new nodes are called worker nodes. They are not created with pre-configurations for applications but will contain all configurations from the admin node. To allow this to work correctly, load balancers need to be added.

This way, you can create a cluster or multiple nodes to deliver the best scenario for your applications.

Let's go take a look at how we set up an application. Okta supports multiple integrations, as follows:

- Cookie applications, which pass cookie content to the app
- Policy applications, which verify policies and grants or deny access
- Proxy applications, which show a simulated access scenario to the application host
- Custom third-party applications, who all have their own specific requirements and setup needs

To understand and give you some basic knowledge of how these apps work, the templated basic header app will be explained in the following section.

Implementing a header-based application

Okay, so now that you have your environment up and running and your Okta org is set up as an **Identity Provider** (**IdP**), you are ready for the next step. Let's add a sample header application:

1. Start by logging in to the Access Gateway admin console.
2. Click **Applications**, then **+Add**.
3. On the left, you have an overview of the different types of apps that you can add. Click on **Access Gateway Sample Header**, then the **Create** button in the top-right corner.

With this, you will open the add application wizard:

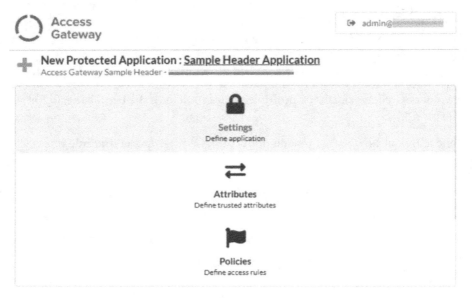

Figure 9.1 – Wizard to add an application in the Access Gateway admin portal

Let's start by clicking on **Settings**, and enter the following information:

- **Label**: The application name, as it would appear on a tile on the Okta dashboard.

- **Public domain**: Your domain-specific URL to access the application, which must be added to the DNS settings.

- **Protected Web Source**: The protected web source's URL.

- **Post login URL**: As an option, you can set the URL used for redirect after successful authentication.

- **Groups**: In this field, you set the Okta groups that have access.

- **Description**: Here, you can set an optional description.

You can click **Show**, in **Service Provider Metadata**, if you want to see or download the metadata. After that, you can set advanced settings as well:

- **Browser Session Expiration**: This setting makes the application session expire with the browser's session. By default, this setting is disabled.

- **Idle Session Duration**: This setting retracts the application session if a user is idle for this duration. By default, this is set to 1 hour.

- **Maximum Session Duration**: With this session, you set the maximum application session duration. By default, this is set to 8 hours, and if you set it to 0, you disable the max session timeout.

- **Deep Linking**: This setting dynamically redirects the browser to the application URI after sign in. By default, this is enabled, and if you disable it, you would be redirected to the post-login URL after signing in.

- **Enforce Deep linking Domain**: Access Gateway allows deep links sharing the domain name when this setting is enabled. By default, it's enabled.

- **Content Rewrite**: By default, Access Gateway tries to rewrite URLs and redirects in the application HTML content.

- **Host header**: You can enable this so that Access Gateway sends the host header to the backend application.

- **Certificate Type**: This is where you create a host-only certificate or a wild card. By default, it's enabled.

- **Debug mode**: This setting puts the app into debug mode, which is good for initial setup and troubleshooting. By default, it's enabled, but should be disabled in production, since it can have a significant impact on performance and machine usage.

- **Maximum File Upload Size**: In this configuration, you can set the maximum file upload size. By default, it's 1 MB. Entering 0 makes it unlimited.

- **Backend Timeout duration**: Here, you can set the timeout for reading back to backend systems. By default, it's 1 minute.

Then, it's time for attributes. They can be sourced from an Okta tenant or from a data store. You can add, edit, delete, and test the attribute in Access Gateway, and each attribute comes from a specific protected application resource. For each attribute, you get to pick a data store. If you select IdP, you get to enter the field attribute name that you want to source. If you select static, you get to enter the value in Access Gateway. To read more on what data stores you can work with, refer to `https://help.okta.com/en/prod/Content/Topics/Access-Gateway/about-application-attribute-datasources.htm`.

After that, it's time to associate your newly set-up application in Access Gateway to your application's URL. In the Access Gateway admin console, click the **Application** table and then click edit (the pen symbol) next to your newly created header application. In the **Essentials** settings, change the **Public Domain** and **Protected Resource** fields to the actual URLs.

After that, we want to associate the right Okta tenant groups to your new application in Access Gateway. In the **Groups** field, enter the groups that should have access to this application. If you don't have Okta groups that match your needs, create them in the Okta admin console, as instructed in *Chapter 5, Automating Using Life cycle Management*.

If you want to make any changes to the advanced settings, you expand the **Advanced** tab. If you want to add more attributes or policies, you can do so. If you need more information on that, you can read it here: `https://help.okta.com/en/prod/Content/Topics/Access-Gateway/add-generic-header-app.htm`.

So now, we need to test the application. We start by assigning the application to a test user:

1. Log in to your Okta tenant and go into the administrator console.
2. Go to **Applications | Applications** and find your newly created header application.
3. After adding it, go to the **Assignment** tab and assign the application to a test user.
4. Click **Done**.

Now, go back to the Access Gateway admin panel. On the row of your newly created header application, click the go to application icon (arrow through a door) and select **IdP Initiated** from the drop-down list. In the results page that shows, make sure all the attributes look as you expected, then close it.

That's it, you are done setting up your application! Now let's look at what tasks you as an administrator have to manage your Access Gateway setup.

Administrating Okta Access Gateway

After deployment, administrating your setup requires more of you than you might expect using Okta, since there are more elements to take into account, as all of this still runs on your infrastructure, just less than before. That means that you as an admin need to take care of the setup.

Backing up and restoring your Access Gateway deployment is one of the administrative tasks you need to take care of. Creating image-based backups is helpful, as these are complete snapshots of the deployed setup.

Overnight, the Access Gateway admin node will create a backup of your configuration. Through the admin interface, you can view and manage these. It allows you to rename, restore to a previous backup, and store the backup somewhere else.

Access Gateway logs a broad spectrum of events. These can be downloaded to be inspected, just like you might be used to in your Okta syslog, or you can have them forwarded to an external logging system to capture and gather all the logs together.

Access Gateway is capable of being set up with different log levels, if troubleshooting is needed. In a production deployment, using levels that generate a lot of traffic is less preferable.

High availability is, of course, top of the mind if you want to guarantee access to applications for your users. Setting this up requires multiple worker nodes to handle the requests to your apps. Managing these worker nodes is done within the admin node, where the reset keys are configured for them as well.

There are several concepts around high availability; we recommend investigating what fits best in your scenario. You can read more here:
`https://help.okta.com/en/prod/Content/Topics/Access-Gateway/high-availability-concepts.htm`.

Admin renomination is the methodology of adding a new node with the newest version. This new node will take over the work of the admin node and makes sure the process of changing is successfully done. Once this process is done, the new admin node will start to run standalone and decommissioning of the old admin node can take place.

This process consists of several tasks, but at a minimum requires the following:

- A worker node to be appointed the new admin node
- Preparation on the new admin node
- Using the Access Gateway Management console to nominate and connect for renomination
- Having the Management console return to the new admin node and determine its IP address
- Updating DNS entries for the new admin node

For more information on this, please check out Okta's help guide:

`https://help.okta.com/en/prod/Content/Topics/Access-Gateway/rolling-upgrade-perform.htm`

Managing Okta Access Gateway does require some additional features to be managed, as follows:

- Access from Okta Support through a VPN connection
- **Simple Network Management Protocol** (**SNMP**) monitoring for device querying
- Upgrading nodes to the newest versions
- Certificate management
- Network interface management
- Trusted domain management

There might be even more based on your setup, infrastructure, and environment.

We strongly recommend checking out each of those sections in the Okta help center to understand what you might need to do in your situation:

```
https://help.okta.com/en/prod/Content/Topics/Access-Gateway/
daytoday.htm
```

Summary

This chapter is different than most others, mostly because of the functionality, integrations, and management surrounding Access Gateway. But if it fits your needs, this is definitely one of your steps toward zero trust, even with your legacy on-prem applications. We spoke about the current concept of the WAM, and how Okta wants to bring that into the future. We talked about how to start, roll out, and manage Access Gateway within your own environments. Lastly, we gave a summary on how to implement your first header-based application to get you going with Okta Access Gateway.

You have now reached the end of this book, and we hope you have found it helpful. Regardless of whether you were an Okta novice or you had already worked with Okta, we hope you have learned something new. If you used this book to study for a certificate, we wish you well on your exam. If you have any comments or want to share anything, please reach out to us. Take care and good luck in your Okta endeavors.

Other Books You May Enjoy

If you enjoyed this book, you may be interested in these other books by Packt:

Mastering Identity and Access Management with Microsoft Azure - Second Edition

Jochen Nickel

ISBN: 978-1-78913-230-4

- Apply technical descriptions to your business needs and deployments
- Manage cloud-only, simple, and complex hybrid environments
- Apply correct and efficient monitoring and identity protection strategies
- Design and deploy custom Identity and access management solutions
- Build a complete identity and access management life cycle
- Understand authentication and application publishing mechanisms
- Use and understand the most crucial identity synchronization scenarios

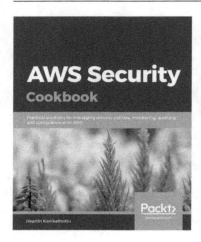

AWS Security Cookbook

Heartin Kanikathottu

ISBN: 978-1-83882-625-3

- Create and manage users, groups, roles, and policies across accounts
- Use AWS Managed Services for logging, monitoring, and auditing
- Check compliance with AWS Managed Services that use machine learning
- Provide security and availability for EC2 instances and applications
- Secure data using symmetric and asymmetric encryption
- Manage user pools and identity pools with federated login

Leave a review - let other readers know what you think

Please share your thoughts on this book with others by leaving a review on the site that you bought it from. If you purchased the book from Amazon, please leave us an honest review on this book's Amazon page. This is vital so that other potential readers can see and use your unbiased opinion to make purchasing decisions, we can understand what our customers think about our products, and our authors can see your feedback on the title that they have worked with Packt to create. It will only take a few minutes of your time, but is valuable to other potential customers, our authors, and Packt. Thank you!

Index

L

layered policies
  creating 109-112
LDAP integration 26-29
Lifecycle Management (LCM) 15, 16, 118
Lightweight Directory Access
    Protocol (LDAP) 20

M

Microsoft AD
  integration 20
Microsoft Installer (MSI) 224
Mobile Device Management
    (MDM) 12, 98
Multi-Factor Authentication
    (MFA) 9, 15, 234
  end users, enrolling in 113
  resetting 113, 114
  settings 94-96
  used, for securing VPN 114-116

N

network zones
  dynamic zone, setting up 103, 105
  IP zone, setting up 102, 103
  setting up 100

O

OIDC Connect applications
  using 80, 81
Okta
  about 4, 5
  exploring 5, 6
  groups, types 39-41

SSO, using with 56
Okta Access Gateway
  administrating 240-242
Okta Access Gateway (OAG) 17
Okta AD agent
  groups, importing with 20-24
  users, importing with 20-24
Okta AD Password Sync agent
  used, for apps login 25, 26
Okta Advanced Server Access 16
Okta, API Access Management
  reference link 203
Okta APIs
  managing 190, 191
  rate limits 200
  reference link 191
  tasks, example 193, 194, 197
  tokens, using 192, 193
  trusted origins, configuring 198, 199
  usage, preparing 191, 192
  using 191
Okta APIs, rate limits
  reference link 200
Okta dashboard
  using 66
Okta Expression Language
  about 135
  attribute magic 137-139
Okta, features
  adaptive multi-factor authentication 15
  discovering 14
  Lifecycle Management (LCM) 15, 16
  multi-factor authentication 15
  single sign-on (SSO) 15
  Universal Directory (UD) 14
Okta groups
  naming 51
  users, creating in AD through 43

Z

www.ingramcontent.com/pod-product-compliance
Lightning Source LLC
LaVergne TN
LVHW081338050326
832903LV00024B/1203